Nations, National Narratives and Communities in the Asia-Pacific

Studies of nationalism have tended to follow familiar theoretical tracks. *Nations, National Narratives and Communities in the Asia-Pacific* offers perspectives that escape these tracks in innovative ways, focusing attention on competing narratives, resistance to the narratives of states and ruling elites, and to the mediums of communication. It is several breaths of fresh air for nationalism studies.

Kevin Hewison, *Director, Carolina Asia Center,*
University of North Carolina, US

Many states in the Asia-Pacific region are not built around a single homogenous people, but rather include many large, varied, different national groups. This book explores how states in the region attempt to develop commonality and a nation and the difficulties that arise. It discusses the consequences that ensue when competing narratives clash, and examines the nature of resistance to dominant narratives which arise. It considers the problems in a wide range of countries in the region, including Indonesia, Malaysia, Singapore, Hong Kong, Korea, Australia and New Zealand.

Norman Vasu is an Assistant Professor in the S. Rajaratnam School of International Studies at Nanyang Technological University.

Yolanda Chin is a Research Fellow in the S. Rajaratnam School of International Studies at Nanyang Technological University.

Kam-yee Law is an Associate Professor in the Department of Social Sciences at the Hong Kong Institute of Education.

Comparative development and policy in Asia series

Series Editors:

Ka Ho Mok
Faculty of Social Sciences, The University of Hong Kong, China
Rachel Murphy
Oxford University, UK
Yongjin Zhang
Centre for East Asian Studies, University of Bristol, UK

Nations, National Narratives and Communities in the Asia-Pacific

Edited by Norman Vasu, Yolanda Chin and Kam-yee Law

Routledge
Taylor & Francis Group

LONDON AND NEW YORK

First published 2014
by Routledge
2 Park Square, Milton Park, Abingdon, Oxfordshire OX14 4RN

and by Routledge
711 Third Avenue, New York, NY 10017

First issued in paperback 2016

Routledge is an imprint of the Taylor & Francis Group, an informa business

British Library Cataloguing in Publication Data
A catalogue record for this book is available from the British Library

Library of Congress Cataloging in Publication Data
Nations, national narratives and communities in the Asia-Pacific/edited by Norman Vasu, Yolanda Chin and Kam-yee Law
    pages cm. – (Comparative development and policy in Asia series; 14)
    Includes bibliographical references and index.
    1. Cultural pluralism–Asia. 2. Cultural pluralism–Pacific Area. 3. Nationalism–Asia. 4. Nationalism–Pacific Area. 5. Ethnicity–Political aspects–Asia. 6. Ethnicity–Political aspects–Pacific Area. I. Vasu, Norman, editor of compilation. II. Chin, Yolanda, editor of compilation. III. Luo, Jinyi, editor of compilation.
    HN655.2.M84N38 2013
    305.800959–dc23

                                                                    2013011793

ISBN 13: 978-1-138-65355-9 (pbk)
ISBN 13: 978-0-415-81972-5 (hbk)

Typeset in Times New Roman
by Wearset Ltd, Boldon, Tyne and Wear

Contents

Figures

Tables

Contributors

Allen Bartley is a sociologist and senior lecturer in the School of Counselling, Human Services and Social Work at the University of Auckland, New Zealand. He migrated to New Zealand from the US in 1992. His primary research interests include 1.5-generation migrants and transnationalism, ethnic politics in New Zealand and transgenerational ethnic identity. Current work includes a study of overseas-qualified social workers practising in New Zealand, and the development of transnational professional spaces. His most recent publication in this field is 'Transnational social workers: Making the profession a transnational professional space', published in the *International Journal of Population Research* in 2012.

Hikmat Budiman is the founder and chairperson of the Jakarta-based Interseksi Foundation (http://interseksi.org), a non-profit organization established in 2003 dedicated to building a tolerant and critical society in Indonesia. The foundation has conducted researches and published books on the issues of democracy, citizenship and minority rights in Indonesia.

Yolanda Chin is Research Fellow and Coordinator of the Social Resilience programme at the Centre for Excellence for National Security (CENS), S. Rajaratnam School of International Studies (RSIS), Nanyang Technological University, Singapore. She holds a BA in Sociology and European Studies from the National University of Singapore and an MSc in International Relations from Nanyang Technological University. Prior to joining RSIS in 2006, she was a secondary school teacher of history, social studies and English from 1999 to 2004. She also taught at the National Institute of Education, Singapore from 2005 to 2006 on Singaporean history and social studies education. Her research interest is in national security and social cohesion in multicultural societies.

Catriona Elder is an Associate Professor in the Department of Sociology and Social Policy at the University of Sydney. Her research interests are in the broad field of race relations and national identity. In 2007 her book *Being Australian: Narratives of National Identity* was published (Allen & Unwin). Recently she published, with Keith Moore, an edited collection *New Voices,*

New Visions: Challenging Australian Identities and Legacies (Cambridge Scholars Publishing, 2012). At the moment she is undertaking a research project on representations of history and race relations on Australian television from the 1970s to the present. She has published chapters on reality television and re-enactment (for example, '*Outback House*, Land and Belonging in (Television) Re-enactment' in Vanessa Agnew and Jonathan Lamb (eds) *Settler and Creole Re-enactment*, Palgrave 2009) and is completing a book on history and the mini-series.

Daniel P.S. Goh is Associate Professor in the Department of Sociology at the National University of Singapore. He graduated with a BSc and a Masters in Social Sciences from the National University of Singapore, and received his PhD in sociology from the University of Michigan, Ann Arbor, US. His research interests are in culture and state formation, race and multiculturalism, heritage and urban redevelopment in Asia. His publications include the co-edited book, *Race and Multiculturalism in Malaysia and Singapore* (Routledge, 2009), and articles on the politics of urbanism and multiculturalism in the *British Journal of Sociology, Space and Culture* and *Inter-Asia Cultural Studies*.

Ho Shu Huang is an Associate Research Fellow at the Institute of Defence and Strategic Studies (IDSS), S. Rajaratnam School of International Studies (RSIS), Nanyang Technological University (NTU). He has a BA (Hons) in History from the National University of Singapore (NUS), as well as an MSc in Strategic Studies from RSIS. His research interest is in military sociology, particularly how the military profession relates to, and functions within, broader society. Prior to joining RSIS, Shu Huang worked for the Singapore Armed Forces (SAF) to set up the Army Museum of Singapore. His affiliation with the SAF continues to this day, though now in the realm of professional military education where he is involved in officer education.

Inchoon Kim is a Sociologist and Research Professor at the Institute of East and West Studies, Yonsei University in Seoul, South Korea. She obtained her PhD from the University of Michigan, Ann Arbor, and has been lecturing and conducting research at Yonsei University since 1997. She specializes in political sociology, labour and welfare issues, women's studies and European studies. Kim's current research interests are multiculturalism, democratic corporatism and social compromise issues in globalized South Korea.

Lai Chee Kien is Assistant Professor in the Department of Architecture, National University of Singapore. He is a registered architect, and graduated from the National University of Singapore with an M Arch by research (1996), and then a PhD in History of Architecture and Urban Design from the University of California, Berkeley (2005). His research interests focus on histories of art, architecture, settlements, urbanism and landscapes in Southeast Asia. His publications include *A Brief History of Malayan Art* (Milestone Millennium Press, 1999) and *Building Merdeka: Independence Architecture in Kuala Lumpur, 1957–1966* (Galeri Petronas, 2007).

Law, Kam-yee received an MA in Developing Areas Studies from the University of Hull (UK) and a PhD in Political Sociology from the City University of Hong Kong. He is currently Associate Professor in the Department of Social Sciences, the Hong Kong Institute of Education, and also the Executive Editor of the *Hong Kong Journal of Social Sciences*. He recently co-authored with Lee Kim-ming a number of papers on the issue of social marginalization in Hong Kong, including 'Citizenship, Economy and Social Exclusion: Mainland Chinese immigrants in Hong Kong' in the *Journal of Contemporary Asia* and 'Socio-political embeddings of South Asian ethnic minorities' economic situations in Hong Kong' in the *Journal of Contemporary China*. He is also the editor of *The Chinese Cultural Revolution Reconsidered: Beyond Purge and Holocaust* (Palgrave Macmillan, 2003) and *Behind the Miracle: Deconstructing the East Asian Modernization* (Oxford University Press, 1997).

Lee, Kim-ming received his M.Phil in Sociology from the Chinese University of Hong Kong and is currently Lecturer in the Division of Social Studies at the Community College of City University, City University of Hong Kong. In recent years he has published extensively on the issue of social marginalization in Hong Kong, including 'Immigration controls, life-course coordination, and livelihood strategies: A study of families living across the Mainland–Hong Kong border' in the *Journal of Family and Economic Issues*, 'Marginalized workers in postindustrial Hong Kong' in the *Journal of Comparative Asian Development*; *A Qualitative Research on Hong Kong Marginal Workers: Trap, Exclusion and the Way Out* (Oxfam Hong Kong, 1996) and *The Economy of Hong Kong in Non-economic Perspectives* ((co-edited with Law Kam-yee, Oxford University Press, 2004).

Norman Vasu is Assistant Professor and Deputy Head at the Centre of Excellence for National Security, S. Rajaratnam School of International Studies (RSIS), Nanyang Technological University, Singapore. He obtained an MA from the University of Glasgow in 1998 and an MSc in International Relations from the London School of Economics in 1999. In 2004, he received his doctorate in International Politics from the University of Wales at Aberystwyth. He has been a tutor at the Department of International Politics at the University of Wales, Aberystwyth; lecturer on International Relations for the Centre for Widening Participation and Social Inclusion at the same university; a Post-Doctoral Fellow with the Institute of Defence and Strategic Studies, Nanyang Technological University, Singapore; and a Fulbright Fellow at Arizona State University. His research interest is in national security issues pertaining to the social fabric.

Introduction

Un/settled narrations – Nationalism in the Asia-Pacific

Norman Vasu, Yolanda Chin and Kam-yee Law

National narratives – or the stories that nations convey to connect their past, present and future – are powerful and necessary tools in shaping national identity. Within such narratives, the 'nation' as a concept seeks to moderate diversity via the creation of a coherent unity that may sometimes appear to rely heavily on an essentialized narrative while at other times appear to be less so. Yet, regardless of ontological firmness, this is arguably a mere blanket over the differences that truly exist within and between communities. In these spaces lie endless pockets of identificational ambiguities continuously in need of discovery and critical discussion. This volume of investigative and exploratory essays aims to critically interrogate this nebulous space of adaptation, negotiation and re-conceptualization of national identity by addressing the following questions: can nation states construct commonality via the discourse of nationalism while accommodating inter-communal differences? Who shapes the agenda and where are the sites of resistance? Do contending accounts of what a nation stands for work for or against the nation-building project?

National narratives and theories of nationalism

Theories on nationalism in general may be divided into three camps – the primordial, perennial and modern. While all three differ from each other in varying degrees based on their view on the origins of nations, all three regardless share a common thread – for there to be a nation, there has to be a national narrative. Stories have to be told on how 'we the people' are or have become a distinct group from others. Dependent upon specific theories, some narratives are extremely essentialized while other narratives are markedly less so.

With regard to primordialist theories on nationalism, such theories trace the origins of nations back to antiquity and hold nations to be natural ontologically real entities. An example of such primordialist views may be found in the work of Pierre van den Berghe.[1] Following van den Berghe, natural selection favours 'nepotistic' behaviour as organisms contribute to their own 'inclusive fitness' by favouring kin.[2] Building on this belief, the social boundary of ethnicity is created by communities through 'preferential endogamy and physically by territoriality', which then further develops into nationalistic sentiment.[3] This particular conception of nationalism as a natural phenomenon has found expression most obviously in the nationalism of the Third Reich in Germany and in the nationalism arguably expressed in modern China with the conception of Chinese-ness as Han.

In extreme opposition to such a conception of the nation lies the modernist camp. Though a diverse group, modernist theories on nationalism have a theoretical family resemblance by sharing the view that nations are the products of modernity. For example, for Ernest Gellner, 'nationalism is not the awakening of nations to self-consciousness: it invents nations where they do not exist'.[4] According to Gellner, the industrialization experienced during the transition to modernity demanded individuals to be mobile as well as have the ability to communicate with one another. Thus, individuals had to be socialized into the same 'high culture' for 'contextless communication' for industrialization to take place.[5] This socialization led to the creation of nations – a creation that saw reproduction around the world as other societies employed the same social tools to create the commonality required to industrialize. Another proponent of the modernist nationalist position is of course Benedict Anderson.[6] Anderson's oft-cited quote maintains that the nation is 'an imagined political community – and imagined as both inherently limited and sovereign'.[7] The nation has to be imagined as the 'members of even the smallest nation will never know most of their follow-members, meet them, or even hear them, yet in the minds of each lives the image of their communication'.[8] Displaying the family resemblance of all within the modernist camp where nationalism is a product of modernity, Anderson is of the view that the imagined nation arose from the development of print capitalism. Capitalist entrepreneurs printed their books in the vernacular languages (instead of the more exclusionary script languages, such as Latin) in order to maximize circulation. Following from this, as readers speaking various local dialects became able to understand each other so a common discourse emerged. Irrespective of theories or theorists in the modernist camp, however, commonality is still shared with the primordialists – a narrative, albeit imagined, is constructed and disseminated amongst those of the same nation. This narrative facilitates feelings of commonality and the othering of those on the 'outside'.

Finally, perhaps best located between the primordialists and modernists, perennialist theories of nationalism while rejecting the ontological absoluteness of the nation found in primordialism do acknowledge that nations emerge from 'felt kinship ties' that may be considered perennial.[9] For the perennialists, the emergence of nations is grounded in 'ethnic persistence' where the nation is the modern equivalent of a pre-modern ethnic identity.[10] Myths and symbols – and, it should be added, the narratives that permit their transmission and absorption – explain the endurance of ethnic identification in modern times.[11] This reasoning supports Anthony Smith's position that the nation is 'a named human population sharing a historic territory, common myths and historical memories, a mass public culture, a common economy and common legal rights and duties for all its members'.[12]

Significantly, it is no accident that this volume, while acknowledging the importance of such theorizing, has avoided becoming entangled in the grand debates of the nationalism canon. Recognizing that there is no consensus between and within the primordialist, perennialist and modernist camps on the origins of the nation, this volume has chosen instead to perhaps more fruitfully explore the narratives of the nation and the resistance and problems that arise from particular narratives. If nations are indeed an amalgamation of diverse individuals with competing aspirations, then nation-building projects aimed at homogenizing difference when conducted poorly are likely to elicit resistance and discontent rather than unity. In the absence of a consensus regarding what a nation stands for, national identity formation is a quest for an elusive end and hence a never-ending work-in-progress. National identity is thus not static but constantly defined and redefined by individuals and communities within the nation. In this respect, national narratives serve as platforms of social mediation for this ongoing dialogue and negotiation between myriad segments of society seeking to articulate their aspirations of what their country, as an extension of themselves, stands for.

As a tool of communication, national narratives in this collection of essays are not limited to the conventional state attempts to construct a common historical narrative to develop a sense of belonging but will include analyses of the manner in which a nation's values and identity is reified in the formulation of cultural policies. The extent to which alternative narratives are permitted to join and influence the discussion on national identities will then be assessed.

While there are many important works on the topic of nationalism per se and nationalism in Asia specifically, there has yet to be a collection of thought-provoking pieces that encompasses a comprehensive overview of nationalism from a multidisciplinary viewpoint that deals with both state narratives and counter-narratives in the Asia-Pacific. This combination of experiences and strategies of both the powerful and the relatively less powerful within this book facilitates a better understanding of nationalism's impact on both and is probably a key contribution of this collection. It distinguishes itself from other works in at least three ways: (1) it captures the crucial state narratives of a wide range of states in the Asia-Pacific that are not normally found in one volume while providing an assessment of the key policies that have been put in place in order to generate feelings towards the nation; (2) it presents a critical analysis of counter-narratives that seek to resist, reformulate or review state-offered perspectives; and (3) it offers an analysis of mediums of communication often overlooked in currently available volumes on nationalism such as comics and murals. These three vistas on the topic of nationalism in the Asia-Pacific enable the unique perspective of the comprehensive collection of essays in this single volume.

Following from this, this volume explores the tensions between contending visions of the nation by juxtaposing state-sanctioned official narratives and civic counter-narratives.

Narrating nation/s

This book is divided into three broad themes: (1) the attempt to develop commonality and the nation by the state and the difficulties that arise; (2) the fallout when competing narratives clash; and (3) the modes of resistance to dominant narratives.

With regard to the first theme, Ho Shu Huang, in his examination of the commemoration of military heroes in the Singaporean national narrative, addresses the limitations of scripting war heroes in Singapore's official history anchored in the patriotic sacrifices of 'the great, the dramatic, and the distant' national heroes under exceptionally harsh and tumultuous circumstances. On the one hand, national heroes, who personify the key values of a nation, such as Major General Lim Bo Seng who fought during the Second World War, may humanize and consolidate a national narrative by serving as reference points for citizens to vicariously relive a shared past. Moreover, they also convey to the citizens the state's expectation of how they should respond in the face of a national crisis. However, Ho notes that this approach to imbuing a sense of national pride is problematic not only because it is a highly selective scripting of the identified heroes' character and war efforts to fit the intended narrative that is larger than life and difficult to emulate. More importantly, the protracted absence of war and the significant alteration in the nature of warfare over the years call for the inclusion of military heroes in the national imagination who have made sacrifices motivated by camaraderie and patriotism in the line of duty during peace time. Citing the example of Second Lieutenant Tay Siow Kai who, in 1970, lost his life when a live grenade exploded in his hands as he tried to save the life of a recruit and corporal under his command, Ho argues that even though Tay's act of bravery occurred during a military training session rather than an actual war, his actions were not only as heroic as Lim's during the Second World War but are also likely to inspire all able-bodied Singaporean males for whom National Service is compulsory.

Following from Ho, and questioning the key role played by print capitalism in Benedict Anderson's theory of nationalism in creating the imagined nation, Lai Chee Kien problematizes such a medium of communication owing to its assumption that the majority of the population is literate. How, then, can newly independent multicultural states with a culturally fragmented populace that has yet to attain general literacy in their unifying national language communicate a common national narrative? Lai offers an analysis of the manner in which the post-independence government of Malaysia employed pictorial imagery, namely a series of state-commissioned murals installed on prominent national buildings between 1957 and 1969, to depict state-sanctioned national heroes and aspirations of modernity and national unity for the masses. Nevertheless, such an endeavour at reifying specific interpretations of history and culture that does not square with the lived reality of the masses may ring hollow, as evidenced in the eruption of serious ethnic riots in 1969 despite deliberate depictions of ethnic harmony in the murals.

Continuing from Ho and Lai and moving on to the second theme of the book, Daniel PS Goh, Allen Bartley, Kam-yee Law and Kim-ming Lee and finally Inchoon Kim in employing the experiences of Singapore, New Zealand, Hong Kong and the Republic of Korea, respectively, discuss and assess the consequences of competing narratives of the nation.

Daniel P.S. Goh, in his assessment of the resilience of Singaporean multiculturalism, suggests that the government lacks a well-articulated narrative of a model of multiculturalism that Singapore should strive for. This lack has unwittingly encumbered Singapore's ability to articulate a narrative of itself as a stable multicultural nation. Rather than a coherent vision of a multicultural society to aspire to as an end in itself, he argues that policies shaping Singapore's multicultural identity are driven by the government's desire to preserve short-term stability by preventing Singapore from becoming either an assimilative multicultural state characterized by low political representation and high intercultural interaction or a neoliberal state with high political representation and low intercultural interaction. This is achieved by implementing piecemeal policies to guide society away from developing into either state model, which then results in a tendency for the nation's multicultural complexion to alternate between the two. This in turn impedes the potential for a 'multicultural utopia' to grow into a 'historical possibility'; such a fruition requires it to be high in political participation and intercultural interaction – and the state is ambivalent about both policies. Consequently, the unstable multicultural system perpetuates the state's anxiety regarding the difficulty of forging a multicultural national identity.

Expanding on the issue pertaining to a clash of national narratives, Allen Bartley, in his chapter on multiculturalism in New Zealand, examines the challenges faced by the state in balancing the aspiration of an increasing number of ethnic minorities for inclusive citizenship and resistance to them. The tension lies between the tendency for proponents of New Zealand as a bicultural nation as opposed to a multicultural one to view both narratives as mutually exclusive. The policy of biculturalism officially recognizes the indigenous status of the marginalized Maori and the guarantee of a special relationship between the Maori and the Crown (namely, New Zealanders of British descent) enshrined in the 1840 Treaty of Waitangi; the policy of multiculturalism extends the state's commitment to addressing the unequal socio-economic opportunities faced by non-Maori ethnic minorities vis-à-vis the dominant citizens of British descent. Critics of multiculturalism are of the opinion that the policy is a 'dishonest' and 'reactionary' position to reduce the status of the Maori from a treaty partner to 'just one more ethnic minority', whereas advocates of the policy point to the alienation of the Pacific peoples, non-European and non-Polynesian migrants to New Zealand as a result of the policy of biculturalism. Bartley argues that a resolution to the tension between biculturalism and multiculturalism requires that the two policies are not taken to be binary opposites but instead that biculturalism is conceived as the framework within which multiculturalism may be realized.

Unlike Goh and Bartley, who both assess the effect of competing national narratives on those that may be considered nationals, both Kam-yee Law and

Kim-ming Lee and Inchoon Kim develop the issue of competing national narratives to consider its effects on those considered 'Others' who are within the nation. In the case of Hong Kong, Kim-ming Lee and Kam-yee Law analyse the Hong Kong state's attempt to shed its colonial past and develop a national identity that reflects its new close political and economic ties with China. This objective was pursued through a policy of Sinicization premised on 'the recollection, reinvention and rediscovery of historical and cultural ties between Hong Kong and China'. An examination of the manner in which the Sinicization policy discriminates and excludes two separate segments of Hong Kong society – ethnic minorities and Chinese from Mainland China – demonstrates the challenges faced by the state in defining a national identity that accommodates cultural diversity. On the one hand, the non-White ethnic minorities, namely those of Southeast Asian and South Asian descent, are marginalized as Chinese neonationalism results in the denial of citizenship to ethnic minorities. On the other hand, the goal of cultivating close ties between China and Hong Kong has been impeded by an existing prejudice which sees Mainland Chinese as culturally inferior social parasites, resulting in their treatment as another discriminated against minority. This has been attributed in part to Hong Kong citizens' perception of the cultural superiority of the British colonizers rather than the Chinese. As a result, the negative stereotype of the Mainland Chinese serves to secure a second place for the Hong Kong citizens in the nation's racial hierarchy. Hence the failure of the state's efforts to develop a postcolonial national identity by distancing itself from the British and aligning itself to Mainland China underscores the complexity in the deliberate engineering of nationhood.

Similar issues are grappled with in Inchoon Kim's piece on the Republic of Korea. Kim's case study of South Korea provides insights into how a culturally homogenous society grapples with its national identity as the population becomes increasingly culturally diverse. While South Korea's national identity has traditionally been built on the notion of a 'nation unified by one bloodline', this narrative is increasingly being challenged by the nascent presence of a culturally distinct non-Korean population as a result of the country's reliance on foreign labour and inter-marriage between Koreans and non-Koreans. Kim locates two sources of resistance and anxiety pertaining to the debate over national identity. First, the recognition of the rights of ethnic minorities unsettles a segment of society which fears that cultural pluralism will dilute the Korean way of life. Second, the aversion to cultural diversity is exacerbated by the government's immigration policy, which discriminates against migrant workers from developing countries and inadvertently formulates a prejudice against ethnic foreigners based on racial markers, namely the colour of their skin. While the state recognizes the importance of cultivating a multicultural society in the current milieu, its efforts are met with resistance from cultural nationalists. Following from this, Kim argues that the multicultural agenda can be forwarded if the discourse on national identity is recast from a notion of race to that of inclusive democratic principles that is gaining traction among South Koreans.

Finally, Catriona Elder and Hikmat Budiman, in discussing the experience of Australia and Indonesia, respectively, reveal insights into the modes of resistance to dominant narratives that fail to capture all of the nation. Elder explores the tension between contending narratives of Australian identity that reflect the unsettled relations between the indigenous and non-indigenous population through the case study of the use of space in the Parliamentary Zone in Canberra; namely, the Aboriginal Tent Embassy and Reconciliation Place. The organic development of the Aboriginal Tent Embassy from a protest by indigenous activists to government policies on land rights in 1972 to an established symbolic site of resistance is noteworthy for two reasons. First, the equivocal response of the state in which, on the one hand, it refuses to confer the Embassy the status of an authorized structure within the Parliamentary Zone but, on the other hand, is willing to list it on the Register of the National Estate as a social heritage site, underscores a tension that lies between the gatekeepers of the dominant discourse. Second, the state's decision in the late 1990s to develop a new commemorative site called Reconciliation Place in the Parliamentary Zone to affirm [Australia's] commitment to the cause of reconciliation [between the indigenous and non-indigenous Australians] as an important national priority has been interpreted in some quarters as the state's endeavour to recognize and include alternative voices in the national narrative. However, its detractors criticize it as a veiled attempt to undermine the Embassy as an authentic site of resistance. In this respect, the ongoing negotiation over Australian identity embodied in these two monuments reflects the unsettled nature of nationalism in Australia.

Echoing the difficulty in constructing a narrative that has traction with all in Elder's chapter, Hikmat Budiman examines the resistance of ethno-religious minorities towards the state's attempt to construct unity via reducing the complexity of managing the rich diversity of cultures and religions of the nation. This is carried out by limiting the compulsory identification of its citizens to one of the five official religions. His comparative analysis of different responses of the ethnic minorities and their consequences underscores the interaction of cultural pride and state–citizen power dynamics in the negotiation of national identity. In the case of the *ToWana* (which translates as 'people from the forest'), their refusal to conform to any of the official religions denies them recognition as citizens and in turn access to state-sponsored social services and the right to settle in government villages. In a bid to accommodate the state policy of imposing cultural uniformity, the *Kajang* community officially subscribed to Islam. However, by practising a form of Islam that is distinct from the Muslim majority, they faced pressure to conform to the mainstream teachings, which included demands that they discard their ancestral rituals and cultural practices. Another community, the *ToWani Tolotong*, which practises a form of Islam, strategically chose Hinduism rather than Islam as their official religion to avoid scrutiny by mainstream Islamic followers. In this manner, they have succeeded in protecting their cultural heritage in practice, although not in name.

Un/settled narratives

In effect, the final two chapters bring the book back full circle – the continual cycle of narration and re-narration unfolds in an almost Hegalian-like dialectic with thesis, antithesis, synthesis. National narratives emerge, alternative conceptions arise in response, resistance begins and the process repeats itself. Nations will certainly differ in their experiences of this process – some will experience more rapid narrative generation and renewal while some will approach such narrative contestations far more peacefully than others. Regardless, in agreement with Anderson, it is perhaps unnecessary to discuss the authenticity of the imagined and far more fruitful to understand why, who and what is being said about who and how one belongs.

Notes

1 Pierre van den Burghe, *The Ethnic Phenomenon* (London: Praeger, 1987).
2 Ibid., pp. 18, 35.
3 Ibid., pp. 24–25.
4 Ernest Gellner, *Thought and Change* (London: Weidenfeld and Nicholson, 1965), p. 168.
5 Ernest Gellner, *Nations and Nationalism* (Oxford: Blackwell, 2006), p. 134.
6 Benedict Anderson, *Imagined Communities* (London: Verso, 2006).
7 Ibid., p. 6.
8 Ibid.
9 Walker Conner, *Ethnonationalism: The Quest for Identity* (Princeton, NJ: Princeton University Press, 1994), p. 202.
10 Anthony D. Smith, *Nationalism and Modernism* (New York: Routledge, 1998), p. 181; John Armstrong, *Nations before Nationalism* (Chapel Hill: University of North Carolina Press, 1983), pp. 4–7.
11 Anthony D. Smith, *The Ethnic Origins of Identity* (Oxford: Blackwell, 1986), p. 15.
12 Anthony D. Smith, *National Identity* (Harmondsworth: Penguin, 1991), p. 14.

References

Anderson, Benedict. *Imagined Communities* (London: Verso, 2006).
Burghe, Pierre van den. *The Ethnic Phenomena* (London: Praeger, 1987).
Gellner, Ernest. *Thought and Change* (London: Weidenfeld and Nicholson, 1965).
Gellner, Ernest. *Nations and Nationalism* (Oxford: Blackwell, 2006).
Smith, Anthony D. *The Ethnic Origins of Identity* (Oxford: Blackwell, 1986).
Walker, Conner. *Ethnonationalism: The Quest for Identity* (Princeton, NJ: Princeton University Press, 1994).

Part I

Constructing commonality and the nation

1 Rethinking the who, what and when

Why not Singaporean military heroes?[1]

Ho Shu Huang

Singapore's national narrative, in its present form generally referred to as the Singapore Story, serves the nation building project by providing 'the backdrop which makes sense of [Singapore's] present ... showing what external dangers to watch out for, and where our domestic fault lines lie'.[2]

Although 'not history for its own sake',[3] this national narrative is still written by utilizing the historian's basic questions of who, what and when to explain Singapore's success against vast odds.[4] The answers are typically derived from a small pool of historically significant 'great men' (and women) who acted with distinction and agency during earlier events of political flux or dramatic crisis. The bulk of 'The Singapore Story – Overcoming the Odds', a multi-million dollar exhibition put up in 1998 as part of Singapore's then newly launched National Education (NE) effort, represented such an approach. Although narrated by a granddaughter–grandfather pair, ostensibly common Singaporeans, the history presented in the exhibition focused on the agency of leading historical figures in Singapore as it faced one challenge after another from its birth to the present.[5] Such an overarching narrative, however, has a tendency to assume a finite, timeless constitution, particularly in intellectual interpretation. This is problematic as the mind of the national narrative's target audience, Singaporeans, does not remain static; it develops intellectually, like a maturing individual. With increasing levels of education and global exposure, Singaporeans' understanding of themselves has become more sophisticated and critical over time. The rising interest in counter-narratives in Singaporean history is a clear example.[6]

This chapter does not seek to add to the discussion that there are opposing sides, or perspectives, to the Singapore Story, but accepts that the intellectual essence of the incumbent Singapore Story is currently hegemonic, and will be so for some time to come. Rather, through an examination of the commemoration of military heroes (or lack of) in the Singaporean national narrative, this chapter identifies two practical problems the Singapore Story, as it is currently scripted, faces when used in nation building. It first argues that narrowly scoping the basic historical terms of person (who), event (what) and period (when) to include only the great, dramatic and the distant, limits the scripting of the national narrative to merely a narrow band of the past, at the expense of the rest of the colourful spectrum. Such an approach, homage to Thomas Carlyle's 'Great Man' view of history, provides recognizable anchors to the Singapore Story for the easy consumption of the masses. Yet, this constrained approach also occasionally twists historical facts to fit the process, a glaring abuse of history that can undermine the legitimacy of the national narrative.

Furthermore, the lack of diversity in approaching the Singapore Story can inadvertently disengage Singaporeans, especially as new chapters are written. This chapter also posits that in order to avoid this disinterest, the stories of those who are not immediately associated with the nation as a concept, what Albert Lau refers to as the 'underside' of history,[7] also have to be included. By injecting the comparatively insignificant stories of heroic Singapore Armed Forces (SAF) soldiers into the Singapore Story, a pool of citizens who have interestingly been overlooked despite the profession's association with the production of great personalities, it is hoped the field of history of Singapore will no longer be 'disappointingly barren and non trodden by Singapore's home scholars'.[8] Doing so will help shift the framing of the national narrative away from the overstated 'whiggish telos of economic development, progress, modernity and modernisation'[9] by incorporating the subaltern into the Singapore Story as well.

This is important. As younger generations become increasingly wary of the existing Singapore Story as merely a propaganda tool of the People's Action Party (PAP) government, and as new chapters of the national narrative have to be written about a comparatively less tumultuous present, this fixation with the larger-than-life personality and the historically grand event may be detrimental to NE in the long term. Almost four decades ago, the *National Pioneer*, the monthly newsletter of the SAF already noted that responses to NE would correspond to how well it reflected the 'nature and character' of the present.[10] How the national narrative is constructed has to address younger Singaporeans who are more interested in a relatable past of the average citizen than one that focuses almost exclusively on the grand person or event. The *epistemes* of the Singapore Story have to be broadened to include the perspective of the subaltern, as well as explore lower-level personalities and historical events from a recent past. For the Singapore Story to remain usable, the who, what and when questions have to be cast in broader directions, not just upwards but downwards too.

Dismantling the existing mould of the great, the dramatic and the distant

That history is a powerful tool in nation building cannot be ignored. Hong Lysa puts this task in more precise terms: 'The history that a state tells of itself, and the degree of its success in getting its citizens to embrace that history as their own, are ... central to the process of its nation-building.'[11] This dynamic nexus between the past, present and future through the historical text has been engaged variously by Singaporeans of different stripes and agendas, especially by academic historians whose bread and butter lies precisely in this realm of historical interpretation, contestation and presentation. Summarizing this burden, Wang Gungwu notes that Asian historians can no longer afford to pursue history for its own sake, but find themselves compelled to write national histories for their country's nation-building efforts, an expected professional contribution.[12] And so, responsible historians have.

In Singapore, however, the lead author of the dominant component of the national narrative was not a historian, but its first Prime Minister, Lee Kuan Yew. Lee's two-volume memoirs, generally referred to by the first volume's abridged title, *The Singapore Story*, has become just that, despite Lee's claim otherwise.[13] His memoirs, Lee wrote, were penned to inform younger Singaporeans just how difficult it was for Singapore to survive in the tumultuous post-war years with few resources, and how despite these odds, Singapore, through good governance, still managed to steer itself to success.[14] This heroic narrative of achievement against tremendous odds has now become the preamble to any part of the Singapore Story.[15] The unbroken dominance of the PAP in Singaporean politics, of whom Lee was a founder, makes this unsurprising.[16]

Singaporean historians are thus confronted with how to further the national narrative within Lee's hegemonic heroic-survivalist rubric. Expectedly, there exists a tension between the historian's ethos of objectivity and completeness, and the need of a state to be selective in what it recalls in its national narrative. This debate on the politics of inclusion and exclusion, appropriation or rejection, has been ably explored in the recent edited volume, *The Scripting of a National History: Singapore and Its Pasts*, by Hong and Huang Jianli.

How the basic historical components of this debated past – person, event and period – are defined, however, has received far less critical attention. The methodology and structure in the engineering of the national narrative is fundamentally important as the shape of a national narrative depends as much on what the historical framework allows in, as what the authors of the story decide to include. In the current Singapore Story, the historical actor must have been a great man (or woman) of history whose contributions were far-reaching.[17] An event worthy of a place in the national narrative must be dramatic, and have equally dramatic consequences. Historical periods worth considering must be from an earlier past that is notably removed from the present. The result is a national narrative that has a very narrow range of characters from precise events and periods. For example, Loh Kah Seng observes that the tumultuous period of the 1950s and 1960s, the 'most compelling chapter of the "Singapore Story"', has been 'authorised primarily by the personal experiences of the PAP Old Guard'.[18] In sum, the Singapore Story is a dramatic one of the endeavours of the elite from a period that has already passed; a conclusive narrative of victory by the victors.[19]

Singaporean author Gopal Baratham notes how the way the Singapore Story is written reminds him of how he was taught British imperial history. That history, taught through the victorious 'heroism of brigands like Drake, Clive and Warren Hastings', was unbalanced as it was exclusionary. Yet his main critique of this approach lies in the omission of the counter-narratives of the defeated, but only those so considered within the existing Gramscian framework of the great, the dramatic and the distant. Returning to the Singapore Story, Baratham uses the example of the lack of attention paid to the protests by the *Barisan Sosialis* (the 'defeated') against the 1962 Singapore National Referendum on merger with Malaysia to illustrate his point.[20] No issue was taken with that framework itself, one that aligns itself with Carlyle's now unfashionable 'Great Man' approach to history. While usefully suggesting that the Singapore Story should be scripted from a wider perspective, Baratham merely implies the net should be cast more widely laterally, rather than vertically to include other actors from below and, additionally, from less dramatic events and periods too.

Controversial challenges to the Singapore Story often continue to accept this narrow assumption of the parameters of these historical parts of the great, the dramatic and the distant, with interest remaining mainly in the larger issue of how power politics determines the representation of that elite band of history: should Lim Chin Siong, who split from the PAP to form the *Barisan Sosialis* opposition party, and is demonized in the Singapore Story, be accorded the same status of anti-colonial patriot as Lee Kwan Yew?[21] Was Singapore really ejected from Malaysia, or did the PAP actually have a larger than acknowledged role in the 1965 separation?[22] Should the Singapore Story actually begin before Sir Stamford Raffles' arrival in 1819?[23] These are but a few examples of new historical investigations within old structural demarcations.

The Singapore military hero, too, is cut from this rigid mould. Major General Lim Bo Seng, 'Singapore's best known war hero',[24] epitomizes the result of such a selection process: he was an educated, British-trained, anti-Japanese resistance fighter who was a successful businessman before the war. Compromised by traitors, Lim suffered a brutal, but heroic death at the hands of the Japanese for not divulging the names of his comrades. Lim was martyred during the Japanese Occupation, a period removed from the present. Lim's heroism is beyond reproach, but his actual nationality and *Weltanschauung* make his appropriateness in the Singapore Story debatable. More importantly, his dramatic presence in the national narrative, guaranteed by the narrow selection process he was chosen through, eclipses the stories of other Singapore military heroes. Ignored because they were ordinary Singaporeans who acted heroically in a comparatively insignificant event from a recent past, they may in fact have a better claim to the paramount position of military hero Lim currently occupies.

The myth of the Singapore(an?) war hero, Major General Lim Bo Seng

National heroes, individuals who personify the key values of a country, naturally serve a useful role in elaborating the national narrative. They humanize and consolidate a national story, acting as points through which citizens from the present can vicariously relive a shared past, drawing them closer to it.

As Chan Heng Chee once put it, heroes 'are like the garlic in the oil when you fry a dish. You can have it without, but the flavour, the punch, isn't there.'[25] In 2008, Lui Tuck Yew, the Senior Minister of State for Education and

Information, Communications and the Arts, acknowledged this importance of national heroes and reiterated that the experiences of national heroes serve to unite a multicultural Singapore, and enhance its identity.[26] Lui was elaborating on a fundamental point made earlier, in 1991, by George Yeo, then Minister for Information and the Arts, who stated the need to identify and commemorate great historical figures more pragmatically. Stable societies always need heroes to look up to, and they are therefore vital to the soul of the nation, Yeo then concluded. Without such a soul, its citizens would see the country as merely a hotel, where no roots are planted.[27]

Interestingly, though, Singapore still has no officially declared national heroes. In 1999, then-Prime Minister Goh Chok Tong admitted 'a country needs national heroes', yet acknowledged Singapore had not officially recognized any, though worthy candidates did exist. Singapore, he concluded, 'would do this at an appropriate time' – a time that apparently has yet to come.[28] For war heroes, however, state sanction is seemingly unnecessary. Singaporeans unanimously commemorate Major General Lim Bo Seng as a national hero, even if he is not officially recognized as one. After all, war is the ultimate crucible of hero construction, where personalities, beyond reproach because their patriotic sacrifices are made under abnormally hard and often violent circumstances, can be singled out as perfect citizens whose lives are worthy of emulation.[29] Furthermore, Singapore, a victim of awful circumstances resulting from the inadequacy of the British defence of the island during the Second World War, now places strenuous emphasis on self-reliance, especially in defence. The national strategic psyche instinctively searches for a concise reminder of this need, and Lim conveniently fulfils it. It reminds citizens of the importance of preserving peace through the backdrop of Lim's story, and reminds them of the standards they should aspire to should the country be tested in conflict.

Lim ran his family's brick and biscuit business in Malaya before the outbreak of the Second World War. In the years of hostility between China and Japan, he was steadfastly anti-Japanese and supported various resistance efforts on the mainland. As he fled Malaya from the advancing Japanese, he decided to resist the Japanese actively as a soldier, and no longer merely passively as a fund-raising businessman.[30] He would later join the British guerrilla group, Force 136, and was eventually deployed behind enemy lines in Japanese-held Malaya. He died in Japanese captivity on 29 June 1944, refusing to divulge the names of his comrades even under torture and starvation, thus allowing them to escape a fate similar to his.

In recognition of his selflessness and heroism in the face of such inescapable adversity, Lim has been variously referred to as 'Singapore's greatest Second World War hero', and 'just about the only larger-than-life hero we have right now'.[31] Two memorials have been dedicated in his memory, and a street was named after him.[32] On the fiftieth anniversary of his death in 1994, the Singaporean broadsheet *The Straits Times* featured multiple tributes commemorating his heroism and sacrifice.[33] Students are still moved to tears and inspired by his story, and his name automatically comes to mind alongside other Singaporean national figures such as 'Benjamin Sheares, Yusof Ishak, Goh Keng Swee and Lee Kuan Yew'.[34]

His appropriation as a Singapore war hero, however, is problematic on three counts. First, accepting Lim as a Singapore war hero sets a standard that is difficult to follow. His shadow looms so large and his story is so dramatic that it presently limits the arena from which military heroes are selected for inclusion in the Singapore Story to war alone. For a country that has known no war since its independence, any Singapore military hero from after the Second World War naturally cannot be a war hero. As the SAF moves into the twenty-first century with more realistic training, as well as an expanded non-war fighting role, heroism in the military has to be accordingly recognized in areas beyond the traditional crucible of such behaviour, the battlefield. Peace looks set to be the locus of the creation of Singapore*an*, not just Singapore, military heroes for subsequent chapters of the Singapore Story.

Second, there is a discernible discomfort in emphasizing Japan's aggression during the Japanese Occupation in the Singapore Story, the vital context in which Lim's story as a patriotic and selfless war hero must be told to have the necessary impact. Some argue that the Japanese Occupation has in fact become 'Singapore's missing war', or that memories of it in the Singapore Story are skewed because of contemporary concerns.[35] Although contemporary Japan has reformed and now shuns imperialism, it has yet to come to terms with its history of aggression in the same complete way that Germany has with its Nazi past. As Japan is now a major global economic powerhouse and an important trading partner, Singapore has opted to remain uncontroversial and undemanding in how the Japanese Occupation is presented in the Singapore Story, a stark contrast to the challenges other Asian victims such as Korea and China have mounted against Japan in their national narratives.[36] While Japanese inhumanity is included in the Singapore Story, the ineptitude of the British and Singapore's vulnerability seem to be the main aspects of Singapore's past vis-à-vis the Second World War that are prudently emphasized instead.[37] MG Lim thus remains a Singapore war hero who is popularly commemorated, but overt official sanction remains difficult because of contemporary sensitivities.[38]

Finally, the accuracy of how Lim is honoured is questionable. The distinction between a Singapore and Singaporean military hero is an important one. It is commonly observed that Lim is labelled a Singapore war hero, as opposed to a Singapore*an* one. The former label could still be accurate, but the latter, not. Lim was not Singaporean, but part of the Chinese diaspora residing in colonial Singapore; independent Singapore did not yet exist.[39] He was trained by the British, and posthumously commissioned a major general by the Kuomingtang (KMT). His association with Singapore and eventual death in Malaya, possibly seen by him as merely an overseas battlefield, was in a sense purely incidental. To the PAP government, that Lim was not Singaporean (Singapore did not yet exist) and was actually employed by the British, makes him ineligible as an officially acknowledged national hero, where Singaporean nationality is presumably a requirement. In this regard, as Goh put it in 1999, Lim 'cannot compare with freedom fighter José Rizal, whom the Filipinos regard as the father of modern Philippines'.[40] Recognizing Lim's utility in enhancing the heroic-survivalist Singapore Story, the PAP government, however, has not protested his inappropriate appropriation into the Singapore Story, despite his lack of Singaporean citizenship.

In fact, it is acquiescent to the process. That Lim is often labelled a Singapore war hero, not a Singapore*an* one, also suggests where the agency in ascribing him that honour lies. The adjective 'Singapore' has been externally imposed on Lim by the Singapore Story and those who shape it. 'Singaporean war hero', on the other hand, can only be ascribed to a true citizen of Singapore, if it is to be used accurately. Thus, that label is organically determined by the individual's citizenship. In this regard, Lim cannot be considered Singaporean, whose roots and future were tied to Singapore. It is likely Lim saw himself a Chinese nationalist patriot instead – the norm for overseas Chinese during the period of Sino-Japanese conflict.[41] In all probability, he would have preferred to be remembered as a Chinese war hero. By conferring on him the posthumous rank of major general after the war, the KMT government certainly saw him as one. As Hong and Huang conclude, Lim was simply a 'brave and civic-minded' individual 'who happened to function in Singapore'.[42] The best the Singapore Story can do, then, is to claim Lim as a Singapore war hero retrospectively by emphasizing his links to Singapore, glorifying how his sacrifice benefited the country, but underplaying the fact that his heart may actually have pined for a different motherland.

This distinction between Singapore and Singapore*an* war hero, however, is not always clear. Lim's story in the Singapore national narrative is told in such a way as to make him appear to be a *bona fide* Singaporean martyr to an uncritical audience, an impression that has seemingly become common historical knowledge in Singapore. How Lim was commemorated on the fiftieth anniversary of his death is particularly instructive. A ceremony at his memorial at the Esplanade was described by its organizer, The Singapore Chinese Chamber of Commerce and Industry (SCCCI), as 'Singapore's way of marking a hero's contribution to his country during World War II'.[43] Lim had now become Singaporean. More tellingly, a tribute in *The Straits Times* singled him out as a source of inspiration for younger Singaporeans, for 'men like Maj-Gen Lim took responsibility for the destiny of a people [Singaporeans] under Japanese subjugation'. Demonstrating the full process of this (mis)appropriation, the tribute concluded that Singaporeans, were fortunate to have a personality such as Lim, implicitly Singaporean in the article, to admire.[44]

Moving away from 'foreign talent': Conscripting the local military hero[45]

When scrutinized carefully, Lim's place as a Singapore war hero thus looks more contentious than the Singapore Story makes it out to be. He, however, continues to loom large in the Singaporean historical consciousness because it is informed by a national narrative that emphasizes the big and the grand. Lim fits that mould perfectly, which makes his appropriation as a national military hero so easy. This overwhelming consensus regarding the appropriation of Lim as a war hero has unfortunately eclipsed other Singaporeans who have heroically served in uniform.

Consider these two narratives:

> Many people remember Major-General Lim Bo Seng as the man who chose to die at the hands of his Japanese torturers rather than expose his anti-Japanese guerrilla comrades.[46]

> On that unfortunate day [26 Aug 1970],... [Second Lieutenant Tay Siow Kai of] the Singapore Armed Forces was killed after a live grenade exploded in his hands as he tried to save the life of a recruit and corporal under his command.[47]

Lim and Second Lieutenant (2LT) Tay both acted bravely in times of crisis – Lim in war, and Tay during a military training accident. Both were incontestably, and fatally, heroic. Far fewer, however, remember who Tay was, let alone honour him as they do Lim. In recognition of Tay's gallant act, a donation drive organized shortly after his death raised $583 for his family, a sum that was only slightly more than his monthly army allowance of $480. The memory of Tay's heroic deed was soon forgotten. It was only after a remarkably similar training mishap almost 40 years later, in 2008, when another conscript officer saved the life of a recruit, that Tay's name was recalled from the depths of Singapore history. Even then, interest did not amount to more than a solitary newspaper article.[48]

The hitherto noted framework of history that values the great, the dramatic and the distant arguably plays a key role in the exclusion of Tay's story from the national narrative. Tay was not a 'great' individual till his heroic act, but merely a nondescript young Singaporean man serving his National Service, like hundreds of other men his age. Even after his death, he still remained largely unremembered. The training accident which led to his death, while dramatic on its own, was broadly, historically insignificant – it had no bearing on Singapore's present, or future. Finally, the year of Tay's death, 1970, was the beginning of Singapore's present, not a removed past. It marked the start of a stable, modern Singapore, when optimism was beginning to displace the fear and uncertainty that followed separation from Malaysia, and Britain's surprise 'East of Suez' announcement of an earlier-than-anticipated withdrawal from Singapore. Decades of growth leading to the present would follow, development that was aided by a peaceful national environ that has left the racial and political strife of the preceding years behind. In sum, Tay's story does not fit the current mould that the Singapore Story is cast from, even though he is unquestionably a Singapore*an* military hero.

It is time the Singapore*an* military hero, as opposed to a Singapore war hero, is written into the Singapore Story, particularly as the passing of time urges the addition of new chapters. The conscript nature of the SAF, for one, guarantees an instant, appreciative audience. With National Service, served mainly in the military, compulsory for all able-bodied male Singaporeans, the act of a heroic brother-in-arms will resonate with a significant section of Singapore's population. It is currently estimated that the SAF's mobilized strength is approximately 350,000, a figure that excludes those who have already been retired from their National Service cycle.[49] The number of Singaporeans with personal military experience is therefore actually far larger. Lim's story may adequately deliver the messages of righteousness and patriotism, but there can be no better courier of such a message than a fellow SAF soldier who acted heroically while in the service of his own country, Singapore.

Ronald Krebs argues that the military serves as the 'school of the nation' for it is an important vehicle for spreading desirable social values, one that has served the important nation-building role since ancient Greece.[50] Such a function is undisputed among governments and scholars alike.[51] This is certainly acknowledged in Singapore too, for NEXUS, formerly the Central National Education Office (CNEO), is administered by the Ministry of Defence (MINDEF), its head a serving senior officer in the SAF.[52] Set up in 1971 as the National Education Branch 'to get buy-in for National Service and inculcate loyalty to the nation', NEXUS now provides the 'strategic planning, direction and coordination of the NE initiatives' in Singapore.[53] In essence, it is one of the main arbiters of the Singapore Story, which explains the strong security slant to Singapore's national narrative. If the military does indeed play an important role in nation building by providing useful mechanisms, and in the case of NEXUS, entire programmes, to spread collective notions of national identity, Singaporean military heroes could have a larger role to play in the national narrative. This is all the more convenient in geographically small Singapore, with its consistently large defence budget and the omniscience of military National Service.

The SAF certainly does not lack military heroes. Tay's tremendous act of bravery may have unfortunately escaped official recognition, but the SAF has recognized other conspicuous acts of gallantry in recent years. Singaporean law allows four medals to be awarded to members of SAF for acts of bravery – the Bintang Temasek (Star of Temasek), Pingat Kehormatan (Medal of Honour), Pingat Gagah Perkasa (Tentara) (SAF Conspicuous Gallantry Medal) and the Pingat Jasa Perwira (Tentara) (SAF Medal for Distinguished Act).[54] The latter was incepted in 1997 to acknowledge 'individuals who have performed an act or series of acts of courage in hazardous circumstances without regard for personal safety'.[55] It is the only medal that has publicized recipients, possibly because the first three are awarded for bravery in war, though this has not been officially declared.

In the 15 years since its introduction in 1997, the Pingat Jasa Perwira (Tentara) has been awarded to six SAF servicemen. First Sergeant (1SG) Teo Boon Hong, First Warrant Officer (1WO) Mohinder Singh and Lieutenant Colonel (LTC) Toh Boh Kwee received the award for acts of heroism following an overseas training accident that occurred in New Zealand. Captain (CPT) Kok

Yin Khong and LTC Lo Yong Poo received the medal for rescuing fellow peace-keepers while under fire during United Nations missions in Kuwait and Afghanistan, respectively. The sixth and most recent recipient, 2LT Kok Khew Fai, shielded a recruit from a grenade blast during a training accident, a mishap that was similar to the one that had claimed Tay's life 38 years earlier.[56] Through their individual acts, each medal recipient showed the same values of sacrifice, bravery and selflessness that Lim embodied. As role models for Singaporeans, they too deserve equal place in the national narrative. War should no longer be the only criterion for acknowledging heroism.

War, the traditional 'well-spring of heroic individuals',[57] is also becoming a rarity. Such was the trauma of the Japanese Occupation that the fifth of six key messages of the NE programme is 'We must ourselves defend Singapore', recognition that 'no one else is responsible for our security and well-being'.[58] In the Singapore Story, that particular war therefore serves the unitary purpose of reminding younger generations to be on guard and interested in defence always, even during peace-time.[59] The memory of Lim's heroism is invoked because it emphasizes this point well. It also fits with the Singapore Story's overall account of the country's survival against almost insurmountable odds. On the other hand, why each of the six recipients of the Pingat Jasa Perwira (Tentara) was commended better reflects the reality of the strategic environment of Singapore that current and future chapters of the Singapore Story will have to account for. War, in these chapters, will feature minutely, if at all.

Admittedly, Teo, Singh and Toh received their medals for gallantry during an accident that was conducted to prepare them for possible war in the future. In that sense, war, albeit rather abstractly, will always still claim a place as Singapore's national narrative develops. What, however, draws more attention is where the training was conducted – New Zealand. That the military exercise was conducted in partnership with the New Zealand Army, in their country, shifts the emphasis away from the preparation for war specifically, to the globalized nature of contemporary Singapore, where international links are valued, and the geographic notion of national space expanded. That a New Zealand Army officer, Lieutenant Leroy Forest, was also conferred the Pingat Jasa Perwira (Tentara) for bravery during the accident also highlights this. The military thus acts as a conduit of diplomacy, its role expanded beyond just war fighting specifically. This is better shown by where and why CPT Kok and Lo acted heroically. Both were serving overseas on behalf of the United Nations, part of contingents of peacekeepers that Singapore, as a responsible global citizen, contributed to. Military heroes can, and should be, drawn from this new strategic context of Operations Other Than War (OOTW), rather than strictly war, even if that is what is intuitively (and perhaps romantically) associated with the military. The Singapore Story, therefore, has to take into account what some have described as the dawn of the postmodern military, where armed forces take on missions that are not usually thought to be military in nature.[60] With National Service already a uniquely Singaporean institution, deeply woven into the country's social fabric, and globalization entrenched in the national psyche, it thus makes better sense for Singaporean military heroes to be chosen from the SAF, even if they do not fit the mould of the great, dramatic and distant that the current Singapore Story framework demands.[61]

The need to replace this elitist approach to scripting the national narrative is urgent, especially as it is used in the NE programme. NE was in part originally conceived as a response to a survey conducted by a local newspaper, and subsequently verified by a larger one by the Ministry of Education, which revealed a stark lack of knowledge among Singaporean students of the country's early years as a fledgling independent nation. Owing to its greater emphasis in the school curriculum, Singaporean students had a better understanding of Singapore's pre-independence past. In an effort to shore up Singaporeans' understanding of 'the basic facts of how we became a nation', the history, moral education and social studies syllabi were revamped to accord greater attention to the post-independence years of nation building. This shift in focus to hitherto sidelined history, however, was just one prong of the National Education programme that was officially launched in 1997. Through other activities, greater emphasis was placed on how newly acquired 'book knowledge' could help Singaporeans connect themselves inextricably to the country, both in the heart, and by internalizing set values such as patriotism, social cohesion, self-sufficiency, meritocracy and perseverance.[62] As then-Prime Minister Goh Chok Tong put it, NE 'is an exercise to develop instincts that become part of the psyche of every child. It must engender a shared sense of nationhood, an understanding of how our past is relevant to our present and future.'[63] NE is thus a means to use selections from history to build the Singaporean character. Despite its reasonable intentions, this attempt to systematize the construction of the Singapore citizen has not been problem-free. The programme is increasingly ignored, or even rejected, by Singaporeans. Its usefulness in achieving its nation-building ambitions is therefore now questionable.

Chua Beng Huat suggests the indifference towards NE may ironically be the result of the programme being too successful, having made the current Singapore Story 'everyday knowledge', or 'common sense' to Singaporeans, so much so that continued representations of it have become 'tedious' and 'boring'. Inadvertently, the apparent hegemony of the national narrative has therefore resulted in a lack of interest among Singaporeans in investigating how the Singapore Story, as a narrative, is written.[64] Why bother if there is, after all, only one version?

Singaporean youth, however, are more critical. Some dismiss NE because they perceive it to be a nefarious programme of mass indoctrination organized by the PAP government. A survey recently revealed that 40 per cent of pupils interviewed felt that the National Education messages from Singapore history classes – the Singapore Story in a pedagogic form – were 'government propaganda', a criticism the Ministry of Education accepts, though it points to poor implementation rather than NE itself as the source of this cynicism.[65] A group of students even told the Minister of State for Education that National Education was boring because it was propaganda![66] However, perhaps fearing that they too would one day, like their elders, uncritically accept it as 'everyday knowledge', the group pondered if now was the 'time to look more searchingly at different sides to the Singapore Story'. Yet, reflecting the hegemony of the framework of the great, the dramatic and the distant, they still used an examination of history from the side of the '*Barisan Sosialis* activists and communists' as an example of looking at the Singapore Story from a fresh perspective.

More interesting, however, is a parallel curiousness among other young Singaporeans who wish to find out more about comparatively insignificant details of the Singapore Story, such as who designed the state flag or composed the national anthem. 'The 'history' that such young Singaporeans claimed to 'crave for', Hong observed of this phenomenon, 'was supplementary rather than alternative, and in the form of vignettes rather than analyses of Rajaratnam or Toh Chin Chye...'.[67] While history in the Singapore Story does not have to be revisionist or radically reconfigured, younger Singaporeans demand that how the Singapore Story is scoped, and what is considered for inclusion, be expanded broadly. Recognizing this interest, the National Heritage Board released a children's book in 2008 chronicling the contributions of 'lesser-known heroes of Singapore', the theme of that year's National HeritageFest.[68]

More specific to NE, the Committee on National Education reported in 2007 that feedback received suggested that interaction with those who could share first-hand accounts of Singapore's history, including 'SAF veterans', could animate the facts from history textbooks and therefore make NE more effective.[69] To that end, the committee's report proposed that the Singapore Story in NE be personalized by telling the stories of Singaporeans who 'contributed to Singapore society in different ways'. These personalities did not necessarily have to be members of the 'old guard', but commoners such as Hamida Ismail, a nurse who fell fatally ill from Severe Acute Respiratory Syndrome (SARS) while on duty during the global outbreak in 2003.[70] In this regard, those who were awarded the Pingat Jasa Perwira (Tentara) may be better symbols than MG Lim in the eyes of younger Singaporeans searching for new stories from Singapore's past because historical anecdotes of the commoner are apparently what Singaporean youths are now interested in. Whether the NE programme, and therefore the Singapore Story, will explore such a path, however, remains to be seen.

Conclusion

The Singapore Story has long been framed by the great person, the dramatic event and the distant period. This chapter has turned its attention away from the usual discussion of the politics of inclusion and exclusion within these hegemonic categories by looking instead at the problems this framework presents in the first place. As has been shown, Singaporeans with heroic credentials are excluded from the Singapore Story because they do not meet the inflexible requirements of the current structure of the Singaporean national narrative. At the same time, the ascendance of Lim Bo Seng, Singapore's best-known war hero, to such a position in the Singapore Story is also contentious. While this title may, *prima facie*, appear legitimate, Lim was neither Singaporean nor did he sacrifice his life for Singapore specifically. If he is to be used as the personification of patriotism, then Lim's actual nationality and political views are of fundamental importance. Yet, they are played down in the Singapore Story, his mainland Chinese nationalist leanings an inconvenient truth that would contradict the retrospective claim that he was a true Singapore patriot who saw the island as his homeland. Labelling Lim a Singapore war hero is still accurate in that it reflects who appropriated him as one. On the other hand, what that label also implies – that he was fighting for Singapore specifically – is mythical. The half-truth that Lim is a Singapore war hero in the fullest sense, however, continues to be perpetuated because it conveniently fits into the mould of the great, the dramatic and the distant, at the expense of the recognition of lesser-known Singaporean military heroes such as Tay. Thus, victims of exclusion from the Singapore national narrative are not only those who challenge or diminish the dominant Singapore Story with alternate accounts, a topic that is already vigorously debated in historiographic discourse on Singapore history, but also those from below, the cast of ordinary Singaporeans, especially those whose stories come from a past that tethers closer to the now than the then. Singapore's indigenous military heroes, common citizens only recently accorded such an honour for bravery in historically insignificant events, have thus been forgotten by the Singapore Story. Although it has been observed that 'the best heroes are the dead ones and the longer they have been dead, the more heroic they can be made out to be', recent Singaporean military heroes may, in effect, actually be more suitable candidates to personify the values of selflessness, sacrifice and bravery that Lim has long been the face of in the Singapore Story.[71]

As symbols, these military heroes, all Singaporean and all from its indigenous military, the SAF, may be more effective in uniting Singaporeans in appreciation of a common, relatable heritage. In particular, CPT Kok and 2LTs Tay and Kok are particularly appropriate candidates as they all were, or still are, national servicemen, citizen soldiers who put the rest of their lives on hold to serve the nation militarily with distinction, and are thereby examples worthy of emulation. With the awareness of the military already deeply hemmed into the Singaporean social fabric by the institution of National Service, the importance of defence and security in the NE programme and its coordination by MINDEF's NEXUS, these heroes can easily be incorporated into the national narrative. The NE programme, the main vehicle of the national narrative, needs to be rejuvenated for it is fast becoming seen as irrelevant to Singaporeans. This sense of irrelevance ironically is demonstrated from two extremely different perspectives: disinterest on the part of older Singaporeans because the Singapore Story has become hegemonic common sense and is therefore boring, and suspicion on the part of restless Singaporean youths who note the omissions in the national narrative and view the NE programme as government propaganda. Historical vignettes and anecdotes seem to be what young Singaporeans desire to see more of, but are denied because they are presently omitted by the narrowly scoped Singapore Story.

If the Singapore Story is to be used in nation building, its success will be determined by how well the general population relates to it. As the historical distance between the characters from the Singapore Story and the present extends, and the Singapore of the past becomes even more unrecognizable when placed next to the Singapore of the future, the risk of disinterest in it among future generations of Singaporeans will increase if the framework of the great, dramatic and distant continues to be used. It is therefore time to re-ask the questions of who, what and when and to record new answers from Singapore's 'history of the inside'.[72] To that end, conscripting new Singapore*an* military heroes for the Singapore Story offers a convenient place to start.

Notes

1 This paper was originally presented at *The Nation: Narratives and Community* workshop organized by the Centre for Excellence in National Security (CENS), S. Rajaratnam School of International Studies (RSIS) on 2 March 2009. Since then, others have also argued for a more deliberate commemoration of Singapore's own military heroes. See, for example, Samuel Chan, 'Making Things Right: Retrospective Honours for Distinguished Acts', *RSIS Commentaries* No. 38/2012 and K. C. Vijayan, 'Honour our Fallen National Servicemen', *The Straits Times*, 20 May 2012.
2 'Why We Need National Education', *The Straits Times*, 20 May 1997.
3 Ibid.
4 E. H. Carr argues that it is the 'why' question which matters the most in history. But the basis of a good answer to that question is always assembled from the answers to this triad of questions. See E. H. Carr, *What is History?* (London: Macmillan, 1961).
5 A virtual form of this exhibition can still be viewed online at www.sg/explore/multi-media_story.htm.
6 See, for example, Derek Heng, ed. *New Perspectives and Sources on the History of Singapore: A Multi-disciplinary Approach* (Singapore: National Library Board, 2006); Hong Lysa and Huang Jianli, *The Scripting of a National History: Singapore and Its Pasts* (Singapore: NUS Press, 2008).
7 Albert Lau, 'The National Past and the Writing of the History of Singapore', in Ban Kah Choon, Anne Pakir and Tong Chee Kong, eds. *Imagining Singapore* (Singapore: Eastern Universities Press, 2004), p. 50.
8 Loh Kah Seng, 'Rethinking Singapore's History from Below: Traditional Culture and Kinship in an Immigrant Society', in Derek Heng, ed. *New Perspectives and Sources on the History of Singapore*, p. 31.
9 C. J. W.-L. Wee, 'Our Island Story: Economic Development and the National Narrative in Singapore', in Abu Talib Ahmad and Tan Liok Eee, eds. *New Terrains in Southeast Asian History* (Singapore: Singapore University Press, 2003), p. 141.
10 Lim Swee Cheong, 'Problems Underlying National Education Today', *National Pioneer*, 9 February 1971, p. 1.
11 Hong Lysa and Huang Jianli, *The Scripting of a National History: Singapore and Its Pasts* (Singapore: NUS Press, 2008), p. 1.
12 Wang Gungwu, 'Contemporary and National History: A Double Challenge', in Wang Gungwu, ed. *Nation-building: Five Southeast Asian Histories* (Singapore: ISEAS Publications, 2005), p. 5.
13 Lee Kuan Yew, *The Singapore Story: Memoirs of Lee Kuan Yew* (Singapore: Marshall Cavendish Editions and The Straits Times Press, 1998), p. 8.
14 Lee Kuan Yew, *From Third World to First: The Singapore Story: 1965–2000* (Singapore: Times Media Private Limited, 2000), pp. 11–13.

15 Alistair Chew, 'The Proxy Arena: Singapore Education History as a Clash of Contending Global Perspectives', in Derek Heng, ed. *New Perspectives and Sources on the History of Singapore: A Multi-disciplinary Approach* (Singapore: National Library Board, 2006), p. 56.

16 Lau, 'The National Past', 44.

17 C. J. W.-L. Wee notes that the Singapore national narrative 'often foregrounds elite personalities ... and often sees the making of the nation-state as an idealist venture in which the indigenous bourgeoisie lead their people from subjugation to freedom' ('Our Island Story', p. 142).

18 Loh Kah Seng, 'Within the Singapore Story: The Use and Narrative of History in Singapore'. *Crossroads* 12, no. 2 (1998): 1.

19 Loh Kah Seng, 'Within the Singapore Story', p. 14, and 'Rethinking Singapore's History from Below', p. 31.

20 Gopal Baratham, 'Letter – Who Will Recount the Objective Truth?', *The Straits Times*, 22 May 1997.

21 Hong and Huang, *The Scripting of a National History*, p. 232.

22 Even theatre has been usefully employed to further this debate. In 2005, the play *Separation 40*, jointly staged by theatre companies in Singapore and Malaysia, contested the account of separation in the Singapore Story.

23 An interesting example of this is an exchange of letters in *The Straits Times* Forum. See Gilles Massot, 'Singapore History Began Long Before Raffles', *The Straits Times*, 16 November 2005; Derek Heng, 'How to Incorporate Our Indigenous Past', *The Straits Times*, 21 November 2005; Lim Siok Peng, 'Singapore History Before Raffles: Heritage Board Creates Awareness of Early Years', *The Straits Times*, 21 November 2005.

24 See Clara Show, *Lim Bo Seng: Singapore's Best Known War Hero* (Singapore: Asiapac, 1998).

25 Chua Mui Hoong, 'We Don't Need Another Hero, or Do We?', *The Straits Times*, 9 August 1991.

26 Lui Tuck Yew, 'Opening Address at Singapore HeritageFest 2008' (Speech, Causeway Point Shopping Centre, 12 July 2008).

27 George Yeo, 'Civic Society – Between the Family and the State', in V. Mohan, ed. *Inaugural NUSS Lecture: Civic Society* (Singapore: National University of Singapore Society, 1991), p. 7.

28 Goh Chok Tong, 'Whither Singapore?' (Speech, Nanyang Technological University, 11 May 1999).

29 Hong and Huang, *The Scripting of a National Narrative*, p. 169.

30 'In Memoriam: From Family Man to Fighter', *The Straits Times*, 30 June 1994.

31 Ray Tyers, *Singapore: Then and Now*, Volume 2 (Singapore: University Education Press, 1976), p. 516; Yeong Ah Seng, 'Where are the Heroes of Singapore?', *The Straits Times*, 29 June 1994.

32 MG Lim was buried with full military honours at a ceremony near MacRitchie Reservoir, where his remains are still interred. In 1954, a public memorial describing his heroic actions was erected at the Esplanade. Two years later, a road was named in his honour. Victor R. Savage and Brenda S. A. Yeoh, *Toponymics: A Study of Singapore Street Names* (Singapore: Eastern Universities Press, 2003), p. 57.

33 See, for example, 'Lim Bo Seng: A Hero's Death, 50 Years On', 'He Was Like a Father to Me, says Brother', *The Straits Times*, 28 June 1994; Yeong Ah Seng, 'Where are the Heroes of Singapore', *The Straits Times*, 29 June 1994; Dominic Nathan, 'A Tribute to Lim Bo Seng', 'In memoriam: From Family Man to Fighter', 'Lim Bo Seng Remembered', *The Straits Times*, 30 June 1994; Chen Bing-Yan, 'Letter – How about a Ceremony for our Unsung Heroes', *The Straits Times*, 1 July 1994.

34 'War Memoirs Inspire Essay Excellence from Students', *The Straits Times*, 6 August 1996; Ephraim Loy, 'Life Stories to Inspire', *The Straits Times*, 24 July 2006.

35 For a full treatment of this concern, see Asad-ul Iqbal Latif, 'Singapore's Missing War', in David Koh, ed. *Legacies of World War II in South and East Asia* (Singapore: ISEAS Publishing, 2007); Diana Wong, 'Memory Suppression and Memory Production: The Japanese Occupation of Singapore', in T. Fujitani, Geoffrey M. White and Lisa Yoneyama, eds. *Perilous Memories: The Asia-Pacific War(s)* (Durham, NC: Duke University Press, 2001).

36 Latif, 'Singapore's Missing War', pp. 96–98.

37 Wong, 'Memory Suppression and Production', pp. 232–234.

38 Admittedly, then-Minister for Information and the Arts George Yeo laid a wreath at Lim's memorial on the fiftieth anniversary of his death. Such official involvement in the commemoration of Lim has since stopped, perhaps because of caution arising from the resurgence of anti-Japanese sentiment from the mid-1990s onwards over the lack of acknowledgement of Japan's war-time past in Japanese school textbooks. These disputes are generally referred to as the 'Japanese Textbook Controversies'.

39 Hong and Huang explore this in greater detail; see *The Scripting of a National History*, pp. 163, 169–171.

40 Ibid., 169.

41 Eugene K. B. Tan, 'The Majority's Sacrifices and Yearnings', in Leo Suryadinata and Wang Gunwu, eds. *Ethnic Relations and Nation-building in Southeast Asia* (Singapore: ISEAS Publications, 2004), p. 182; Goh Chor Boon and Saravanan Gopinathan, 'History Education and the Construction of National Identity in Singapore, 1945–2000', in Edward Vickers and Alisa Jones, eds. *History Education and National Identity in East Asia*, 1st edn. (Abingdon: Routledge, 2005), p. 219.

42 Hong and Huang, *The Scripting of a National History*, p. 171.

43 'Lim Bo Seng: A Hero's Death, 50 Years On'.

44 Yeo, 'Where are the heroes of Singapore?'.

45 Hong and Huang wryly observe that popularly acknowledged national heroes of Singapore, such as Lim Bo Seng, were technically foreigners, the 'original "foreign talent"'; see *The Scripting of a National History*, p. 169.

46 'He was Like a Father to Me'.

47 David Boey, 'Let Us Honour Our SAF Heroes: Stories of Bravery by Our Men in Green Must be Passed On', *Today*, 9 September 2008.

48 Ibid.

49 Tim Huxley, *Defending the Lion City* (Crows Nest, NSW: Allen & Unwin, 2000), p. 93.

50 Ronald R. Krebs, *Fighting for Rights: Military Service and the Politics of Citizenship* (Ithaca, NY: Cornell University Press, 2006), p. 1.

51 Ibid., p. 2.

52 The director of NEXUS is typically an SAF colonel. By comparison, the heads of Army, Air Force and Navy recruitment in the SAF Careers Centre are only majors, indicative of NEXUS' scope of responsibilities and, more significantly, importance.

53 'NEXUS – About Us' (2009). Available from NEXUS (Central National Education Office), Singapore, at www.nexus.gov.sg/imindef/mindef_websites/topics/nexus/about_us.html.

54 'Prime Minister's Office – Info on Medals' (2008). Available from Prime Minister's Office, Info on Medals. At www.pmo.gov.sg/NationalHonoursandAwards/Infoon-Medals/Info+on+Medals.htm.

55 'MINDEF – News – SAF Medal for Distinguished Act (14 Jul 97)'. Available from MINDEF News Releases, at www.totaldefence.sg/imindef/news_and_events/nr/1997/jul/14jul97_nr2.html.

56 'Cyberpioneer – People – A Selfless Hero in Time of Need (October 2008)'. Available from Cyberpioneer, at www.mindef.gov.sg/imindef/publications/cyberpioneer/people/2008/oct08_people.html.

57 Hong and Huang, *The Scripting of a National History*, p. 163.

58 Ministry of Education – Committee on National Education, *Report of the Committee on National Education* (Singapore: Ministry of Education, 2007), p. 23.
59 Cindy Chou, *Beyond the Empires: Memories Untold* (Singapore: National Heritage Board, 1995), p. i.
60 Charles C. Moskos, John Allen Williams and David R. Segal, 'Armed Forces After the Cold War', in Charles C. Moskos, John Allen Williams and David R. Segal, eds. *The Postmodern Military: Armed Forces After the Cold War* (New York: Oxford University Press, 2000), p. 2.
61 Boey, 'Let Us Honour Our SAF Heroes'.
62 Goh Chok Tong, 'Prepare Our Children for the New Century: Teach Them Well' (Speech at the Harbour Pavilion World Trade Centre, 8 September 1996). The six NE messages imply these values: (1) Singapore is our homeland; this is where we belong, (2) We must preserve racial and religious harmony, (3) We must uphold meritocracy and incorruptibility, (4) No one owes Singapore a living, (5) We must ourselves defend Singapore, and (6) We have confidence in our future.
63 Ibid.
64 Hong and Huang, *The Scripting of a National History*, p. x.
65 Ministry of Education – Committee on National Education, *Report of the Committee on National Education*, p. 14.
66 Hong and Huang, *The Scripting of a National History*, p. 231.
67 Ibid., pp. 231–233.
68 Benita Aw Yeong, 'Secret Heroes among Us,' *The Straits Times*, 17 August 2008.
69 Ministry of Education – Committee on National Education, *Report of the Committee on National Education*, p. 15.
70 Ibid., p. 53.
71 Chua, 'We Don't Need Another Hero, or Do We?'.
72 Loh, 'Rethinking Singapore's History from Below', p. 31.

References

Aw Yeong, Benita. 'Secret Heroes among Us,' *The Straits Times*, 17 August 2008.
Baratham, Gopal. 'Letter – Who Will Recount the Objective Truth?', *The Straits Times*, 22 May 1997.
Boey, David. 'Let Us Honour Our SAF Heroes: Stories of Bravery by Our Men in Green Must be Passed On', *Today*, 9 September 2008.
Carr, E. H. *What is History?* (London: Macmillan, 1961).
Chan, Samuel. 'Making Things Right: Retrospective Honours for Distinguished Acts', *RSIS Commentaries* No. 38/2012.
Chen, Bing-Yan. 'Letter – How about a Ceremony for our Unsung Heroes', *The Straits Times*, 1 July 1994.
Chew, Alistair. 'The Proxy Arena: Singapore Education History as a Clash of Contending Global Perspectives', in Derek Heng Thiam Soon, ed. *New Perspectives and Sources on the History of Singapore: A Multi-disciplinary Approach* (Singapore: National Library Board, 2006), pp. 55–64.
Chou, Cindy. *Beyond the Empires: Memories Untold* (Singapore: National Heritage Board, 1995).
Chua Mui Hoong. 'We Don't Need Another Hero, or Do We?', *The Straits Times*, 9 August 1991.
'Cyberpioneer – People – A Selfless Hero in Time of Need (October 2008)'. Available at www.mindef.gov.sg/imindef/publications/cyberpioneer/people/2008/oct08_people.html.

Hong, Lysa and Huang Jianli. *The Scripting of a National History: Singapore and Its Pasts* (Singapore: NUS Press, 2008).

Goh Chok Tong. 'Prepare Our Children for the New Century: Teach Them Well'. Speech at Harbour Pavilion World Trade Centre, 8 September 1996.

Goh Chok Tong. 'Whither Singapore?'. Speech at Nanyang Technological University, 11 May 1999.

Goh Chor Boon and Saravanan Gopinathan. 'History Education and the Construction of National Identity in Singapore, 1945–2000', in Edward Vickers and Alisa Jones, eds. *History Education and National Identity in East Asia*, 1st edn (Abingdon: Routledge, 2005), pp. 203–225.

Heng, Derek. 'How to Incorporate Our Indigenous Past', *The Straits Times*, 21 November 2005.

Huxley, Tim. *Defending the Lion City* (Crows Nest, NSW: Allen & Unwin, 2000).

Krebs, Ronald R. *Fighting for Rights: Military Service and the Politics of Citizenship* (Ithaca, NY: Cornell University Press, 2006).

Latif, Asad-ul Iqbal. 'Singapore's Missing War', in David Koh, ed. *Legacies of World War II in South and East Asia* (Singapore: ISEAS Publishing, 2007), pp. 92–103.

Lau, Albert. 'The National Past and the Writing of the History of Singapore', in Ban Kah choon, Anne Pakir and Tong Chee Kong, eds. *Imagining Singapore* (Singapore: Eastern Universities Press, 2004) pp. 34–53.

Lee Kuan Yew. *From Third World to First: The Singapore Story: 1965–2000* (Singapore: Times Media Private Limited, 2000).

Lee Kuan Yew. *The Singapore Story: Memoirs of Lee Kuan Yew* (Singapore: Marshall Cavendish Editions and The Straits Times Press, 1998).

Lim, Siok Peng. 'Singapore History Before Raffles: Heritage Board Creates Awareness of Early Years', *The Straits Times*, 21 November 2005.

Lim Swee Cheong. 'Problems Underlying National Education Today', *National Pioneer*, 9 February 1971.

Loh Kah Seng. 'Rethinking Singapore's History from Below: Traditional Culture and Kinship in an Immigrant Society', in Derek Heng Thiam Soon, ed. *New Perspectives and Sources on the History of Singapore: A Multi-disciplinary Approach* (Singapore: National Library Board, 2006), pp. 55–64.

Loh Kah Seng. 'Within the Singapore Story: The Use and Narrative of History in Singapore', *Crossroads* 12, no. 2 (1998): 1–21.

Loy, Ephraim. 'Life Stories to Inspire', *The Straits Times*, 24 July 2006.

Lui Tuck Yew. 'Opening Address at Singapore HeritageFest 2008'. Speech at the Causeway Point Shopping Centre, 12 July 2008.

Massot, Gilles. 'Singapore History Began Long Before Raffles', *The Straits Times*, 16 November 2005.

'MINDEF – News – SAF Medal for Distinguished Act (14 July 97)'. Available from MINDEF News Releases, at www.totaldefence.sg/imindef/news_and_events/nr/1997/jul/14jul97_nr2.html.

Ministry of Education – Committee on National Education. *Report of the Committee on National Education* (Singapore: Ministry of Education, 2007).

Moskos, Charles C., Williams, John Allen and Segal, David R. 'Armed Forces after the Cold War', in Charles C. Moskos, John Allen Williams and David R. Segal, eds. *The Postmodern Military: Armed Forces After the Cold War* (New York: Oxford University Press, 2000), pp. 1–13.

Nathan, Dominic. 'A Tribute to Lim Bo Seng', *The Straits Times*, 30 June 1994.

NEXUS (Central National Education Office, Singapore). 'About Us' (2009). Available at www.nexus.gov.sg/imindef/mindef_websites/topics/nexus/about_us.html.

Prime Minister's Office. 'Prime Minister's Office – Info on Medals' (2008) Available at www.pmo.gov.sg/NationalHonoursandAwards/InfoonMedals/Info+on+Medals.htm.

Savage, Victor R. and Brenda S. A. Yeoh. *Toponymics: A Study of Singapore Street Names* (Singapore: Eastern Universities Press, 2003).

Show, Clara. *Lim Bo Seng: Singapore's Best Known War Hero* (Singapore: Asiapac, 1998).

Straits Times, The. 'He Was Like a Father to Me, says Brother', 28 June 1994.

Straits Times, The. 'Lim Bo Seng: A Hero's Death, 50 Years On', 28 June 1994.

Straits Times, The. 'In Memoriam: From Family Man to Fighter', 30 June 1994.

Straits Times, The. 'Lim Bo Seng Remembered', 30 June 1994.

Straits Times, The. 'War Memoirs Inspire Essay Excellence from Students', 6 August 1996.

Tan, Eugene K. B. 'The Majority's Sacrifices and Yearnings', in Leo Suryadinata and Wang Gunwu, eds. *Ethnic Relations and Nation-building in Southeast Asia* (Singapore: ISEAS Publications, 2004), pp. 168–206.

Tyers, Ray. *Singapore: Then and Now*, Volume 2 (Singapore: University Education Press, 1976).

Vijayan, K. C. 'Honour Our Fallen National Servicemen,' *The Straits Times*, 20 May 2012.

Wang Gungwu. 'Contemporary and National History: A Double Challenge', in Wang Gungwu, ed. *Nation-building: Five Southeast Asian Histories* (Singapore: ISEAS Publications, 2005), pp. 1–20.

Wee, C. J. W.-L. 'Our Island Story: Economic Development and the National Narrative in Singapore', in Abu Talib Ahmad and Tan Liok Eee, eds. *New Terrains in Southeast Asian History* (Singapore: Singapore University Press, 2003), pp. 141–167.

Wong, Diana. 'Memory Suppression and Memory Production: The Japanese Occupation of Singapore', in T. Fujitani, Geoffrey M. White and Lisa Yoneyama, eds. *Perilous Memories: The Asia-Pacific War(s)* (Durham, NC: Duke University Press, 2001), pp. 218–238.

Yeo, George. 'Civic Society – Between the Family and the State', in V. Mohan, ed. *Inaugural NUSS Lecture: Civic Society* (Singapore: National University of Singapore Society, 1991), pp. 5–16.

Yeong, Ah Seng. 'Where are the Heroes of Singapore?', *The Straits Times*, 29 June 1994.

2 The nation and its murals

A reading of figural images in Malaysia, 1957–1969

Lai Chee Kien

In *The Wretched of the Earth*, Frantz Fanon discussed the various psyches produced in the postcolonial nation by its new 'indigenous' government and
citizens, and how these may precipitate the resultant cultures and their extent
forms. Besides identifying the struggles between colonial forces and native intellectuals during those time periods, he highlighted a group of 'native artists and
architects' whose task was to represent the new nation and new citizen and give
form and shape to those national cultures.[1] These artists and architects would
interpret mainly state aspirations or projections through literature, art, dance,
theatre, architecture and other forms of expression for its citizens as well as formulate larger external projections to outsiders. For each decolonizing nation, the
discourse informed the choice of artists, the contexts in which representations
were made and the content matter of the works themselves in response to the
exigencies of this 'new nation'. In this chapter I explore the national cultural
productions at the time of Independence in Malaya/Malaysia from 1957 to 1969.
The contexts of these productions as wall murals are examined to assess how
they were intended to give form to aspects of national identity, national narratives and the national citizen. I argue that a serial reading of the mural form that
was prevalent in 1960s Malaysia can provide the medium through which the
nation was actively imagined.

Race and the postcolonial citizen

As a country, ethnicity has consistently entered Malaysia's histories and politics
as an important consideration. Historian Cheah Boon Kheng has described how
the first few leaders of post-war Malaya, notably Onn Jaafar and Tunku Abdul
Rahman, oscillated politically between Malay nationalism and a more inclusive
multi-ethnic/plural nationalism for its constitutive populations.[2] The racially distinct categories of Malay, Chinese and Indian had been created by British colonizers to specify labour for colonial commerce and simultaneously dictate the
governance of the various groups through spatial segregation and differentiated
social policies.[3] The categories had obviously been inadequate in denoting the
diversity of subgroups and *mestizo* ones within these categories and also did not
account for their interactions.[4]

After the war, pending imminent British departure, the experiment of creating a Malayan Union in 1946 that sought to provide equal citizenship status to all its inhabitants was rejected by the Malay groups. This sparked the first awakenings of Malay nationalism, the formation of an ethnically-Malay political party (UMNO) and claims of primary sovereignty status for the Malays in what is generally acknowledged as *Tanah Melayu* (Land of the Malays). The claims of original settlement by the Malays on the Malay Peninsula, however, also met with challenges. The heralding of a *bumiputra* (sons of the soil) Malay people created tension with other claimants such as the Orang Asli or 'original peoples', who had long lived and continue to dwell in the interior forests and mountains. Archaeological excavations in the northern parts of the peninsula had also yielded evidence of early Indianized settlements on both the north-western and north-eastern coasts as far back as the second century.[5]

In 1955, Tunku Abdul Rahman rose to become the leader of a plural political party known as the Alliance Party to contest the first federal elections in Malaya. His own United Malays National Organisation (UMNO) party was combined with the Malayan Chinese Association (MCA) and the Malayan Indian Congress (MIC) to represent the three largest racial groups in the land. On securing a resounding majority victory in the elections, Tunku Abdul Rahman, as the nation's first prime minister, proclaimed that: 'No one can say it is a Malay government. It is an all-community government, a microcosm of the people of Malaya.'[6] The pronouncement revealed a concern with racial issues at the core of national issues, but at the same time quelled allegations that racial chauvinism partial to the majority Malay population would be the basis of indigenous governance of the new nation.

Much later, the decision by the Tunku to create a Greater Malaysia out of the remaining British colonies in Southeast Asia in 1963 drew opposition from Indonesia and resistance from the Philippines. Once again, ethnic calculations undergirded the new geopolitical entity's conception. By incorporating Singapore and its predominantly Chinese population into the Federation, Malaysia would share the island's desirable and advantageous port and defence facilities, and mute the potential communist threat in the erstwhile British colony. However the merger would also increase the Chinese population to 44 per cent in comparison to the 42 per cent Malay population.[7] The alleviation of this problem lay in the absorption of Brunei, North Borneo and Sarawak on the island of Borneo as 'East Malaysia' to increase the ratio of Malays to 41.5 per cent and decrease that of the Chinese to 38 per cent.[8] At the same time, more indigenous groups such as the Kadazandusun, Iban and Dayak entered the fray.[9] Ethnic mapping across a continuously changing geographical landscape subsequent to this period increased in complexity, especially with the separation of Singapore from the Federation in 1965.

The constitutive parties within the Alliance Party coalition remained, however, largely racially and operationally distinct. Apart from political affiliation and Cabinet formation, the three parties did little to ensure ethnic commingling amongst members of its respective echelons across the country. The

legitimacy of the groups within the Alliance to represent the various ethnic communities was often questioned, leading to subsequent party fractures and new
offshoots. On the ground, the geography of Kuala Lumpur had also reflected a
racially divided landscape as a result of the colonial policy of segregation. The
capital city had originally been established in the mid-nineteenth century by tin
miners who were largely Chinese, and whose populations grew exponentially
over the years to form the city's main residential ethnic group. This number was
complemented by Indian communities in adjacent towns and plantations, various
Malay settlements on the fringes of the city centre, and other minor ethnicities,
including descendents of European settlers. By the end of the 1960s, there were
more than half a million people in the city, but the communal ratios for its population were not significantly altered.

The ethnic divisions as presented in the nascent nation, as well as the segreg-
ated landscape of Malaysia's capital city, would later exacerbate dormant communal tensions between the different groups. On 13 May 1969, racially
motivated riots erupted in the capital city following a national election, resulting
in hundreds of deaths and much destruction of property. While the repercussions
of similar clashes were also experienced in several other cities in the country, the
fiercest confrontations occurred in Kuala Lumpur over several days when a government largely paralyzed by the events was unable to contain the violence and
destruction. Parliament resumed only in February 1971, along with a change of
prime minister, and soon afterwards the New Economic Policy (NEP) was introduced as part of the Second Malaysia Plan. The various principles were to have
wide-ranging social and political impacts that shape the country to this day.

The study of Malaysia's history between 1957 and 1969 is thus crucial to
understanding the extent and framework of decolonization and nationalism in a
Southeast Asian nation. The cultural production of nationhood, as Fanon has
proposed, was 'a vigorous style, alive with rhythms, stuck through and through
with bursting life; ...full of color, [but also] bronzed, sunbaked, and violent'.[10]
Cheah has argued that there were ferments of both Malay nationalism and
'multi-cultural Malaya' pluralism during the first decade of the nation's political
life, but the prime minister delayed the full implementation of the 'Malay nation
state' for the purpose of consolidating and imagining it as 'nation'.[11] Given
Fanon's prediction of form and the presence of plural nationalisms, what were
the forms of expression in Malaysia of the time and how was the nation's population portrayed in them or projected from them?

Expressions of art and architecture in independent Malaya

With the advent of independence, the government in Malaya capitalized on its
strong export-based economy, established a public works programme and
encouraged civil fervour to construct infrastructural and national projects
throughout the peninsula, especially in the capital city of Kuala Lumpur. These
monuments included a language agency, a national mosque, a university, a
museum, a memorial, two stadiums and a parliament house, all of which, it was

hoped, would serve as symbols of liberation and disengagement from the colonial predecessors and as catalysts to ferment new national imaginings. They served to metrofit and to raise it to the status of city, but were also a means to project state aspirations, especially of physical development and the attainment of democracy, to both its peoples and the international arena. In 1963, the Agong personally called on its citizens to construe the buildings as representing their host institutions and values, serving as important bases to foster their citizenship.

The modernist architecture employed for the national buildings in Kuala Lumpur affirmed the ease in transfer of trans-Atlantic architectural ideologies as emblematic of achieving 'modernity' in the 1950s and 1960s. Such modernist idioms and forms as eventually employed, however, were translated and hybridized rather than wholesale adoptions or adaptations of Western ones. The buildings' specific contexts and milieu, climatic demands, existing labour conditions and construction technologies, availability of building materials, and the architects and engineers themselves, played a role in transducing and creating a modern architectural language that veered from the tenets of Western modern architecture. The designers grappled formally with primary notions of postcoloniality, modernity, tradition and religion to spatialize expressions for celebration, congregation and commemoration. The suitability of introducing, incorporating or interpreting 'pre-existing tradition' to these built structures became a major contention in discourse about national architecture or an 'apt' national style. Much of this debate surrounded the manner in which the buildings were conceived and designed, or their fecundity as national symbols.

The interpellation of the subject of nation onto national culture was a project graduated in different forms for postcolonial Southeast Asian states. The new national buildings were, naturally, visual signs towards which a common, national gaze might be directed. In Kuala Lumpur, the visual consumption of the national projects did not terminate with their physical forms, or solely as presented architecture. Such buildings and monuments were converted into images that were disseminated through art, posters, stamps, currency notes, school textbooks, print images and film and television images. These images entered the lives of the national citizen through their quotidian use, visual consumption and as personal memory. Besides architecture, the citizen living in Malaya in the 1950s and 1960s was also immersed in an environment where art and popular culture, such as dance, theatre and film, constantly invited them to construe their existence as a national person. The mural form became an important feature of such buildings, evidenced by their frequent installation onto prominent wall surfaces, on exteriors or interiors. These offer space in which art and architecture, as well as issues of 'tradition' in relation to 'modernity', may be inscribed, read, contested or discussed.

As in architecture, for formal visual art practices, Malaysia also questioned the meaning of 'modern' in relation to pre-existing traditions at the momentous period of independence. In *Merdeka Makes Art, or Does It?*, T. K. Sabapathy outlined the various contesting forces at work in the realm of art production in

Malaysia during this period.[12] One group cherished the cathartic, expressive freedom and connections to modernity that were afforded by Abstract Expressionism, which was hailed as 'avant garde modern art'. Another group employed a painterly realism to transform, in Sabapathy's words, 'the mundane into images of mythical splendour in the belief that a newly emergent nation should be embodied in heroic imagery'.[13] Within the space of state-sponsored murals, artists who were commissioned or won competitions had to confront state or institutional aspirations head on, and mediate or translate onto the large-scale canvasses such political or social ideas. Regardless of their racial background or artistic affiliation, these artists answered the clarion call with figurative painting in some form or other, to render and portray aspects of the emergent national citizen and the nation's communities.

At one level, the inclusion of pictorial imagery and the extent of their employment revealed the reluctance of modernist architecture practitioners to expunge such imagery and ornament to conform to purist modernist aesthetics, forms, and spaces. At another, it showed how difficult it was for new national cultures and identities to be divorced entirely from their precolonial or premodern figurations and imagery, especially if there had been an enduring historical legacy of such representations. As an intersecting medium between art and architecture, the murals warrant our reading as a form that was significantly expressed nationally at a crucial period in the development of the nation of Malaysia to register the 'unconscious energies' of the emergent nation.

In the early premodern histories of Southeast Asia, there had been precedents to figuration in public art and architecture. Hindu–Buddhist complexes, such as Borobudur, Angkor Wat and the Bayon, conspicuously incorporated sculpture and relief elements to extol social, religious and political abidance. In colonial Malaya, figural imagery had long been present in religious buildings, such as *jataka* paintings in Buddhist temples, painted murals in Chinese ancestral temples, sculpted figurines in Hindu temples and stained glass panels in Christian or Catholic cathedrals. The British colonials were also prone to continuing this practice through similar depictions on memorials and civic buildings in Malaya and Singapore, including bas-relief, murals and sculpture for the main railway stations in Singapore and Malaysia. The national murals are a departure from these various forms in that figurations are no longer only in support of these religious or economic ideologies but are now co-opted into projective 'national' ideologies.

In professional discourses and debates in relation to the development of a modern 'Malayan' architecture, the inclusion or exclusion of imagery and ornament were issues. Such debates involved mostly overseas-trained practitioners and localized expatriates who naturally looked to prevalent trans-Atlantic models and perceived their secondary transmittance to developing nations as desirable corollaries of progress and Western modernity. The issues of formal interpretation, attention to local climate and conditions and use of materials and workmanship ranked high within that discourse. After the period of high modernism, even its most fervent operator – Le Corbusier – 'lapsed' into the use of imagery in buildings such as the Chandigarh complex in India. Figuration as transposed/ abstracted from traditional referents, or installed as murals or sculpture elsewhere in the world, were looked upon as alleviating the harsher aspects of modernist architecture or as ameliorating its transfer to new local milieus. Writing about the design of the Singapore Conference Hall and Trade Union House of 1963, Tan Kok Meng describes the incorporation of multicolour glass mosaics in its internal walls, based on abstracted patterns of interwoven mats of the Malays that use *pandanus* leaves, amidst the designers' refined understanding of volumetric, planar and environmental spaces.[14] The building had been designed by UK-trained local architects who returned to lead the profession in private practice and architectural education in Malaya and Singapore, and who were unabashedly regarded as the best champions of a universal, modernist architectural idiom, albeit filtered occidentally.[15] Tan discerned this situation as the presence of an 'other' that resisted the instrumentation of the modernist architectural language and prevented a foreclosure to discussions of post-independent architectural identities in Singapore and Malaya.[16]

Murals as state projects

The most impressive precedents for the use of large-scale murals for state projects may be found in Mexico and the United States from the 1920s to the 1940s. After the Mexican Revolution of the 1920s, Mexico produced artists whose murals became specific and vital forms of national expression. Diego Rivera, its most prolific exponent, participated in many state mural projects, including the famous 'History of Mexico' in Mexico City's National Palace, for which complex tableaux of figures, objects and locations were juxtaposed to narrate in pictorial form the social, political and religious changes from the time of the Aztecs right up to Rivera's own time.[17] Later, he rendered his individualistic and idiosyncratic views and projections of history, technology and politics in many mural commissions in the United States, including a controversial one for the RCA Building at Rockefeller Center in New York in 1933.[18]

Under Franklin Roosevelt's 'New Deal', the US Congress passed Acts legislating several billion dollars' worth of public works projects aimed at relieving unemployment during the Great Depression. These led to the Public Works of Art Project (PWAP) and the Works Progress Administration Federal Art Project (WPA/FAP).[19] Between 1933 and 1943, the programmes sponsored and produced 2,566 murals, among other media, which were based on various themes of history, social and cultural life, technology and economic production.[20]

We may explore the depiction of the new post-war Malayan nation through its mural production. During the 1960s, murals in Kuala Lumpur served the various purposes of projecting institutional or state 'messages' to a larger intended public. The first public one may have been the wall mural by Pauline Old at the Sungei Besi Airport built in 1956, a year before the country's independence. Commissions and competitions were also subsequently organized by state or other institutions such as the Arts Council for major public buildings in the city, for example banks, commercial companies and even schools and palaces. Four murals or mural sets installed onto national buildings are explored in this chapter as representing state murals. They are those on the Dewan Bahasa dan Pustaka (Literature and Language Agency), the Stadium Negara (National Stadium), the Muzium Negara (National Museum) and the Parliament House. These were commissioned by the state during a burst of fervour for murals carrying messages to project on to citizens.

The first huge public mural to be installed on national buildings in Kuala Lumpur was a composition by Ismail Mustam for the Dewan Bahasa dan Pustaka in 1961 (see Figure 2.1).[21] The Alliance government set up the agency first as the Balai Pustaka (Literature Agency) in 1956 and then constitutionally enacted Malay as the national language the following year. The setting up of the agency was the fulfilment of a campaign pledge made at the first federal elections of 1955, and sought to reinstate, develop and promote the use of Malay as the national language for literature, art and culture. English, instead of Malay, had been the dominant administrative and educational language under the colonial British administration and a redress was perceived as necessary after independence.[22]

The building had a T-shaped plan, formally connecting a low auditorium/cultural hall that can accommodate 1,000 persons, to a six-storey linear administrative block for a library and reading rooms, an archive and offices for translation, editing and language promotion. The slab block, with its uncompromising modernist idiom of a vertically segmented façade and modular panels and windows,

Figure 2.1 The Dewan Bahasa dan Pustaka with its central mural (by artist Ismail Mustam) at Edinburgh Circus.

was likened to 'a United Nations building in miniature'.[23] Notwithstanding its somewhat awkward conjunction, the building was introduced to the national public as incorporating 'Malay features': a roof garden sheltered by a canopy to symbolize 'outspread umbrellas and national dignity', and abstracted triangular and rectangular patterns constructed on both sides of the auditorium akin to traditional sarong motifs.[24]

The 65 × 25 ft glazed mosaic mural was the result of a design competition won by Ismail Mustam.[25] As it was prominently installed on the front façade of the building facing a roundabout, both the building and the mural became landmarks.[26] The official title of the mural was 'The Malayan Way of Life and the National Language', and it sought to herald both the agency's functions and aspirations.[27] At the centre of the mural is a group of five semi-abstract standing figures, nominally depicting a Sikh, Indian, Malay, Chinese and Eurasian perusing an open book with a stylized *daun lontar* (*lontar* palm leaf).[28] This central group is placed within an irregular green background that radiates diagonally towards its four corners to divide pictorial space into four other areas. The remaining areas are used to project multi-racial commingling in religious, cultural, educational, agricultural, industrial and technological activities. The message is easy to grasp: the use of a common language actualizes the idealized national space of Malaysia despite the citizens' different ethnic backgrounds.

The next set of murals was designed for the indoor stadium, Stadium Negara, and would explore figural representation of the new nation in a similar manner (see Figure 2.2). As the construction of the stadium neared completion in December 1961, a competition was organized by the Arts Council for designs for two large murals, each measuring 32 × 8 ft for the upper foyer of its main entrance, and two smaller ones measuring 18 × 7 ft for the side entrance vestibules.[29] The themes were set as Malayan folklore for the larger murals and sports for the smaller ones. The larger mural commissions in landscape format were won by two Chinese artists: Yee Chin Ming and Phoon Poh Hong.[30] Both attempted to portray Malayan life and culture with pictorial spaces saturated with the depiction of human figures from different ethnicities, attested by their costumes.[31] Yee's mural was segmented into eight equal vertical panels subdivided by thin white lines.[32] This time, 25 semi-abstract figures were distributed within the space of the panels, depicting the three main races in the midst of economic or social activity. In the other, Phoon's 22 human figures were shown

Figure 2.2 Mural design by Phoon Poh Hong for the Stadium Negara.

engaged in cultural activities, and inhabiting a seemingly contiguous background connected by overlapping rectangles across the horizontal space of the mural.[33]

On closer examination, other aspects of the murals' figuration were evident. Both artists appeared to have faithfully reflected Malaysia's existing ethnic ratios, using decreasing percentages of Malays, Chinese and then Indians, while minority groups such as the Orang Asli, Straits Chinese and Eurasians were absent. The groups of figures were also clustered within their own race groups in both murals, rather than shown to be interacting with one another, so much so that Malays, Chinese and Indians could be visually distinguished as separate groups on the mural surfaces. The four central panels of Yee's mural depicted Malays, with Chinese and Indian figures located on the four remaining panels on each side of the 'Malay' group. In Phoon's composition, 'Malay' figures inhabited the left half of the mural, and the other two races took up the right half.

Yet another competition for two more murals, each measuring 115×20 ft was organized by the Prime Minister's Department for the National Museum in June 1962. The two decorative murals were to be executed in Italian glass mosaic and had been planned by its architect, Ho Kok Hoe, to adorn the external walls of the galleries that face a major road (see Figure 2.3).[34] Cheong Laitong's entry was eventually selected out of five submissions by preselected artists.[35] The themes for the murals were 'Episodes of Malayan history' and 'Malayan crafts and craftsmen'.[36] At the outset, the artists were provided with a list of historical 'episodes' together with a set of historical photographs for reference.[37] The subject matter for the 'crafts' panel was less specific, but required the competitors to depict those representing Malayan culture.

The events and their time frames for the 'history' mural were as follows:[38]

1 Hindu–Buddhist period in North Malaya, 12th century
2 Admiral Cheng Ho's visit to Malacca, 1409
3 Hang Tuah–Hang Jebat duel, *c.*1475
4 Portuguese attack on Malacca, 1511
5 Bugis warrior princes at Johore, 1720
6 North Malaya–Thai connections, 1840
7 Signing of the Pangkor Treaty, 1874
8 Arrival of first railway train in Kuala Lumpur, 1886
9 Early planting of rubber in the Federation, 1900
10 Japanese Occupation, 1941
11 Merdeka, 1957

When the 'history' mural was eventually installed, the onlooker would read the events chronologically from right to left, as if reading a classical Islamic or Chinese text. Mubin Sheppard, the museum director, had a hand in determining and inscribing the 'chapters' of the nation's history and furnishing numeric dates for the selected events. Notably, the selection did not commence with the history of the Malaccan sultanate, but the settlement in the northern peninsula by Hindu–Buddhist settlers from Eastern Indian states.[39] Cheong depicted each episode with a group of human figures engaged in activity linked with the episode's theme, and endowed each with related and accompanying images as well. His eventual design for the 'crafts' panel depicted semi-abstract figures engaged in processes of 'handloom weaving, basket-making, brassware, *kris* and silverware [crafting], boat building, woodcarving, carpentry, pottery, leatherwork, batik and decorative kites [making]',[40] inspired by similar scenes he had witnessed on visits to the east coast of peninsular Malaya before and during the competition period.[41]

As a set of murals for a national building, these pieces show some problems if we conduct a close reading of their figurations and comparative representations of national history. While a cast of multi-ethnic characters – including British and Japanese – was used to reconstruct the events in the mural with the historical narrative, national cultural production (crafts) on the other mural comprised only crafts by Malays from the country's east coast, specifically the two coastal areas of Kelantan and Trengganu.[42] The state's representative statement and enactment of national history and national culture thus appeared to have been authored by different racial groups.[43]

The new Parliament House, which was nearing completion in 1963, was by far the most potent symbol of political democracy to be constructed in Malaysia. The architect responsible for its design, Ivor Shipley, sought at the outset to incorporate murals and sculpture into the buildings.[44] A major mural painting was planned for installation in the interior gable wall above the Speaker's platform inside the House of Representatives. He commissioned Chuah Thean Teng, an artist based in Penang and known for his innovation of a genre of painting incorporating batik printing techniques, to design several options to fit into the triangular gable wall measuring 60 ft at the base and 80 ft in height.[45] The selected design featured 52 human figures depicted in costume engaged in all manner of cultural activities. The figures or groups of figures themselves were distributed within an ochre-coloured background.[46] Though inhabited by a large number of figures in Malay dress, the racial composition in the mural seemingly

Figure 2.3 Mural competition entry submitted by artist Cheong Laitong for the Culture Gallery (above) and History Gallery (below) for the Muzium Negara (National Museum) (source: reproduced by permission of Cheong Laitong).

reflected the complexity of racial diversity in everyday Malaya, which was soon to be enlarged to include the peoples of Singapore and Borneo in 1963 as Malaysia. Distinguishable Malay, Chinese and Indian figures were evident, but also figures costumed as Orang Asli, and of Thai, Iban and Dayak races. All the figures are making music, dancing and moving as if synchronously resonating within the common space of the mural (see Figure 2.4).

However, the mural, along with other planned art and sculptures, was ultimately not installed at the Parliament House, thwarted by an external committee set up to decide upon their suitability.[47] Merits of the mural design aside, it was left to conjecture why such a potent visual and ethnic representation was not used in the most national of spaces. Was Chuah's mural depiction too proximate and truthful a representation of the real, multi-racial Malaysian people and nation in 1963?

Figure 2.4 Proposed mural design by artist Chuah Thean Teng for the House of Representatives, Parliament House. The design depicting comingling multi-ethnic groups was not installed.

In the four sets of murals, we can perceive the reliance on human figures as the main subject matter to capture or portray state-projected ideologies on buildings. The Dewan Bahasa dan Pustaka mural extolled the importance, but also the eventual dominance of the Malay language in the service of a plural society. The stadium murals were attempts at capturing the three ethnicities, but eventually these were grouped as official ratios and spatially registered as distinct and separate. The National Museum simplified a history involving different ethnic players, but culturally promoted specific Malay groups. The proposed mural for the House of Representatives at the Parliament House attempted to project that plurality, but was ultimately not installed. Collectively, they may support Cheah Boon Kheng's views regarding the oscillation between the two political stances of Malay and Malayan nationalism, through their cultural productions.

The Hang Tuah-Hang Jebat discourse

In order to examine Cheah's observations further, we need to discuss the Hang Tuah and Hang Jebat discourse as it also featured prominently in cultural productions of various forms. Their ethnicity had been nominated as Malay in literature, but there have also been doubts about these identities. As happened in other Southeast Asian nations, precolonial historical narratives were recalled for structuring the new national narrative and the concomitant creation of heroes in Malaysia. In the *Sĕjarah Mĕlayu* (*The Malay Annals*) written in 1536 AD, both Hang Tuah and Hang Jebat belonged to a group of noblemen warriors serving Sultan Mansur in Malacca. The Malaccan sultan ordered Hang Tuah's execution when he was reportedly carrying on an intrigue with a court lady, but was sheltered by the *bendahara* (a position akin to grand vizier or chief minister) and was moved out of the court.[48] Another nobleman, Hang Kasturi, attempted to avenge his friend by barricading the sultan's palace in defiance. Having no other recourse left to him, the *bendahara* brought Hang Tuah out of hiding, assuring the sultan that he was the only person capable of defeating Hang Kasturi. An epic duel between friends ensued and Hang Tuah killed Hang Kasturi. He was then promoted to the position of *laksamana* and led various military and naval expeditions before dying *c.*1500.[49]

Around 1700 AD, another work of classical Malay literature was written: *Hikayat Hang Tuah* or *The Epic Tale of Hang Tuah*. In this version, Hang Tuah is eulogized as the Malay man par excellence: he was ideal man, warrior and citizen, and lived throughout the entire 110 years of precolonial Malacca. His acquired weapon, a dagger or *kris* named Taming Sari, made him invincible. He is still calumniated in the story and sheltered by an elder statesman. Another nobleman, Hang Jebat (and not Hang Kasturi as in *Sĕjarah Mĕlayu*), makes himself master of the palace and is finally killed when Hang Tuah emerges and duels with him. Towards the end of the *Hikayat*, both the sultan's headgear and Hang Tuah's dagger are lost in a misadventure, and both men disappear in mysterious circumstances when the Portuguese invade and capture Malacca. In this version of the story, Hang Tuah was elevated to mythical proportions and ascribed as representative citizen of the entire period of precolonial Malacca.

The reappearance and adaptation of the narrative for the third time draws us into the historical fray of independence in Malaya and demonstrates how the text became important for state agents in re-inscribing political and popular culture. Mubin Sheppard, an Irish-born colonial servant in the Malayan civil service, published the first English translation of the narrative in 1949, after having initiated the project while interned at Changi Prison during the Second World War.[50] Before the war, Sheppard was British adviser to Negri Sembilan and had the opportunity to stage plays, musicals and a pageant commemorating the coronation of Queen Elizabeth and write versions of Malaya's history.[51] *The Adventures of Hang Tuah* was adapted freely from both the *Sĕjarah* and the *Hikayat*, although Sheppard purportedly exercised 'an author's discretion' in deciding between conflicting accounts and data, including the choice of Hang Jebat over Hang Kasturi.[52] Sheppard also abandoned the chronologies suggested by the previous texts for a sequence based on what he determined as 'the History of Malaya'. The work was popular and there were four editions and one reprint by 1960. Notably, this was the first text that provided a printed image of Hang Tuah.[53] This 'reincarnation' had a seemingly prescient ending: while asking the hand in marriage of a magical princess on behalf of the sultan of Malacca, Hang Tuah alone entered the princess's mountain cave dwelling. Soon afterwards, a representative of the princess appeared to bid his entourage's return to Malacca without Hang Tuah, as he would become immortal and watch over the land. Returning his dagger to them, she said: 'Take back his *kris* to Malacca, and let it be preserved for all time. In some far distant century the day may dawn when he will come again to claim it.'[54]

In the meantime, Sheppard would transform himself from a colonial civil servant into a postcolonial one serving the new government. He converted to Islam, and among other projects, set up various institutions for culture and heritage, including the National Museum, the National Archives and the National Art Gallery, and became the de facto cultural adviser for the new prime minister and nation.[55] He published fervently on subjects of history and culture, with many books on Malay heritage to his credit. The versions of his Hang Tuah narrative would now be translated from his text into other popular media.

His next post during the Emergency brought him to the capital city and an opportunity to stage a water pageant in Kuala Lumpur's Lake Gardens as part of a Festival of Malay Culture in July 1956. Sheppard produced the entire show and chose to showcase the Malacca sultanate and concentrated so much on the Malay hero that the prime minister remembered it afterwards as the 'Hang Tuah pageant'.[56] A year later, the Merdeka Historical Exhibition was staged at the Chinese Assembly Hall by the Malayan Historical Society as part of the Independence celebrations.[57] Once again, Sheppard was the instrumental contributor and determined the overall layout plan. The first exhibit that greeted visitors was titled 'Military Forces 15th to 20th Century' and comprised several soldier figures from various Malay Regiments attired in different military uniforms and looking up towards Hang Tuah – the consummate fifteenth-century warrior.[58] This exhibition thus conjoined historical warriors during the feudal period in Malacca with the Malay Regiment of the contemporary period.

Hang Tuah was also cited on various occasions in the historical period leading up to the nation's independence.   In December 1955, the press media celebrated the spirit of Hang Tuah after the British made secessions to independence just before negotiation talks by the Alliance Party with communist leaders in Baling.[59] In the same year, a Malay film was made by Malay Film Productions entitled *Hang Tuah*, starring popular actor P. Ramlee in the title role. The budget was close to one million dollars, and was the first local film shot in Eastman colour.[60] The film's narrative was based on Sheppard's textual version and commenced with five young friends defeating a gang of pirates and venturing to Gunung Ledang (Mount Ophir) in search of a guru who would teach them martial arts and magic.[61] They are subsequently inducted into the sultan's service, and the story's climax featured the duel between Tuah and Jebat. With normalcy returning to Malacca after Jebat's death, Hang Tuah contemplates the moral dilemma he faces, that of killing his friend but restoring the state, in the final scene by ruminating: 'Was Jebat right   or was I right?'

Released in January 1956, the film was screened all over the country and seven million people are estimated to have seen it.[62] It brought the issue of citizenship to the larger public through the perspectives of the two protagonists: Hang Tuah's blind and logically unsound loyalty to the state and Hang Jebat's outrage (*amok*) at the injustices committed against his friend and Malay society at large. Against the backdrop of the transfer of colonial power and the new government's uncertain battle with communism, Malayans were ambivalent regarding the choice of a hero to rally behind. As the title of the film suggested, and in many other government-linked cultural productions, the state promoted the role of Hang Tuah over that of Hang Jebat. Hang Tuah demonstrated unstinting loyalty to the Malaccan sultanate even if injustice had been inflicted on him – a useful legitimizing metaphor to placate various state sultans in light of a new multi-racial government and imminent British departure.[63] More importantly, the narrative restated and legitimized the need for an intervening class of warriors and, now, the military, to mediate and serve the interests of the sultans, the government and the people. Lastly, Hang Tuah was useful as a projective role model from the past to embody attributes of the new Malayan citizen, as he maintained the ethos, mentality and characteristics of the Malay identity.[64]

The increasing recognition of Hang Jebat's actions as 'the other' and as an equally legitimate form of citizenship was perhaps indicated by the number of local *sandiwara* and theatre performances that began to focus on him instead of Hang Tuah. As if in response, a Malay film bearing the title *Hang Jebat* was produced by Cathay-Keris in 1961.[65] It condensed the time frame of the narrative and began with an irate sultan declaring that 'Hang Tuah must be killed', with the assumption that the audience was able to enter the story at that juncture and understand what had occurred before that moment. Given ample time within the film, the protagonists were better developed and contrasted, but the film similarly climaxed with the duel and Jebat's death, although like the *Hang Tuah* film, the leads were portrayed as monogamous and their lives sanitized of the sexual intrigues implicated in the earlier texts. The film was so popular that it almost paid for its production within ten days.[66]

A wider audience that included historians, sociologists, dramatists, poets and film directors was increasingly in support of this bifurcation and the coexistence of Hang Jebat as an alternate hero or model.[67] Kassim Ahmad's 1959 dissertation at the University of Malaya, 'Characterization in Hikayat Hang Tuah', noted the simplification and standardization of all other narrative characters to herald no central hero but, rather, a binary construct between Hang Tuah and Hang Jebat, and ignited the debate academically.[68] In 1961, Ismail Mustam, the artist for the Dewan Bahasa mural, painted *The Last Fight – Hang Tuah & Hang Jebat*. It depicted the two in combat from an overhead vantage point, without identifying the warriors or hinting at the outcome of the duel.[69] The two are shown engaged within a circular arena of white and yellow, outside of which are pointed shards piercing through the ground plane, suggestive of spear tips penetrating from below the floorboards by a participating public. In these new accounts and texts, there was thus a conscious downplaying of the status of Hang Tuah, who was increasingly characterized as 'the lackey of the establishment', in favour of two possible narratives, or the existence of two, rather than one, hero figure. The heralding of Hang Jebat as a new 'modern' Malay hero required the citizen to judge for him or herself.[70]

In the meantime, either as hero narratives or as binary opposites, the two characters and their roles were further scrutinized by widening publics through media that now included many spheres of popular culture such as *sandiwara* (a form of drama), *bangsawan* (a form of Malay theatre) and comics. The Literature and Language Agency published many expositions on the topic, including simplified versions for primary and secondary school textbooks. Symbols and aspects from that era entered everyday and political life. In Malay politics, the party flag for the United Malays National Organization (UMNO) was designed to incorporate 'the colours of Hang Tuah, the sovereignty of the rulers, and the dominance of Islam in the Malay world'.[71] The eventual design featured a *kris*, a Malay dagger that is often invested with magic and power. *Silat*, the form of martial arts employed by the feudal heroes, became attributed to them and enjoyed a large following.[72] Years later two perpendicular roads near two national symbols – the Merdeka Stadium and the Literary and Language Agency – Jalan Shaw and Davidson Road, were renamed Jalan Hang Tuah and Jalan Hang Jebat, respectively.[73]

As the new National Museum (*Muzium Negara*) was nearing completion in 1962, Sheppard as museums director began curating its contents to fill two galleries divided under general themes of history and culture. The history gallery was now bifurcated into two longitudinal bays to distinguish between political and economic histories, unlike the undifferentiated Merdeka Historical Exhibition in 1957. Exhibits with new subject headings were added to the 1957 list, but like in 1957, the history bay concluded with the urban development of Kuala Lumpur. The three 'pre-colonial exhibits' of Malacca, Penang and Kedah (exhibit numbers 6, 7 and 9 in 1957) were joined by the previously omitted

Sri Vijaya, Riau-Johore and Perak civilizations. These were preceded by four archaeological exhibits and two on agricultural settlements. Compared with the 1957 exhibition's focus on rubber and tin, the museum's 'Economic History' bay included new exhibits on silver, brass, forestry, fishing, rice and textiles, supplemented by woodcarving, mats and basketry, and pottery. At the end of this bay was an entrance that led to a separate gallery about the lives and arte-facts of the indigenous peoples (Orang Asli). Thus, although the external wall mural of the museum's History Gallery listed one chronology of Malayan histor-ical events, the actual exhibits inside it described and displayed slightly different versions.

Hang Tuah would feature inside the History Gallery as a special feature. A seven-foot high, bronze-coated plaster figure of Hang Tuah, set in relief within an 8 × 8 feet timber frame, was conceived as early as January 1962 as one of the main features for the National Museum.[74] It was located centrally at the end of the political history bay and the section on the history of the Malacca sultanate, to 'dominate ... Malayan history'[75] in Sheppard's words. The life-size standing figure faced the viewer entering the gallery, his right hand clutching the hilt of a *kris* at his waist as if ready for action and his left holding another *kris* at the scabbard. A perimeter foliate border enclosed the scenes while a similar foliate line divided the frame horizontally into two bands behind the hero at the level of his knees. The background relief in the upper band showed the peak of Mount Ophir, while the two smaller reliefs in the lower band indicated significant vignettes from the hero's life: the five youths training with the *guru* at Mount Ophir's caves on the left, and the five defending the village against two men who had gone *amok*, on the right.[76] A phrase attributed to Hang Tuah, 'Ta' Melayu Hilang Di Dunia' (the Malays will not perish from the earth) was inscribed beneath the top border.

The first visual illustration of Hang Tuah in Sheppard's 1949 book was con-sidered 'too gentle' in appearance and he now looked to the First Malay Infantry Regiment to locate ideal models for the museum exhibit.[77] He needed an image that would portray 'the honesty, loyalty and drive in Malay character', and which could educate the visiting public as an ideal character projection.[78] He arranged for the First Malay Regiment to be assembled on their camp parade grounds and inspected each soldier for suitable facial features, together with Waveney Jenkins, the designated sculptor. Eventually, the two chosen soldiers posed for Jenkins, who merged their features into one composite Hang Tuah figure. Various consultants and museum staff provided advice on suitable clothing styles and pattern designs, as well as choices of regalia such as headgear and *kris*. Sheppard then required further adjustments when Jenkins finished the composition, to include drawn brows and aquiline noses so that the image was 'fiercer'.[79] While Cheong's 'history' mural on the museum's outer walls depicted the battle between Hang Tuah and Hang Jebat, this specially commissioned portrayal of Hang Tuah inside the gallery highlighted the official preference for Hang Tuah.

Over the years, the narrative has been etched into the national psyche to the extent that the country has variously refocused on it in times of political leadership crises.[80] This was particularly significant around the time of the May 1969 riots and the subsequent implementation of the New Economic Policy, and more recently, when Mahathir Mohammad characterized his former deputy prime minister as a 'disloyal warrior ... [who] used his power to have illicit sex', leading to his sacking and arrest in 1998.[81] The temporal characterization of Hang Tuah as a national hero up till 1959, and thereafter the establishment of Hang Jebat as a modern hero fighting against feudalism, colonialism and governmental indiscretions remains to this day.[82]

Re-enacting history and culture

The state's identification with Hang Tuah through Sheppard's orchestration had the consent of Tunku Abdul Rahman, the first prime minister. As *Bapa Malaysia* (Father of Malaysia), he commissioned the national buildings onto which the murals were installed. The buildings and murals changed the physical appearance of the capital city so much that Sheppard remarked how 'these landmarks are so much part of the local landscape that few can remember how featureless the town was before the genius of Tunku embellished the capital with evidence of his own imagination'.[83] As premier, but also a hereditary prince of Kedah, Tunku Abdul Rahman constructed symbolic images, as well as connected his personal life to that of the new nation which now identified with historic Malacca and its heroes.

Leading and representing the Alliance Party, Tunku negotiated independence from the British in London. After the Merdeka agreement was signed in London on 9 February 1956 to coincide with his fifty-third birthday, the mission arrived in Singapore eight days later. The next morning, he chose to fly to Malacca, rather than Kuala Lumpur, the capital city, to announce his success in attaining independence to the people of Malaya. He arrived at the city's *padang* wearing simple Malay headdress and clothes. 'Malaya,' he said, would soon 'regain the independence usurped by a foreign power more than four hundred years ago'.[84] Raising his *kris* with his left hand in the air, he led the crowd of about 50,000 people in chanting 'Merdeka!' ('Freedom!'). It was as if, as the finale in Sheppard's version had foretold – a reincarnated Hang Tuah had returned to Malacca to liberate his people after four centuries of colonization. In later remembrances of the Malacca declaration, the Tunku invoked the link with that hero, claiming: 'I never expected to be given the Kris of Hang Tuah, Malacca's legendary hero'.[85]

Besides being the site of Portuguese, Dutch and British colonization, the reference to Malacca in the crucial independence period would also reinstate the nation's legitimacy and primacy in the Malay world. The identification of the new nation state with Malacca not only forced a connection with the sultanate's history, but also emphasized its historical differentiation from Java, which was now in post-war Indonesia. Leonard Andaya has pointed out that, although the history and geography of 'Melayu' included the Melayu of present-day Indonesia and the Philippines, the textual creation of the *Sĕjarah* and *Hikayat* reaffirmed Malacca's centrality as 'the ultimate measure of all things Melayu'. It also spatially defined the phrase, '*Tanah Melayu*' (Land of Melayu), to refer specifically to the peninsula of Malaya.[86] The Tunku would return to the very same *padang* in Malacca in March 1963, this time to announce that the ideal date for the inauguration of the geographically enlarged Greater Malaysia was to be 10 July 1963, the anniversary of the first invasion of Malacca by the Portuguese in 1511.[87]

Conclusions

Benedict Anderson's seminal work, *Imagined Communities: Reflections on the Origins and Spread of Nationalism*, argued the importance of creating 'horizontal-secular, transverse-time' and print capitalism in the imagining of national communities.[88] In post-independence Malaya/Malaysia, such a time period intersected both precolonial and colonial time frames, respectively, for the history of the Malacca sultanate, as well as the plural communities formed through British colonization. By privileging English-language education and subjugating Malay, as well as other vernacular languages, the newspapers and novels in Malaysia did not quite enable the imagining of a particular national community through print capitalism. There was also no acknowledged 'great novel' in English or its indigenous languages.

Instead, murals on commissioned national buildings attempted to serve that role for the emergent community that had yet to attain general literacy in their forebear's tongues. In the interceding decade-dateline before *Bahasa Melayu*'s primary use in education and administration, figural images, rather than the print medium, created an alternative language that could be circulated through such national spaces. Depicted on murals or as visual media, these sought to evoke a similar 'horizontal-secular, transverse-time' and to generate national fervour. It is no surprise that the first large-scale mural in Kuala Lumpur was created on the external wall of the Dewan Bahasa dan Pustaka, the National Language and Literary Agency, to advertise the new language besides its own role of textual production. The murals on the four national buildings indicated local sentiments regarding oscillations between Malay and a more plural nationalism.

The recreation of a state-sanctioned hero for crafting a national narrative took the form of re-establishing the central role of Hang Tuah, a folk hero from the Malacca sultanate in the associative history of the Malays in peninsula Malaya. The development of a separate hero, Hang Jebat, derived from the same narrative origin, created two heroes whose intertwined relationships and actions became an important dual-narrative between the state and its people. The dissemination of information on Hang Jebat in the 1960s was made possible through popular forms of media such as film, art, *bangsawan*, comics and popular literature, rather than the official forms, such as the murals, sculpture and so on that heightened Hang Tuah's position. In place of a 'great novel' and print capitalism, the narrative and counter-narrative to galvanize the state and its people in Malaysia nationally was recalled from the past and occurred in particular non-print formats to approximate that 'horizontal-secular transverse-time'. Throughout this process, the figural representations of both Hang Tuah and Hang Jebat also had to be developed by both the state and other authors for a public whose own language had to be recast after decolonization.

Notes

1 Frantz Fanon, *The Wretched of the Earth* (New York: Grove Press, 1968), pp. 224–225.
2 Cheah Boon Kheng, *Malaysia: The Making of a Nation* (Singapore: Institute of Southeast Asian Studies, 2002), Chapters 1–3.
3 Using Hirschman's work in the Federation of Malaya, Anderson argued that the construction of simplistic categories such as Malay or Malaysian was arbitrary and problematic, and ultimately developed into clearly racial categories. Benedict Anderson, *Imagined Communities: Reflections on the Origins and Spread of Nationalism* (London: Verso, 1991), pp. 164–165.
4 For example, the Malay, Indian or Chinese groups each have distinct dialect subgroups. There are *mestizo* groups such as the Straits-born Chinese (Malay-Chinese), Eurasian and Thai–Malay groups at the northern borders. The minority groups are equally diverse and include those of Portuguese, Dutch and Armenian parentage, etc.
5 See Michael Tweedie, *Prehistoric Malaya* (Singapore: D. Moore, 1955); Alastair Lamb, *Chandi Bukit Batu Pahat* (Singapore: Eastern University Press, 1960).
6 Tunku Abdul Rahman, 'On the Road to Nationhood', in *The Straits Times Annual for 1957* (Singapore: The Straits Times Press, 1957), p. 4. He was widely regarded as the 'Father of Malaysia' and had several other appellations such as 'Father of the Nation' (*Bapa Negara*) and 'Father of Peace' (*Bapa Keamanan*).
7 The racial dynamics are well described in George Kahin, *Southeast Asia: A Testament* (London: RoutledgeCurzon, 2003), pp. 158–176.
8 Figures from *Time* LXXXI, no. 15, 12 April 1963, pp. 36–37. Brunei pulled out a few months before the actual merger.
9 Sarawak and Sabah are on the island of Borneo, which has historical and geographical characteristics of 'Island Southeast Asia' rather than of 'Mainland Southeast Asia', unlike the peninsula. The indigenous peoples of Borneo are also distinct from the 'aborigines' in the peninsula.
10 Frantz Fanon, 'On National Culture', in *The Wretched of the Earth*, p. 220.
11 Cheah Boon Kheng, *Malaysia*, pp. 76–77.
12 T. K. Sabapathy, 'Merdeka Makes Art, or Does it?', in T. K. Sabapathy, ed. *Vision and Idea: Relooking Modern Malaysian Art* (Kuala Lumpur: National Art Gallery, 1994), pp. 51–76.
13 The group, comprising mainly Malay artists, began as Majlis Kesenian Melayu in 1956 and was subsequently renamed Angkatan Pelukis Semenanjung. Sabapathy, 'Merdeka Makes Art, or Does it?', pp. 57–61; Marco Hsü, *A Brief History of Malayan Art* (translated and expanded by Lai Chee Kien) (Singapore: Millennium Books, 1999), p. 119. Fanon was of the opinion that 'after independence [the native painter's] anxiety to rejoin his people will confine him to the most detailed representation of reality'. Fanon, *The Wretched of the Earth*, p. 225.
14 Tan Kok Meng, 'Critical Weave: Interwoven Identities in the Singapore Conference Hall'. *Journal of South East Asian Architecture* 4, no. 1 (2000): 17–23.
15 The architectural team was a Malayan architect co-partnership, and originally comprised two architects trained in London and one in Manchester.
16 Tan Kok Meng, 'Critical Weave', pp. 22–23.
17 The mural was painted from 1929 to 1935.

18 Irene Herner, 'Diego Rivera: Paradise Lost in Rockefeller Center Revisited', in Juan Coronel Rivera, Fausto Ramirez, William H. Robinson, Dawn Ades and Paul Karlstrom, eds. *Diego Rivera, Art and Revolution* (Mexico City: Conaculta, 1999), pp. 247–258. The work, titled *Man at the Crossroads with Hope and High Vision to the Choosing of a New and Better Future*, explored Rivera's complex political readings. Herner noted how Lenin was portrayed as gathering workers' hands in his as a criticism of capitalism, but other elements condemned Stalinist Communism and Nazi Fascism as well.

19 Heather Becker, 'The Great Depression, the New Deal, and the WPA Federal Art Project,' in Heather Becker ed. *Art for the People: The Rediscovery and Preservation of Progressive- and WPA-era Murals in the Chicago Public Schools, 1904–1943* (San Francisco, CA: Chronicle Books, 2002), pp. 71–78.

20 Andrew Hemingway, 'The Debate on Art and the State in Post-war America', in Francis Ames-Lewis and Piotr Paszkiewicz, eds. *Art and Politics* (Warsaw: Institute of Art 1999), p. 154. Besides the murals, there were 17,744 pieces of sculpture, 108,900 paintings and 11,285 prints.

21 Marco Hsü, *A Brief History of Malayan Art*, p. 126.

22 A clause provided that English could still be used officially for a period of ten years after Merdeka Day. Syed Nasir bin Ismail, 'The Dewan and the National Language,' *A Brief Study of the History of the National Language* (Kuala Lumpur: Dewan Bahasa dan Pustaka, 1962), p. 31; *Malay Mail*, 31 January 1962, p. 5.

23 *Malay Mail*, 23 August 1961, p. 4. The building was described as 'an internal (*sic*, probably 'international-style') building with nuances of monumentality...' in Lilian Tay Ngiom, ed. *80 Years of Architecture in Malaysia* (Kuala Lumpur: Pertubuhan Akitek Malaysia, 2000), p. 91.

24 *Malay Mail*, 23 August 1961, p. 4; *Malay Mail*, 31 January 1962, p. 4.

25 The mural competition drew 44 entries. The winner of the first prize was awarded $1,500, and runners-up Yee Chin Ming and Nik Zainal Abidin each received $250. *Malay Mail*, 2 August 1961, p. 2; *Malay Mail*, 23 August 1961, p. 4.

26 This was Edinburgh Circle, later transformed into an elaborate four-way traffic junction.

27 Y.T. Lee, 'Dewan Bahasa dan Pustaka'. *BINA: Journal of the Federation of Malaya Society of Architects* 5, no. 1 (1964): pp. 22–24.

28 The central multiracial group, besides hinting at the unity of the races through a common language, is a subtle depiction of the Alliance party. Besides the five, East Malaysians, Caucasians and other races were also incorporated. Interview with Ismail Mustam, 24 July 2002.

29 *Malay Mail*, 19 December 1961, p. 5. A prize of $2,000 was offered for each winning large mural, and $1,000 for each of the smaller ones.

30 *Malay Mail*, 22 February 1962, p. 5. The winners were selected from 59 entries submitted by 28 artists.

31 Ibid., p. 18.

32 Some figures or objects overlap across the borders, but the divisions are nonetheless distinctive.

33 Marco Hsü, *A Brief History of Malayan Art*, p. 126.

34 In my interview with Ho Kok Hoe on 21 August 2001, he regarded the incorporation of murals as an act of marrying art with architecture. The construction and installation of the murals were financed by Singaporean millionaire Lee Kong Chian through Ho's contact, since the museum's construction and content curating had exceeded the $1.5 million budget. From Mubin Sheppard, *Taman Budiman: Memoirs of an Unorthodox Civil Servant* (Kuala Lumpur: Heinemann, 1979), pp. 233–234.

35 They were Chen Wen Hsi, Cheong Laitong, Chuah Thean Teng, Mohammad Hoessein Enas and Syed Ahmad Jamal. Email communication from Cheong Laitong to author, 9 April 2002. Cheong was one of the founders of the Wednesday Art Group, a pioneering art society in Kuala Lumpur, and is himself an accomplished artist.

50   *Lai Chee Kien*

36 *Malay Mail*, 14 June 1962, p. 10.
37 Interview with Cheong Laitong, 11 July 2002.
38 *BINA: Journal of the Federation of Malaya Society of Architects* 5, no. 1 (1964): 20. The elements of the serialization were also described in *Malay Mail*, 14 June 1962, p. 10; 24 November 1962, p. 12.
39 The commencement of history from the northern Kedah also legitimized the home state of Prime Minister Tunku Abdul Rahman.
40 Ho Kok Hoe, 'Museum Negara'. *BINA: Journal of the Federation of Malaya Society of Architects* 5, no. 1 (1964): pp. 19–21; *The Straits Times*, 31 August 1963, p. 14.
41 Telephone interview with artist, 28 March 2002. Cheong was then employed in the Malayan Film Unit and his experiences with Malay crafts were enriched by visits to M.A.H.A. exhibitions, as well as by his accompanying film crews to the East Coast to examine the craft production there closely.
42 One or two figures in the panel suggest ties with Thailand, Malaysia's border neighbour to the north, in craft production. While the mural was installed, the nation's politicians rallied for the construction of a Malaysia that would include the people of Borneo with large indigenous groups.
43 Cheong realized the problem with such a portrayal, and submitted an earlier draft without clothing on the figures so as to deflect the 'racial reflection'. This was rejected by the museum and thus sarongs or wraps were eventually used. From an interview with Cheong Laitong, 29 July 2003.
44 Besides seeing those installed in major Kuala Lumpur buildings, Shipley had also visited Chandigrah and remembered Le Corbusier's use of a fabric mural at the court building. From an interview with Ivor Shipley, 2 July 2001.
45 Interview with Ivor Shipley, 1 July 2001.
46 Chuah produced a full-colour painting for the architect. Interview with Chuah Thean Teng. Many art historians have noted Chuah's multi-racial project, including Dolores Wharton. Dolores D. Wharton, *Contemporary Artists of Malaysia: A Biographic Survey* (Petaling Jaya: Asia Society, 1971), pp. 15–16.
47 Interview with Ivor Shipley, 1 July 2001. While approving Chuah's portrayal of 'Malaysian human figures', Shipley was also somewhat disappointed that he had not painted with the abstracted, flowing style he had witnessed in his other paintings.
48 The *bendahara* was the court adviser to the sultan, somewhat like a grand vizier.
49 De Josselin de Jong, 'The Rise and Decline of a National Hero'. *Journal of the Malayan Branch of the Royal Asiatic Society* 38, no. 2 (1965): 140–141. The position of *laksamana* is roughly equivalent to supreme commander or admiral.
50 Mubin Sheppard, *Taman Budiman*, p. 221. In the same year, he published *History of Trengganu*, an east-coast state, begun similarly in prison. However, the first translation of *Hang Tuah* into romanized Indonesian was by Reinder Brons Middel in 1893, and into Malay by William G. Shellabear in 1908. The first version in Dutch was probably in 1906, and a version in German by Hans Overbeck was published in 1922.
51 Mubin Sheppard, *A Short History of Malaya* (Kuala Lumpur: B. T. Fudge, 1953); *Historic Malaya: An Outline History* (Singapore: Eastern University Press, 1959). The latter was first published as a supplement to the *Malayan Historical Journal* in 1956, and became prescribed as a textbook for government examinations in Malay.
52 Mubin Sheppard, 'Author's Note', *The Adventures of Hang Tuah* (Hong Kong: Oxford University Press, 1975), pp. 132–133. Sheppard justified the preference of Hang Jebat by aligning him with similar role characterizations occurring in local *bangsawan* (a form of Malay theatre) performances that he had witnessed. The other text in English that described the story was Ann and Cyril Parkinson's *Heroes of Malaya* (Singapore: D. Moore, 1956), targeted at children, which included Hang Tuah as one of 20 heroes.

53 The image was a lithograph by Kathleen Walker. In later 1950s reprints, this image was redrawn. An image of the hero was also illustrated in Sheppard's *Historic Malaya: An Outline History*, facing p. 10.

54 Mubin Sheppard, *The Adventures of Hang Tuah*, pp. 124–131.

55 Mubin Sheppard wrote his memoirs in 1979, as *Taman Budiman: Memoirs of an Unorthodox Civil Servant*.

56 Mubin Sheppard, *Taman Budiman*, pp. 212–213. He staged a similar pageant on 1 September 1957 as part of the Independence celebrations (p. 222).

57 The exhibition was held from 30 August to 8 September 1957. *Malaya in History* 4, no. 1, Merdeka Historical Exhibition issue.

58 Ibid., p. 4; Mubin Sheppard, *Taman Budiman*, p. 222.

59 T. N. Harper, *The End of Empire and the Making of Malaya* (Cambridge: Cambridge University Press, 1999), p. 347.

60 The parent company, Shaw Brothers, was based in Hong Kong and Singapore. The film was directed by Phani Mujumdar. James Harding and Ahmad Sarji. *P. Ramlee: The Bright Star* (Selangor Darul Ehsan, Malaysia: Pelanduk Publications, 2002, p. 69.

61 The first scene of the film showed a book with the words 'Hang Tuah' inscribed on the cover, and below it, an acknowledgement of Sheppard's authorship.

62 De Josselin de Jong, 'The Rise and Decline of a National Hero', p. 145.

63 According to the *Sejarah Melayu*, Hang Tuah served under the reigns of three Malaccan sultans.

64 T. N. Harper, *The End of Empire and the Making of Malaya*, p. 15; Mubin Sheppard, 'Treasure Trove', p. 56. In a 1989 film titled *Tuah*, the protagonist is shown time-travelling to the contemporary era.

65 *Hang Jebat* (1961), a black and white Cathay-Keris Film directed by Hussain Haniff.

66 De Josselin de Jong, 'The Rise and Decline of a National Hero', p. 147. He also pointed to the fact that Islam stresses self-inspection and is against hero worship, changing the perception of the Tuah–Jebat conflict.

67 T. K. Sabapathy, 'On Vision and Idea: Afterthoughts', in T. K. Sabapathy, ed. *Vision and Idea: Relooking Modern Malaysian Art* (Kuala Lumpur: National Art Gallery, 1994), p. 110.

68 Kassim Ahmad, *Characterization in Hikayat Hang Tuah* (Kuala Lumpur: Dewan Bahasa dan Pustaka, 1964), pp. 48–49. In the chapter analysing Jebat, he hailed his unique non-Western democratic role and termed him 'prophet and hero of Malay nationalism' (p. 33). Although written in 1959, Kassim's work was published only in 1966.

69 Interview with Ismail Mustam, 24 July 2002. The oil painting has also been well contextualized and analysed by T. K. Sabapathy in 'On Vision and Idea', pp. 110–112.

70 Interview with Ismail Mustam, 24 July 2002.

71 From Mohamed Abid, *Reflections of Pre-Independence Malaya* (Subang Jaya, Selangor: Pelanduk Publications, 2003), pp. 74–79. Syed Muhammad Naquib al-Attas was asked by Onn bin Jaafar, the first founder, to design the flag, which was composed of two bands, red over white, superimposed by a green *kris* on a central yellow circle. The red and white colours were related to those that Indonesia had adopted for its own national flag.

72 As discussed in Shaharuddin Maaruf, *Concept of a Hero in Malay Society* (Petaling Jaya, Selangor: Eastern University Press, 1984), pp. 60–73; Ahmad Mustaffa and Wong Kiew Kit, *Silat Melayu: The Malay Art of Attack and Defence* (Oxford, New York and Melbourne: Oxford University Press, 1978), pp. 1–2.

73 Besides road names, buildings were also taking on symbolic forms. A case in point is the Maybank Building by Hijjas Kasturi, the form of which is likened to the Taming Sari of Hang Tuah.

74 Ibid. In his memoirs, Sheppard disclosed that he had planned the bas relief 'from the outset'. From Mubin Sheppard, *Taman Budiman*, p. 228.

75 Mubin Sheppard, 'Treasure Trove', p. 56. The figure is sited so that 'he can be seen from a distance of over 100 feet'.
76 Interview with Waveney Jenkins, 25 March 2004.
77 Ibid. Like the 1957 exhibition, the Malay Regiment is once again associated with Hang Tuah, the mythical hero.
78 The 'ignominy of racial distinction' was a Malay concern during this period of nascent Malay nationalism, as described in Ishak Tadin, 'Dato Onn and Malay Nationalism, 1946–1951'. *Journal of Southeast Asian History* 1, no. 1 (1960): 65. Sheppard noted this phrase as 'Ta' Kan Melayu Hilang di Dunia' in his memoirs, and stated that its installation was 'an indirect appeal to preserve the traditions, character, identity, and wise philosophy of the true Malay in the modern world'. Mubin Sheppard, *Taman Budiman*, p. 228.
79 Ibid. The use of two soldiers instead of one as model alleviated the unease of figural Muslim representations. Besides the Hang Tuah relief, Jenkins, together with museum staff, also made 70 figures for seven dioramas. The bas relief has since been transferred to the National History Museum and designated as its very first exhibit to greet visitors.
80 Analyses have also varied, from those questioning elite feudal legacies and Islamic/universal themes by Shaharuddin Maaruf in *Concept of a Hero in Malay Society*, to feminist ones such as Khoo Gaik Cheng's 'Nationalism and Homoeroticism: A Feminist Reading of the Hang Tuah and Hang Jebat Debate', in Maznah Mohamad and Wong Soak Koon, eds. *Risking Malaysia: Culture, Politics and Identity* (Bangi: Penerbit Universiti Kebangsaan Malaysia, 2001).
81 Ziauddin Sardar, *The Consumption of Kuala Lumpur* (London: Reaktion Books, 2000), pp. 203–209. Ziauddin also described the mutable roles that Mahathir assumed, as both Hang Tuah and Hang Jebat. Mahathir, as a leading member of a group labelled 'ultras', publicly opposed Tunku Abdul Rahman's policies in the 1960s.
82 Khoo Gaik Cheng, *Reclaiming Adat: Contemporary Malaysian Film and Literature* (Vancouver: University of British Columbia Press, 2006), p. 29.
83 Mubin Sheppard, *Tunku, His Life and Times: The Authorized Biography of Tunku Abdul Rahman Putra Al-Haj* (Kuala Lumpur: Pelanduk Publications, 1995), p. 124.
84 Mubin Sheppard, *Tunku: A Pictorial Biography 1903–1957* (Kuala Lumpur: Pelanduk Publications, 1984), pp. 150–151. The spot where he made this speech on 20 February 1956 was consecrated with a monument. In identifying the Portuguese as the 'usurper of independence' in 1511, he averted a direct reference to the British colonizers.
85 Tunku Abdul Rahman Putra, *Looking Back: Monday Musings and Memories* (Kuala Lumpur: Pustaka Antara, 1977), p. 68.
86 Leonard Andaya, 'The Search for the "Origins" of Melayu'. *Journal of Southeast Asian Studies* 32, no. 3 (2001): 71–72. The island of Sumatra was excluded in the *Hikayat* as it was written at a time when the kingdom was challenged by Aceh.
87 *Malay Mail*, 11 March 1963, pp. 1–2. As a result of administrative delays, this date was postponed, first to 31 August 1963 and then to 16 September 1963.
88 Benedict Anderson, *Imagined Communities*, Chapter 3.

References

Abid, Mohamed. *Reflections of Pre-Independence Malaya* (Subang Jaya, Selangor: Pelanduk Publications, 2003).
Ahmad, Kassim. *Characterization in 'Hikayat Hang Tuah'* (Kuala Lumpur: Dewan Bahasa dan Pustaka, 1964).
Andaya, Leonard. 'The Search for the "Origins" of Melayu'. *Journal of Southeast Asian Studies* 32, no. 3 (2001): 315–330.

Anderson, Benedict. *Imagined Communities: Reflections on the Origins and Spread of Nationalism* (London: Verso, 1991).

Becker, Heather. 'The Great Depression, the New Deal, and the WPA Federal Art Project', in Heather Becker, ed. *Art for the People: The Rediscovery and Preservation of Progressive- and WPA-era Murals in the Chicago Public Schools, 1904–1943* (San Francisco, CA: Chronicle Books, 2002).

Cheah, Boon Kheng. *Malaysia: The Making of a Nation* (Singapore: Institute of Southeast Asian Studies, 2002).

De Josselin de Jong. 'The Rise and Decline of a National Hero'. *Journal of the Malayan Branch of the Royal Asiatic Society* 38, no. 2 (1965): 140–155.

Fanon, Frantz. *The Wretched of the Earth* (New York: Grove Press, 1968).

Harper, T. N. *The End of Empire and the Making of Malaya* (Cambridge: Cambridge University Press, 1999).

Hemingway, Andrew. 'The Debate on Art and the State in Post-war America', in Francis Ames-Lewis and Piotr Paszkiewicz, eds. *Art and Politics* (Warsaw: Institute of Art, 1999).

Herner, Irene. 'Diego Rivera: Paradise Lost in Rockefeller Center Revisited', in Juan Coronel Rivera, Fausto Ramirez, William H. Robinson, Dawn Ades and Paul Karlstrom, eds. *Diego Rivera, Art and Revolution* (Mexico City: Conaculta, 1999).

Ho Kok Hoe. 'Museum Negara'. *BINA: Journal of the Federation of Malaya Society of Architects* 5, no. 1 (1964): pp. 19–21.

Hsü, Marco. *A Brief History of Malayan Art* (Translated and expanded by Lai Chee Kien) (Singapore: Millennium Books, 1999).

Kahin, George McTurnin. *Southeast Asia: A Testament* (London: RoutledgeCurzon, 2003).

Khoo, Gaik Cheng. 'Nationalism and Homoeroticism: A Feminist Reading of the Hang Tuah and Hang Jebat Debate', in Maznah Mohamad and Wong Soak Koon, eds. *Risking Malaysia: Culture, Politics and Identity* (Bangi: Penerbit Universiti Kebangsaan Malaysia, 2001).

Khoo, Gaik Cheng. *Reclaiming Adat: Contemporary Malaysian Film and Literature* (Vancouver: University of British Columbia Press, 2006).

Lamb, Alastair. *Chandi Bukit Batu Pahat* (Singapore: Eastern University Press, 1960).

Lee, Y.T. 'Dewan Bahasa dan Pustaka'. *BINA: Journal of the Federation of Malaya Society of Architects* 5, no. 1 (1964): 22–24.

Maaruf, Shaharuddin. *Concept of a Hero in Malay Society* (Petaling Jaya, Selangor: Eastern University Press, 1984).

Malay Mail. 'Ismail, 18 Wins $1,500 Prize in Design Contest', 2 August 1961.

Malay Mail. 'Language Agency Will Have Typically Malay Features', 23 August 1961.

Malay Mail. '$6,000 To Be Offered for 4 Murals', 19 December 1961.

Malay Mail. 'Agency First Housed in a Room in Johore Bahru', 31 January 1962.

Malay Mail. 'A Pupil and Teacher Share Top Honours', 22 February 1962.

Malay Mail. 'Murals for the Museum Based on History and Malayan Art', 14 June 1962.

Malay Mail. 'P.J. Artist Wins $5,000 Design Competition', 24 November 1962.

Malay Mail. 'Greater Malaysia Date Announced', 11 March 1963.

Malaya in History 4, no. 1, Merdeka Historical Exhibition issue.

Mustaffa, Ahmad and Wong Kiew Kit. *Silat Melayu: The Malay Art of Attack and Defence* (Oxford, New York and Melbourne: Oxford University Press, 1978).

Ngiom, Lilian Tay, ed. *80 Years of Architecture in Malaysia* (Kuala Lumpur: Pertubuhan Akitek Malaysia, 2000).

Parkinson, Ann and Cyril Parkinson. *Heroes of Malaya* (Singapore: D. Moore, 1956).

Sabapathy, T. K. *Merdeka Makes Art, or Does it?*, in T. K. Sabapathy, ed. *Vision and Idea: Relooking Modern Malaysian Art* (Kuala Lumpur: National Art Gallery, 1994).

Sardar, Ziauddin. *The Consumption of Kuala Lumpur* (London: Reaktion Books, 2000).

Sheppard, Mubin. *A Short History of Malaya* (Kuala Lumpur: B. T. Fudge, 1953).

Sheppard, Mubin. *Historic Malaya: An Outline History* (Singapore: Eastern University Press, 1959).

Syed Nasir bin Ismail. 'The Dewan and the National Language', in *A Brief Study of the History of the National Language* (Kuala Lumpur: Dewan Bahasa dan Pustaka, 1962).

Sheppard, Mubin. *The Adventures of Hang Tuah* (Hong Kong: Oxford University Press, 1975).

Sheppard, Mubin. *Taman Budiman: Memoirs of an Unorthodox Civil Servant* (Kuala Lumpur: Heinemann, 1979).

Sheppard, Mubin. *Tunku: A Pictorial Biography 1903–1957* (Kuala Lumpur: Pelanduk Publications, 1984).

Sheppard, Mubin. *Tunku, His Life and Times: The Authorized Biography of Tunku Abdul Rahman Putra Al-Haj* (Kuala Lumpur: Pelanduk Publications, 1995).

Straits Times, The, p. 14, 31 August 1963.

Tadin, Ishak. 'Dato Onn and Malay Nationalism, 1946–1951'. *Journal of Southeast Asian History* 1, no. 1 (1960): 56–88.

Tan Kok Meng, 'Critical Weave: Interwoven Identities in the Singapore Conference Hall'. *Journal of South East Asian Architecture* 4, no. 1 (2000): 17–23.

Time. 'The Man Who Would be Prime Minister,' LXXXI, no. 15, 12 April 1963, pp. 36–37.

Tunku Abdul Rahman Putra. 'On the Road to Nationhood', in *The Straits Times Annual for 1957* (Singapore: The Straits Times Press, 1957).

Tunku Abdul Rahman Putra. *Looking Back: Monday Musings and Memories* (Kuala Lumpur: Pustaka Antara, 1977).

Tweedie, Michael Wilmer Forbes. *Prehistoric Malaya* (Singapore: D. Moore, 1955).

Wharton, Dolores D. *Contemporary Artists of Malaysia: A Biographic Survey* (Petaling Jaya: Asia Society, 1971).

Part II
Competing narratives clash

3 Between assimilation and multiculturalism

Social resilience and the governance of diversity in Singapore[1]

Daniel P. S. Goh

Introduction

As a set of principles and beliefs informing the formation of states in ethnically diverse societies, multiculturalism has long taken its conceptual cues from either political philosophy or, less coherently, the pragmatic business of government. This is reflected in social scientific discussions on multiculturalism, where policy deviations from the principles are often explained in terms of the realities faced in governing ethnic pluralism. The case of Singapore provides an abundance of such social scientific studies for this very reason. Singapore is renowned for its successful multicultural governance, yet many of its policies deviate from the liberal principles that have informed the theory of multiculturalism. As such, Singapore's multiracialism, which predates the development of Western multi-culturalism, can easily be offered as a model of a non-Western multiculturalism that works in a plural postcolonial society faced with the legacy of trenchant racialization and the imperative of nation building. After all, the Singaporean system has proved to be resilient in a region where fellow postcolonial neighbours are afflicted by ethnic conflicts and global terrorist threats.

But is Singapore really resilient? If it is, why have the country's political leaders and security technocrats been obsessing with this question? Since 2001, a host of new initiatives have been implemented, for example the setting up of OnePeople.sg to coordinate grass roots efforts promoting racial and religious harmony; and the Community Engagement Programme to foster the readiness and resilience of Singaporeans when it comes to terrorist attacks and ethnic tensions. While this does not mean that the resilience of Singapore's multicultural-ism is suspect, it does suggest that because we do not have a systematic way of knowing and studying the resilience to allow us to even begin suspecting it, the government is taking preventive action in the only way it knows how to – through its bureaucratically managed grassroots networks.

In this chapter, I approach the study of multiculturalism not as political ideo-logy or state policy, but as a complex and non-linear socio-cultural system of institutions of governance that provide for stable relations between evolving ethnic groups with regard to their political, cultural and economic lives. Correspondingly, the dimensions of the system, as I will show by drawing from existing scholarship, are (a) the level of minority political representation, (b) the degree of intercultural interaction, and (c) relative inequality in the costs of ascribed identities. Variations on the first two dimensions, as I will elaborate later, define the three family types of socio-cultural system prevalent in the late twentieth century, with the two types of assimilative and liberal multicultural systems that lie at the heart of debates in Western multiculturalism theory at the extreme ends[2] and in between them, intermediate types I differentiate as postcolonial multicultural systems.[3] Assimilative systems are low in minority political representation and high in intercultural interaction, while liberal multicultural systems are high in the former and low in the latter. Postcolonial multicultural systems have differing degrees of the two variables.

The stability of a system depends on the third dimension of relative inequality in the cost of identities, with higher inequality leading to greater instability of the system because the equitable distribution of socio-economic resources and opportunities is fundamental to the stability of ethnic relations, though it is moderated by the other two variables. This follows what is often called the 'conflict theory' of ethnic relations, which includes Marxist perspectives, such as 'internal colonialism' and 'split labour market' theories and Weberian theories.[4] In particular, this is based on Weber's theoretical view that the competitive economic interests of ethnic groups in specific market conditions take precedence over political and status competition in modern capitalist societies.[5] Political and status competition are linked to the dimensions of minority political representation and intercultural interaction, respectively. When relative equality defines market conditions, ethnic relations become more stable and competition is displaced onto individual competition, which is the goal of proper meritocracies.

Resilience concerns the relationship between the system's stability and other factors. A system's resilience is affected by (1) global processes, particularly neoliberal globalization, of which international events such as the post-2001 War on Terror events are just manifestations of deeper structural processes, and (2) the internal dynamics of governance change, which entail cross-dimensional effects that are often unintended consequences of policies targeted specifically at minority political representation or intercultural interaction, such as the ethnic quota for public housing in Singapore. Resilience, in this sense, is not an absolute ability of a system to return to its original functioning after disturbance by an external event, but *the capacity to reorganize and maintain its stability while undergoing change relative to external processes and internal dynamics.*

This shifts the definition of resilience from a piecemeal preservation of short-term stability to a dynamic consideration of long-term stability. In turn, the redefinition shifts the orientation of resilience analysis from a fundamentally conservative political view to a social scientific basis that allows for objective modelling and testing. It also portends a shift from a managerial or social engineering orientation to an adaptive governance approach that recognizes the complexity of human socio-cultural behaviour and global political cultural processes, which are beyond the capacity of any individual state to master. I will discuss these implications after I, first, outline the dimensions of postcolonial multiculturalism in Singapore as a successful model for the governance of plu-ralist colonial legacies and, second, argue however that the attempts to preserve short-term stability in the face of the internationalization of (neo)liberal multi-culturalism and the internal dynamics tending towards nation-building assimila-tion has made Singapore's postcolonial multicultural system decreasingly resilient.

Dimensions of postcolonial multiculturalism in Singapore

Minority political representation

The question of minority political representation is fundamental in theories of multiculturalism. Theorists of liberal multiculturalism have long argued that the recognition and protection of minority rights is not inherently contra-dictory to the workings of a liberal democracy and may well be a liberal imperative to secure the rights of individuals voluntarily associating and rep-resenting themselves in ethnic groups. Assimilationists, whether of nationalist or liberal stripes, have argued instead that minority rights are only secured within the framework of political representation already defined by the major-ity group. In contrast, postcolonial systems of multiculturalism do not emerge from the interaction between Western political theory and historical con-ditions, but are, in the many senses of the word, overdetermined by history. Postcolonial multicultural systems, such as the multiracial system in Singa-pore, are produced by the convergence of several historical conditions: ethnic pluralism resulting from immigration and the arbitrary drawing of colonial territorial boundaries, pluralist colonial state formation informed by racial theory, and the imperative for nation building after non-revolutionary decolonization.

The key colonial legacies are hardened racial categories of governance and pluralist social institutions constructed in accordance with those racial cat-egories. In Singapore and Malaysia, both successor states of British Malaya, the well-established Chinese–Malay–Indian–Others (CMIO) categories of racial governance were inherited from the British colonial state. These categories func-tioned as the basis of knowledge, produced through data collection instruments such as ethnographic studies[6] and population census,[7] for the governance of the economic division of labour, which steered the migrant Chinese to the urban economy, preserved the Malays as rural, rice-planting smallholders, and migrant Indians as labourers in government-subsidized plantations owned by Europeans.[8] In the colonial legislatures of the Straits Settlements and Federated Malay States, formalized Chinese, Malay, Indian and European representation by private citizens was constitutionally provided for. Parallel to the legislative representa-tion, communal welfare organizations, evolving along ethnically pluralist lines and usually centred on clan, temple and mosque associations, were linked to colonial government support and regulation, in Singapore, through the Secretar-iat of Chinese Affairs and the Mohammedan and Hindu Endowments Board, the latter being the predecessor of the contemporary Majlis Ugama Islam Singapura (Islamic Religious Council of Singapore), Hindu Endowments Board and Hindu Advisory Board.

On achieving independence, the national government of a young postcolonial country is faced with three options – in order of the general level of minority political representation – *assimilate* minorities into the majority group, work towards the *amalgamation* of the racial categories to form a new national identity or keep the pluralist categories as *mosaic* components of the new nation. The first option often leads to ethnic conflicts and ethno-separatist nationalist movements because the colonial situation was already marked by unequal economic distribution across ethnic groups, for example between the better-off comprador and proletarian Chinese and the Malay peasantry in British Malaya, thereby making the assimilation model an inherently unstable option for new postcolonial societies. The second and third options constitute postcolonial multicultural systems whose stability depends on the subsequent inequality of costs of the racial identities ascribed in colonial pluralism.

David Brown's study of the state and ethnic politics in Southeast Asia provides a good survey of the different types of postcolonial socio-cultural systems that are possible.[9] In the case of Burma, the 'ethnocratic state' sought to assimilate minority groups into dominant Burman society and sparked separatist movements. Indonesia's pre-1997 neopatrimonial model and Singapore's corporatist state model both belong to the second option of amalgamation, but are differentiated by the distribution of political and economic resources among the ethnic groups through patronage ties in the former, and through technocratic institutions of the party-state in the latter. The Malaysian model of racial–class fractions organized into coalitional politics reflects the mosaic option.

The difference between the Malaysian and Singaporean models, both postcolonial multicultural models borne out of different approaches to the inherited colonial CMIO pluralism, is that, at least initially, the Malaysian model favoured stronger minority political representation over intercultural interaction, while the Singaporean model favoured stronger interaction over minority representation. This implies that on a continuum from assimilation to liberal multiculturalism, the amalgamation approach exemplified by Singapore's system tended towards assimilation, while Malaysia's mosaic approach is closer to liberal multiculturalism.

That the two are mutually exclusive subtypes of the postcolonial multicultural model is expressed by the tragedy of the intense racial politics of the brief period between 1963 and 1965 when Singapore was part of the Malaysian Federation. The People's Action Party's (PAP) ruling elite of Singapore expressed their amalgamation approach to the CMIO pluralism as a 'Malaysian Malaysia' nation-building project that challenged the 'Malay Malaysia' mosaic approach of the Kuala Lumpur elite. When this entered into the electoral politics of the formally democratic postcolonial state that was still infected by colonial pluralism, the first became racialized as Chinese and the second became racialized as Malay, despite the fact that both sides were supported by multiracial elites.

Months after PAP member and former radical leftist from Singapore, Devan Nair, won an electoral seat in a suburb of Kuala Lumpur in 1964, racial tensions escalated and riots between Chinese and Malay gangs broke out in Singapore. A year later, Singapore left the federation, separation being the only resolution for the tensions created by the two competing postcolonial multiculturalisms. The tensions continued in Malaysia, with opposition parties filling the gap left by the Singaporean elite, but this was resolved in favour of the mosaic approach after the bloody Chinese-Malay riots in May 1969, following the electoral success of a centre-left opposition party championing a variant of the 'Malaysian Malaysia' project.

In the various models of postcolonial multiculturalism, the level of minority political representation is higher than that of an assimilative system because it is formalized in the political system, this formalization being the reason for the mutual exclusion of the amalgamation and mosaic approaches within the postcolonial multicultural models. In Singapore, minority political representation was initially ensured by the PAP's strategy of assiduously recruiting and co-opting Malay and Indian middle-class professionals and business leaders to represent their respective communities. This was later formalized in the Group Representation Constituency system, in which constituencies are grouped together so that teams of legislators with at least one minority group member each are elected to ensure parliamentary representation corresponding to the demographic percentages (in 2011) of 74 per cent Chinese, 13 per cent Malay, 9 per cent Indian and 3 per cent Others.

In addition, the Singapore Constitution provides for the protection of Malay social and economic well-being and interests in the recognition of the Malays' indigenous status in Malaya and the Malay Archipelago region. The Constitution also provides for the establishment of the Presidential Council for Minority Rights to check and prevent discriminatory legislation, and the Presidential Council for Religious Harmony, to advise the government and parliament on matters of religious harmony. Other official institutions connect the executive to communal interests, such as the ethnic 'self-help' welfare groups, religious governance bodies such as those mentioned above for the Muslim and Hindu communities, and myriad interracial and interreligious bodies coordinated by the government's grassroots arm, the People's Association.

Unlike liberal multiculturalism, where different modes of democratic political representation are available to reflect independent group interests, postcolonial multiculturalism models are based on formal arrangements that adhere closely to dominant ideological frameworks, whether on the level of dominant political party organization or state institutions. This formal statist institutionalization permits a minimally effective level of minority political representation, but at the same time limits it. Because the substance of representation is dictated by the dominant national ideology, any representation of interests that are not consistent with the national ideology falls outside institutional politics. This creates inflexibility in the system, which prevents changing minority group interests from being represented.

At the same time, whether the result of patronage politics or ideological selection, co-opted minority leaders tend to lose their capacity to represent minority group interests independently. The emergence of the Association of Muslim Professionals in Singapore made up of middle-class Malay-Muslims and other Muslims in the 1990s is a case in point. The Association's attempt to represent the interests independently of party organization and state institutions was a potential challenge to PAP Malay representatives who have been ineffective in representing the increasingly marginalized Malay community.[10] But the Association was quickly co-opted into the statist framework and allocated a portion of ethnic 'self-help' welfare funds to act as a private counterpart to the official Council for Malay Education (Mendaki), which effectively neutralized the Association's capacity to represent Malay political interests.[11]

Another limitation is the cross-dimensional effects on formal political representation. For example, patronage and pork-barrel politics distribute the economic costs of ascribed identities, but impact directly on the capacity of co-opted communal leaders to represent minority interests. In Singapore, it is not patronage politics, which is more the case in Malaysia, but technocratic considerations with regard to public housing. Public housing is a major service provision of the state; it had approximately 82 per cent of the population living in public housing flats in 2010. After the first allocation by ballot and subsidized sale of a new flat, owners are free to buy and sell in the housing market with relatively few limitations. In 1989, based on resale trends figures according to ethnic group affiliation of buyers, where traditional ethnic preferences for certain locations with historical meanings for them were evident, the PAP government implemented the Ethnic Integration Policy to prevent the formation of ethnic residential enclaves, and to control cross-racial resale transactions to make the residential composition of each block of flats conform to national ethnic proportions.[12] While this may increase the level of intercultural interaction on the microcosmic scale of the neighborhood, it limits the level of minority political representation by preventing minority groups from directly electing their representatives, and effectively putting the Chinese majority in a position to veto minority representatives.[13]

Intercultural interaction

Assimilative socio-cultural systems tend to show high levels of intercultural interaction because the very process of assimilation requires such interactions – of course, in favour of the majority group culture. It may seem contradictory that we find highly ghettoized communities in assimilative societies, for example in France and the United States, but the logic of assimilation is such that resistant communities would be subjected to racial segregation or 'ghettoization'. The balance of assimilation and ghettoization is probably correlated to socio-economic inequality, which I argue, is the key determinant of the stability of socio-cultural systems. In liberal multicultural systems, segregation is usually voluntary and positive for the minority group's preservation of their way of life.

Thus, low intercultural interaction is not necessarily or intrinsically negative. However, segregation in liberal multicultural systems also becomes increasingly involuntary and destabilizing when inequality increases.

In postcolonial multicultural systems, colonial pluralism leaves a legacy of semi-segregation, where, in the famed formula proposed by Furnivall in his study of Burma and the Dutch East Indies, a 'medley of peoples' who 'mix but do not combine', meeting 'only in the market-place' and 'living side by side, but separately, within the same political unit'.[14] With peoples not combining like in assimilative systems, but mixing in common public places unlike in liberal multicultural systems, the level of intercultural interaction in a postcolonial multicultural system can be posited to be between assimilative and liberal multicultural systems. Indeed, evidence from studies of ethnic relations seems to bear this out. Lai's ethnographic study of the Marine Parade housing estate shows that there is a simultaneous 'tendency towards appreciation of heterogeneity and peaceful interaction', on the one hand, and 'intensification of ethnic boundary maintenance and competition', on the other.[15] Two processes of intercultural interaction are happening here. In the public realm, norms of peaceful and politically correct intercultural interaction provide the basis for competitive exchanges between ethnic groups in the marketplace. In the private realm, ethnic groups maintain their way of life through symbolic boundary maintenance, which may give them comparative advantage in the marketplace.

This close association of intercultural interaction and competitive exchanges in the marketplace makes postcolonial multicultural systems similar to assimilative and liberal multicultural systems, in that segregation becomes a destabilizing force in conditions of socio-economic inequality. As the marketplace becomes less competitive because of the unequal distribution of resources, costs and opportunities, the norms for peaceful intercultural interaction lose their function and ethnicity becomes symbolically marked as monopolistic domination and unfair subordination or natural economic success and stigmatizing failure. In such conditions, intensifying intercultural interaction as a result of *social* pluralism – contrary to what cultural studies and liberal scholars who celebrate the decentring or democratizing effects of hybridization say – may be detrimental to ethnic relations.[16]

Thus, in Chua and Kwok's positive appraisal of increased social pluralism as bringing about the liberalization of everyday life in contrast to the autocratic communitarianism of the PAP state, they observe the reverse happening in the Malay-Muslim community, with the tightening of community boundaries and prevalence of general conservatism.[17] This seems to be a defensive move by a marginalized community in the face of increased intercultural interactions in conditions of socio-economic inequality and does not bode well for the multicultural system in Singapore.

Importantly, it is among the Chinese middle classes that social pluralism and intercultural hybridization is becoming more pronounced.[18] I would not be too quick to celebrate this trend because this privileged access to liberating hybridization along racial–class lines reflects the association between intercultural interaction and decreasing competitiveness. Hybridization is increasingly becoming a symbol of cultural distinction used by privileged Chinese middle classes. Besides, state-led creative industries have been actively commoditizing the hybridities, which means that minority cultures are relegated to the peripheries of the lucrative cultural space of the new economy, while the hybridizing social pluralism of the Chinese middle classes gives them a strong state-supported advantage in the marketplace. We need to study the relationship between ethnic pluralism and social pluralism more closely.

Given the above association between intercultural interaction and marketplace competition, it is not surprising that Furnivall advocated a strong role for the colonial state to ensure that ethnic pluralism does not descend into anomic chaos and mob conflict.[19] In fact, one could observe that the postcolonial state in Singapore uses ethnic pluralism as a justification for its interventionist engineering of the spaces and practices of everyday life to socialize the population in the terms of the official CMIO multiracialism. But Furnivall is mistaken, just as colonialism was, in assuming the natural existence of racial differences. Over time, intercultural interaction should lead to depluralization, where ethnic groups become more similar to one another and ultimately amalgamate because of hybridization. Indeed, there is evidence of depluralization in the post-war and immediate post-independence period.[20]

It is not an exaggeration to say that Furnivall's theory introduces an important moral hazard as it is in the state's interest to preserve pluralism and its privileged role as the guarantor of ethnic peace, precisely by interpreting ethnic diversity in the terms of colonial pluralism: that ethnic differences are primordial, immutable, divisive and dangerous. Depluralization would have dissolved both the problem and the purpose of postcolonial multiculturalism and shifted ethnic-based competition in the marketplace to competition based on individual resources and merit. As Benjamin incisively observed, 'Singapore's problems derive largely from the imposition of an essentially divisive ideology upon a relatively uniform cultural reality'.[21] Social scientific surveys have consistently shown that ethnic diversity exists with healthy inter-ethnic ties, strong sentiments of national unity and positive ethnic relations attitudes,[22] suggesting that the problem is not so much ethnic differences per se, but the state's pluralist interpretation and the PAP elites' efforts to engineer social reality to the interpretation.

Therefore, state social engineering introduces contradictions which, if they do not counterproductively create more problems for intercultural interaction, at best do not have any impact on intercultural interaction and waste governmental resources. For example, the residential hollowing out, cosmetic makeover and commercialization of heritage sites such as Chinatown and Kampong Glam that are then used to celebrate the nation's constituent CMIO ethnic cultures, tend to turn ethnically significant living places into dead museum pieces.[23] At the same time, the Ethnic Integration Policy obstructs ethnic residential preferences bcause of certain historical reasons, for example Malays for Eunos, Indians for Sembawang and Chinese for Tiong Bahru, thus denying the function of meaningful places for the sustenance of living ethnic culture. In effect, the state's pluralist world view has led the technocrats to ignore the multiracial composition of both heritage sites and ethnically significant residential locales and the rich intercultural interaction that went on in these mistaken 'ghettoes'.

Similar contradictions appear in language policy, as the 'mother tongue' policy tends to sanitize evolving vernacular ethnic cultures and make them conform to the state's idealization of CMIO cultures, while English is positioned as the language of intercultural interaction.[24] However, attempted technocratic preservation of ethnic cultures has led instead to their formalization and loss of rich ethnic traditions. When the people creatively responded to the imposed linguistic boundaries and evolved a hybrid Singlish that facilitated intercultural interaction, the state launched the 'Speak Good English Movement' to suppress the use of Singlish in the same way that Chinese dialects have been suppressed by the 'Speak Mandarin' campaigns.

Furthermore, state social engineering hardly solves the problem of systemic equilibrium between intercultural interaction and competitive equal opportunities for all ethnic groups. Instead, state social engineering merely introduces unintended cross-dimensional effects that make the system more susceptible to unpredictable destabilization resulting from global processes because it inevitably applies a short-term, reactive and piecemeal view to perceived problems of intercultural interaction. By micro-engineering solutions to systemic problems, the state may be causing the system to become chaotic, with the destabilizing effects not evident until the tipping point is reached or triggered by global events.

In this light, the manufacturing of government-led grassroots inter-racial and inter-religious networks to strengthen resilience through increased intercultural interaction after the 2001 terrorism events is a response to cracks appearing in the system. I am sceptical of the efficacy of this solution because it increases intercultural interaction between community leaders, but does not address the equilibrium between intercultural interaction and competitive equal opportunities. Furthermore, like the other narrowly focused solutions, it would create more cross-dimensional effects on the system with unpredictable results. One possible consequence is that the induction of community and religious leaders into institutions, with an explicit security orientation for quick response to terrorist attacks and which is sponsored by the interior ministry, would cause them to lose their legitimacy with community members or, worse still, make them appear as mere functionaries of the state security apparatus and cause community members to distrust them.

Inequality of costs

Level of socio-economic inequality is the key dimension that determines the stability of a socio-cultural system. Inequality is, of course, a central focus of study in the social sciences. The question for us here is how we conceptualize the aspects of inequality that are relevant to assimilative and multicultural systems. The most intuitive approach is to use the relative socio-economic status of the ethnic groups as measured by wealth or income. But this does not capture the actual relationship between socio-economic inequality and the socio-cultural system. In a socio-cultural system that apportions rights, restrictions and privileges to ethnic groups, the crux of the matter is how these rights, restrictions and privileges affect the comparative advantage of the groups in the marketplace. In this sense, what matters are the different costs exacted from the groups by the assimilative or multicultural system.

An assimilative system is stable – or put another way, the assimilation of minority groups takes place smoothly and with little conflict – when there is low inequality in the costs borne by the majority and minority groups. Increasing instability often causes the system to lose its resilience and leads it to a precarious point of change defined by different values in minority political rights and intercultural interaction. For example, cracks in the French system of assimilation, caused by the ghettoization of citizens of migrant African and Arab descent, have led to minority political mobilization and calls for public recognition of minority cultural spaces and practices, thus increasingly pushing the system to a liberal multicultural configuration. Similarly, liberal multicultural systems are more stable when inequality is low as political and cultural accommodation of minority groups tends not to become a point for ethnic contention and conflict when there is equal access to resources and opportunities. We can compare Canada, Australia and Britain in this manner to understand the increasing level of heightened ethnic tensions, exacerbated by post-2001 terrorism events, destabilizing the system, possibly pushing the British system towards assimilation and the Australian system towards a postcolonial model.

In Singapore's case, Chua rightly argues that the racialization endemic to postcolonial multicultural systems, when subjected to the calculations of the government in terms of national interests, leads to the exaction of unequal costs from different ethnic groups.[25] Chua gives three examples. For the Chinese, cultural homogenization privileging the English language and elevating Mandarin as the exclusive 'mother tongue' has economically disadvantaged the solely Mandarin-speaking and well-educated Chinese and, more so, the solely 'dialect'-speaking and poorly-educated Chinese. The non-conscription of Malays into compulsory military service in the 1960s and 1970s because of putative Singaporean Malay ethnic cultural, religious and kinship links to Malaysia, severely weakened the community's economic position at a time of expanding opportunities as a result of rapid industrialization. Two reasons account for this: a substantial proportion of Malay working men was employed by the British military forces, and their employment was not renewed by the postcolonial government for the new national army, while their sons faced great difficulty securing regular-wage labour because employers were reluctant to hire and train workers who were liable for military call-up at any time.[26] Costs are less apparent for the Indians, except for the glass ceiling in public office, which in any case is applicable, in general, to all non-Chinese. In short, socio-economic costs are incurred simply for being identified as a member of an ascribed racial group.

Chua's examples show the costs incurred directly and one could plausibly rank the groups in terms of incurred, ascriptive costs from low to high in this order: bicultural Chinese, English-speaking Chinese, Indian, Mandarin-speaking Chinese, dialect-speaking Chinese, Malay. But other scholars have pointed out important opportunity costs that are incurred by the non-Chinese communities as a result of policies that distribute unevenly the costs among the Chinese internally. This is because these policies go against the grain of procedural meritocracy by cutting off important opportunities along racial lines. For example, the Special Assistance Plan that provides for very well funded secondary schools catering to the training of bicultural Chinese students effectively excludes able Malay and Indian students from these elite public schools. Arguably, policies favouring the use of Mandarin as a common language for the Chinese marketplace and business transactions have allowed Chinese employers to reject non-Mandarin-speaking job applicants, though the common language of business and government is English. This discriminatory practice has only abated in recent years through 'persuasive' governmental action brought about by a vocal Malay PAP Member of Parliament, Halimah Yacob, who is exceptional for being a female unionist in contrast to the usual profile of co-opted middle-class Malay male technocrats and professionals.

These indirect opportunity costs of ascribed identity mean that Indians are more disadvantaged than Chua has perceived, and one can plausibly differentiate between well-educated English-speaking Indians sharing relatively similar opportunities and advantages as English-speaking Chinese, and poorly-educated non-English-speaking Indians who share similar high costs with Malays. If we consider cross-dimensional effects, the latter group of Indians may be in a worse position because of public housing policies that allocate the lower-end one-/two-room flats to lower-income residents. Thus, Chih observes greater segregation of Indian residents because of their inability to participate in the housing market, and suggests that the ethnic quota policy imposes another constraint on lower-income Indian residents.[27] However, other cross-scale effects worsen the ascriptive costs for Malays. One important effect is the failure to bring multicultural pedagogy to bear on the meritocratic education system when it is obvious that mixed-race classes taught primarily by Chinese teachers bring about unequal results because of unconsciously biased perceptions or culturally biased pedagogy. Malays suffer the brunt of these biases because of pernicious stereotypes, of Malays being by nature or culture lazy and unintelligent, which have survived from the British colonial period.[28]

While the inequality of ascriptive costs primarily characterizes postcolonial multicultural systems, assimilative systems are defined by integration costs, and liberal multicultural systems are defined by exit costs. Integration costs refer to the different prices paid by minority groups in the process of assimilating into the majority culture, and far less commonly, the price paid by the majority group in assimilating the minority group. The costs may be the result of historical cultural differences or structural constraints thrown up by the majority group for various reasons. For example, Asian migrants in the nineteenth-century United

States had to pay a very high price for assimilation compared with European migrants, while the price was exorbitant for blacks during this post-Reconstruction period. Exit costs refer to the price individuals would have to pay to remove themselves from the recognized and protected communal groups in a liberal multicultural system. High exit costs are detrimental to the legitimacy of minority cultural recognition in a liberal democracy and would therefore destabilize the liberal multicultural system.

The type of costs is not exclusive to a system. Though the costs in postcolonial multicultural systems are primarily ascriptive in character, integration and exit costs do matter in shaping the overall structure of cost inequality. Since the 2001 arrests of Jemaah Islamiyah members for allegedly plotting terrorist attacks on US targets in Singapore, increasing governmental pressure has been put on the Malay community to integrate into mainstream society, as Barr and Low observe.[29] But Barr and Low have mistakenly interpreted this as the transformation of the system into a 'programme of assimilation'. They have confused integration and ascriptive costs in their use of educational marginality and the exclusion of Muslim kindergartens from government funding as a case in point – the exclusion applies equally to kindergartens by other religious organizations and is not an assimilative policy targeted at the Malays. The pressure is not on the Malays to submit to Chinese norms or mores, but for Malays to lose their defensive, boundary-maintaining conservatism and increase their intercultural interaction with other groups.

The problem is that this pressure increases the inequality of costs by adding integration costs to the ascriptive costs of socio-economic marginalization Malays already face because the community is expected to drop the defensive conservatism voluntarily, while the marginalization that is the basis of the community's defensive posture is not addressed. Besides, there is little evidence that Malays are less integrated than other groups.[30] The defensive conservatism is directed inwards towards the strengthening of intra-communal bonds, which ameliorates ascriptive costs to some extent, but increases exit costs for individual Malays, and is not directed outwards towards other groups because the community is not in a political position to afford it. Thus, in effect, Malays have to overcompensate for their ascribed identity by working doubly hard, in this case, at intercultural interaction, to prove their loyalty to the country.

Dynamic change and resilience from the 1960s to the 1990s

It is possible to sum up the above discussion of postcolonial multiculturalism in Singapore, in comparison to assimilative and liberal multicultural systems and Malaysia's alternative postcolonial multicultural system, diagrammatically as a diamond-shaped continuum along the dimensions of minority political representation and intercultural interaction. My conjecture that the continuum is diamond shaped is based on the *prima facie* consideration that historically, stable postcolonial multicultural systems have been more diverse than both assimilative and liberal multicultural systems in terms of the two dimensions. The two

subtypes of the amalgamation and mosaic approaches of postcolonial multiculturalism are expressed in the continuum as being situated closer to the assimilative and liberal multicultural systems, respectively – see Figure 3.1.

The shaded zone of very low intercultural interaction and minority political
representation represents the situation of endemic ethnic conflict. Inequality of
costs is captured as determining the stability of the system, which defines the
breadth of the continuum. Stable systems reside within the diamond. Thus, resilience refers to achieving the systemic equilibrium between intercultural interaction and minority political representation within the continuum of stability,
and preventing the system from falling below the continuum and breaking down
into ethnic conflict. Above the continuum are possibilities of high intercultural
interaction and minority representation combinations that do not exist historically, and which are therefore untested multicultural utopias, the stability of
which is unknown. With this specification, we can then discuss the changes in
Singapore's postcolonial multiculturalism as affected by governance decisions
vis-à-vis the internal dynamics of the system and globalization processes, and
hence determine its resilience.

There is no dearth of sociological attempts to define the changes in Singapore's system in terms of historical phases. Writing in the 1980s, Siddique
describes Singaporean multiracialism as a singular and stable CMIO model she
calls 'interactionist', referring to the promotion of intercultural interaction while
preserving the ascribed pluralist boundaries.[31] With the benefit of hindsight,
scholars in the 1990s and 2000s see three to four phases in the development of
the system. Brown points to three phases: ethnic mosaic politics in the years
before independence, meritocratic multiracialism between 1965 and 1980, and
corporatism from the 1980s.[32] Hill and Lian adopt these phases, but criticize
Brown for being reductionistically statist, and argue that the third phase saw the

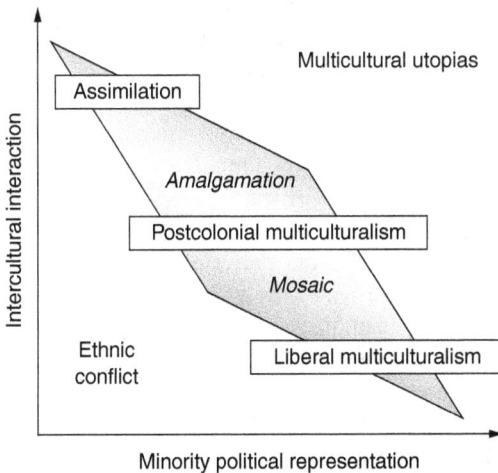

Figure 3.1 Assimilative and multicultural systems in comparative perspective.

first-generation PAP leaders realizing the pluralist model they had developed in the first phase under the historical conditions of mosaic politics, reflecting their economic and political self-confidence after the second phase of nation building accompanying industrialization.[33] Starting with independence in 1965, Vasil adopts almost the same view, though he characterizes the first phase as amalgamation towards an English-speaking Singaporean identity, and the second phase as pluralistic 'Asianising', with a strong Chinese emphasis. He also argues that, with the transfer of power to the second-generation PAP leaders, the 1990s were marked by attempts to assuage the non-Chinese and make the divisive second phase more in tune with the amalgamation thrust of the first phase.[34]

Tan proposes four phases, the first three in line with Vasil's, but he sees the 1990s as experiencing increased ethnic consciousness, rather than the amelioration of divisiveness.[35] Tan's fourth phase, beginning in 2000 and spurred on by the 2001 terrorism events, is more akin to Vasil's proposed third phase of synthesizing pluralism and amalgamation. Tan quotes Prime Minister Goh Chok Tong's 1999 speech – in which he used the metaphor of overlapping four circles to represent the CMIO communities sharing a common Singaporean space, and announced the government would cultivate this common space – as the vision guiding the fourth phase. Importantly, Goh borrowed this vision from a first-generation PAP leader, S. Rajaratnam, who was Minister of Culture when he first articulated the overlapping circles metaphor in 1960.[36] The difference is that Goh emphasized the cultivation of the common space while Rajaratnam advocated its expansion. A few years later, Minister for Community Development and Sports Yaacob Ibrahim reiterated that the government's policy was to combine the 'melting pot' of the first phase and the 'mosaic' of the second phase in what he simply calls 'multiculturalism', where increasing hybridization would be accommodated, if not promoted.[37]

Clearly, the multicultural system in Singapore has not remained static in the past four decades. The problem with the above historical periodizations is that they are not based on clearly stated dimensions defining all the periods, but are intuitively constructed following the general lines of government policy, usually attributing agency to key government leaders. This approach not only introduces problems of different arbitrary interpretations, but also fetishizes the superhuman ability of PAP leaders to engineer the socio-cultural system to their vision, a fetishization that the leaders themselves may advance in public to portray political confidence, but which I doubt they adopt when they are more modestly deliberating the challenges facing them in the policymaking backroom. It is symptomatic that the approaches above tend to rely on political speeches and policy statements for evidence rather than measurable variables. Hill and Lian's criticism of Brown's reductionist statism does not make sense when their approach is even more reductionistic, that is, reducing the state's steering function in the socio-cultural system to the beliefs of political leaders. The periodization approach also does not take into account non-linear shifts through time resulting from global geopolitical changes and the cross-dimensional consequences of state social engineering in previous phases.

At best, the periodization approach may be used as a heuristic to capture major shifts in policy, responding to the social consequences of preceding policies and changes induced by global processes. In such a heuristic analysis, the objectives of governance should be clearly theorized for evaluative analysis. For example, I have argued elsewhere that the objective of national unity can be conceptualized in terms of Durkheim's theory of division of labour and social solidarity;[38] that is, the three phases of government multicultural policies can be seen as reacting to the problems of earlier policy successes by promoting an emotional and knee-jerk 'mechanical solidarity' that is ill suited to the complex socio-economic organization of modern Singaporean society.[39]

In terms of the discussion here, I argue that changes in multicultural governance have been enacted in response to the internal dynamics of amalgamation and the increasing internationalization of neoliberal multiculturalism spurred on by economic globalization and democratization since the 1980s, which accelerated after the end of the Cold War and demise of communism.[40] Because of the latter process, many postcolonial multicultural systems in the Developing World were transformed in order to maintain systemic stability as a result of the social impact of neoliberal globalization on ethnic relations and the socio-economic distribution in these societies. These transformed systems appear in the literature on Latin American political economy as 'neoliberal multiculturalism' or signified by the term, 'postmulticultural'.[41]

The process is conceptualized in my model by the shrinking of the diamond continuum (Figure 3.2), in which the distinction between liberal and postcolonial multicultural systems is being effaced and replaced by neoliberal multiculturalism. When governments around the world deal with the growing inequality of costs that results from globalization by depoliticizing the struggle for minority

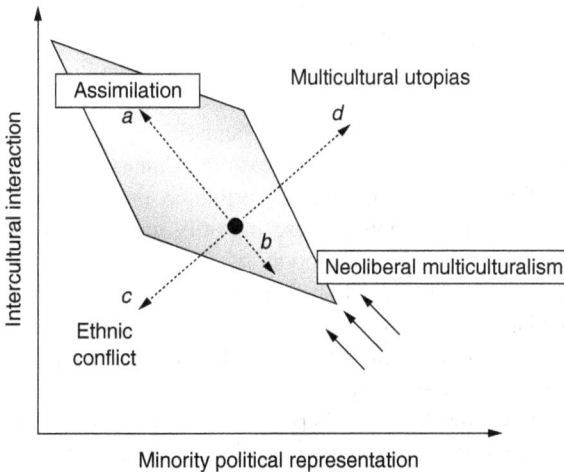

Figure 3.2 Systemic change in Singapore in the context of neoliberal globalization.

rights and commodifying ethnic cultures for global capitalist circuits, they turn political issues arising from the inequality of costs into issues of intercultural communication and appreciation, and reduce the inequality of costs by commercializing ethnic cultures for international tourism or cultural consumption. Stability is thus achieved by increasing intercultural interaction and decreasing minority political representation. Changes in liberal multicultural systems also suggest this process; for example, Gilroy has criticized the British anti-racism movement that began in the 1980s for trivializing 'the struggle against racism' and isolating it 'from other political antagonisms – from the contradiction between capital and labor, from the battle between men and women'.[42]

In the case of Singapore, the change in the multicultural system in the 1980s that scholars agree was a first major period of change was caused, first, by the change in the global landscape as described above and, second, by the internal dynamics of policy shifts responding both to domestic social changes and the changing global landscape. Before the onset of globalization, the system was shifting to its own internal dynamics of nation-building amalgamation and depluralization, and moved towards the assimilative system (vector *a*). Through pluralist lenses, PAP leaders interpreted this as creole deculturalization and sought to arrest the increasing intercultural interaction to prevent the system from becoming what they thought would become an English-based creole-speaking assimilative system – through educational reforms emphasizing moral and ethnic heritage education in the early 1980s. Then, as globalization loomed after Singapore's successful industrialization and integration into the global economy in the early 1980s, the country's multiracial amalgamation system became increasingly precarious as rising costs increased inequality, particularly between the English-speaking Chinese and the rest. A complete neoliberal multicultural solution (vector *b*) was not attractive to the elite as it would entail liberal democratization, which they resisted throughout the 1980s and 1990s, despite strong domestic middle-class and international civil society pressure.

The ruling elite responded with piecemeal institutional solutions to arrest acceleration towards the assimilative system and the slide into neoliberal multiculturalism encroaching from the other side, but cross-dimensional effects created more perturbations. The intensification of Mandarin-language education and public use redistributed the ascriptive costs among the Chinese and stemmed the overall rising inequality somewhat through redistribution among the Chinese groups, but increased the costs for non-Chinese minority groups. The educational reforms, overlapping with the promotion of the Mandarin language, stemmed intensifying intercultural interaction, but brought the system closer to neoliberal multiculturalism with lowered intercultural interaction. Housing ethnic quotas increased intercultural interaction, but lowered minority political representation and increased the inequality of ascriptive costs.

The movement to Confucianize Singapore's political culture to pre-empt liberal democratization pulled the system away from neoliberal multiculturalism, but decreased minority political representation and brought the system closer to the assimilative system. The formalization of minority parliamentary representation through Group Representation Constituencies halted the decline of minority representation, but did little to increase representation or ameliorate the rising ascriptive costs for Malays in particular. Ethnic 'self-help' welfare organizations, with the establishment of Yayasan Mendaki in 1981 to attend to the urgent needs of Malays, and then the Chinese Development Assistance Council and the Singapore Indian Development Association in 1991, were governmental instruments of choice to reduce ascriptive costs through the channelling of a larger proportion of funds to minority groups, but this decreased intercultural interaction in the important nation-building aspect of trans-ethnic collaboration to tackle common social problems.

Thus for more than two decades the PAP leaders have been trying to make the system run to stand still while keeping its footing steady in a shifting global landscape of internationalizing neoliberal multiculturalism. Singapore's system has been kept stable in the short term in the face of change involving assimilation (vector *a* in Figure 3.2) or neoliberal multiculturalism (vector *b*) or ethnic conflict (vector *c*) by the sum of the piecemeal policy actions that have been informed largely by a pluralist worldview. The question is whether this stability comes at the price of long-term resilience.

Adaptive governance in the *fin de siècle* of postcolonial multiculturalism

Contrary to governmental and popular beliefs, I argue that the 2001 terrorism events did not do much to change global trends with regard to multiculturalism. Neoconservative policies associated with the War on Terror on the part of the United States and other Western countries, and the backlash against Muslim minorities in the West, have sharpened the issues concerning the inequality of costs in the assimilative or multicultural systems in these countries. On a wider scale, neoconservatism has only served to highlight the general advance of neoliberal multiculturalism and the decline of various systems of postcolonial multiculturalism in the world. Many postcolonial multicultural systems are unravelling into ethnic conflict, for example Kenya, the Philippines, Pakistan, Iraq and, arguably, Malaysia, because they have not made the transition to neoliberal multiculturalism, which Indonesia and India have been doing with a fair bit of violence in certain hotspots, but with remarkable lack of conflict otherwise, given the ethnic tensions and terror attacks occurring in these countries.

In Singapore, two trends accompanying the international expansion of neoliberal multiculturalism have accelerated in the 2000s, and the 2001 terrorism events have brought into relief the precariousness of the system. The increase of intercultural interaction as a result of global cultural flows has accelerated with the global migratory flows that Singapore is now absolutely dependent on for the functioning of its successfully neoliberalized economy. Governmental control of this immigration through a 'flexible' regime of stratified rights and privileges for differently racialized migrant groups, and the encouragement of the settlement of skilled workers from China and India to maintain the CMIO ethnic proportions, have only introduced more fault lines while doing little to slow down the accelerating intercultural interaction in the system.[43]

Decreasing minority political representation in Singapore has been accompanied by the depoliticization and enculturalization of issues of social and economic justice faced by minority groups. In particular, the government has consistently used the cultural deficit thesis to explain the socio-economic marginality of the Malay community.[44] This turns the inequality of ascriptive costs borne by the Malays into a Malay problem and, in turn, suggests that the government could only help by supporting the community with funds and other institutional resources. The periodic release of governmental reports on the 'progress of the Malay community' since 1980, for example in 2007 by the prime minister himself during his National Day Rally speech, focuses attention on the social and economic issues the community faces from the depoliticized culturalist angle. Rather than treating the issues as national problems caused by structural and institutional inequalities affecting one minority group more than others, the 2007 Report congratulates the community for absolute socio-economic progress, ignores the fact that the relative progress rates show widening income and other achievement gaps and concludes, rather glibly, that the 'progress which has been achieved equips the Malay/Muslim community to tackle these remaining challenges resolutely and decisively'.[45]

Depoliticized enculturalization is also evident during the backlash against the Malay community after the 2001 terrorism events, when the community 'experienced a certain attention that it did not want nor was warranted', as Yaacob Ibrahim put it in his 2003 speech mentioned earlier. In the same speech, the minister asked, 'But, we may want to ask, after more than 30 years of nation-building, why were doubts cast on the Malays?', a question which clearly evoked the ascriptive costs borne by the Malays, but to which he gave the depoliticized culturalist answer, 'Clearly, we had not established sufficient inter-cultural understanding.'[46] Not coincidentally, the speech spelt out the new policy of 'multiculturalism' promoting and supporting increased hybridization.

One is tempted to conclude that the new 'multiculturalism' vision looks very much like neoliberal multiculturalism. But most of the institutional and policy practices that keep the system running on the spot remain and some, like the bicultural education programme, have been further calibrated to update their efficacy. Another possibility is that the government is keeping the system steady to allow it to change 'naturally' to neoliberal multiculturalism, overtaken by the trends of heightening intercultural interaction and declining minority representation. But such an approach is uncharacteristic of the technocratic managers and consummate social engineers of the PAP party-state. Besides, a large part of the political legitimacy of the essentially nationalist PAP resides in its classic postcolonial formula of multiracialism. The post-2001 institutional innovations promoting grassroots inter-racial and inter-religious networking suggest that the technocrats are indeed trying to pull the system away from becoming one of neoliberal multiculturalism. In this light, it is not surprising that, despite conciliatory overtures to an increasingly politicized and vocal gay community, the government has refused to recognize the rights of the sexual minorities and decriminalize homosexual acts between men.

If the system is being pulled away from becoming a neoliberal multicultural system, then in which direction is it heading? The grassroots network initiatives and the position taken against sexual minorities suggest a movement in the direction of an assimilative system (vector *a*), but as past institutional reactions have shown, the government is not too keen to take the system there either. The price may be too high to pay in terms of instability and ethnic conflict, as history has shown that shifts towards assimilation by postcolonial multicultural systems often engender ethno-separatist movements, for example the cases of Burma, the southern Philippines and Sri Lanka. For a city state such as Singapore, it would mean endemic urban ethnic conflict, for example as experienced in the Lebanese civil war. In other words, movement towards assimilation (vector *a*) could easily degenerate into movement towards the zone of ethnic conflict marked by low intercultural interaction and minority political position and high inequality of costs (vector *c*). The safest route, counter-intuitive to the PAP leaders' instincts, would be neoliberal multiculturalism, but the combination of commodified hybridization and rights depoliticization does not appeal to the values and sensibilities rising from the struggles for social justice that animate modern sociocultural systems and postcolonial nationalisms. The safest route is not the most desirable.

Adaptive governance, I argue, borrowing from social-ecological systems theory, is the strategy of the day. Adaptability is defined in social-ecological systems theory as 'the *collective* capacity of the human actors in the system to manage resilience'.[47] This collective capacity is reflexively intentional, in contrast to the natural capacity of the ecological system as a whole to self-organize without intent. In other words, human groups, from farmers to herders to bureaucrats in, say, a savannah, would not go about doing their work individually and automatically with customary practices and rules, but with self-appraising intent orientated towards sustainability and resilience. The difference between the social-ecological and socio-cultural systems is that, here, the system is composed completely and exclusively of human actors, which means that reflexive intentionality is intrinsic to the system. The key word here is 'collective' because the technocratic engineering approach calls for the reflexive intentionality of only the technocratic engineers and, in fact, its success is predicated on the rest of the human actors unreflexively following the signals of institutional incentives and disincentives the engineers input into the system. Adaptive governance, on the other hand, treats reflexive intentionality as the basic code that organizes the social system.[48] In other words, everyone needs to be involved, communicatively and politically to adapt the system to new complexities.

Because reflexive intentionality is intrinsic to the socio-cultural system, adaptive governance is expressed in Figure 3.2 as vector *d*, involving the increase in both intercultural interaction and minority political representation. This is, in fact, counter-intuitive to the current direction of the continuum running from the assimilative to the liberal multicultural systems. There have been moves in the direction of adaptive governance in Singapore under the leadership of Prime Minister Lee Hsien Loong; for example, in the activation of the government-led grassroots networks and coordination between ethnic 'self-help' groups for national and trans-ethnic welfare interventions. If this continues, it bodes well for the reduction of the inequality of costs for both non-Chinese and Chinese (the non-English speaking) minority groups and, therefore, for the overall stability of the system. A matter of urgency that glib culturalist paternalism does not help is the 'at risk' situation faced by many Malay families. High rates of early marriages, teenage pregnancies and single-parent family formation, deindustrialization and low-wage service sector employment, higher rates of drug abuse, indications of unsuccessful residential desegregation[49] and the development of defensive youth subcultures are symptoms of ghettoization and the formation of an ethnic underclass.[50]

A move in the direction of adaptive governance would involve three dimensions. First, the democratization of grass roots institutions, which are heavily bureaucratized and dominated by the political agenda of the ruling party, is needed to expand reflexive intentionality throughout the existing good social infrastructure in Singapore, and realize the citizenry's latent collective capacity. Second, the desecuritization of the new inter-racial and inter-religious grassroots networks and their refocusing on mobilizing the people for community welfare issues would train the collective capacity for proactively decreasing the inequality of costs that is responsible for system instability, rather than train it narrowly for, and reactively to, security events. Third, the recalibration of the ethnic 'self-help', housing ethnic quota, bicultural education, language use and Group Representation Constituency policies in the direction of vector d is called for so that governance would shed its piecemeal and short-term approach and begin to take into account cross-dimensional effects and be holistic in the consideration of the three different dimensions.

By implication, the state would also need to shed its pluralist assumption that ethnic diversity is primordially divisive. Taking a holistic view instead, the state should realize that ethnic diversity ceases to be a threat if minority political representation is positively high and inequality in the cost of ascribed identities minimized. When the other two dimensions are taken care of, ethnic diversity no longer needs to be managed to remain static with contradictory consequences and can be allowed to release its creative energies and fulfil its moral function.

If adaptive governance vis-à-vis internationalizing neoliberal multiculturalism is successful, it is possible that Singapore may create a new type of multicultural system against the grain of the current organization of socio-cultural systems, and which lies in the upper right-hand corner of high intercultural interaction and minority political representation – a successful multicultural utopia that would no longer be a utopia but, rather, a historical possibility and model for other postcolonial multicultural systems in transition. When this happens, the germ of a vision Chua has called 'communitarian democracy',[51] which has guided political innovations in a piecemeal, conservative and pro-ruling party fashion, will come to its proper fruition to serve the real interests of the Singaporean people.

Conclusion

Is Singapore resilient? As I have argued, resilience is relative to the system's internal dynamics and vector of movement in the changing global multicultural landscape. I have posited Singapore's socio-cultural system to be a postcolonial multicultural system with moderate intercultural interaction and minority representation that has seen the rise of the inequality of costs of ascribed identities and has threatened stability in a global context marked by the internationalization of neoliberal multiculturalism and the decline of postcolonial multiculturalism since the 1980s. Thus, I have shown that what scholars have noticed as a shift in governance from the amalgamation to the mosaic approaches of postcolonial multiculturalism in the 1980s reflects institutional innovations to shore up resilience.

But the very institutional innovations that have kept the system resilient have placed the system precariously on the edge of change because of the contradictory effects piecemeal interventions introduce. Consequently, the recovery of stability seems to point towards assimilation or neoliberal multiculturalism. Indeed, the institutional innovations and multicultural policies enacted by the government appear to engage these large-scale changes in these terms, to prevent the Singapore system from becoming either assimilative or neoliberal multicultural. I have argued that an alternative vector of change is possible that goes against the grain of the current organization of socio-cultural systems, and towards higher intercultural interaction and minority political representation, and low inequality of costs for all groups.

For this change to take place, Singapore's political leaders would need a paradigm shift away from the technocratic managerial and social engineering mindset to an adaptive governance orientation. Part of this paradigm shift would be to do away with the conservative valuation of resilience as an absolute moral or public good. In the long run, the creative destruction or non-destructive transformation of a precarious system may serve to build a more resilient system and it is in Singapore's collective capacity to create an alternative system that would better serve the ends of the social, economic and cultural well-being of all groups in the country. In the final analysis, trust will be a crucial factor in determining the future direction of multicultural development in Singapore, but it is not trust between the myriad ethnic groups that is referred to here – it is political leaders who will need to trust the reflexively awakened energies of the diverse groups of people if Singapore is to realize its collective capacity.

Notes

1 This paper was presented at the workshop on '(Un)Problematic Multiculturalism and Social Resilience', Centre of Excellence for National Security, Rajaratnam School of International Studies, February 2008. The paper was not updated to account for events that have taken place between then and August 2012, when the paper was finalized for publication. I believe that my analysis and argument still stand. Please see my other writings on multiculturalism that have been published since 2008 in the *British Journal of Sociology*, *Inter-Asia Cultural Studies* and *Space and Culture*, and in my co-edited book, *Race and Multiculturalism in Malaysia and Singapore*.

2 Charles Taylor, 'The Politics of Recognition', in Amy Gutmann,ed. *Multiculturalism: Examining the Politics of Recognition* (Princeton, NJ: Princeton University Press, 1994); Will Kymlicka, 'Multicultural Citizenship', in Gershon Shafir, ed. *The Citizenship Debates* (Minneapolis: University of Minnesota Press, 1998).

3 Daniel P. S. Goh, 'From Colonial Pluralism to Postcolonial Multiculturalism: Race, State Formation and the Question of Cultural Diversity in Malaysia and Singapore'. *Sociology Compass* 2, no. 1 (2008): 232–252.

4 Harold Wolpe, 'The Theory of Internal Colonialism: The South African Case', in I. Oxaal, T. Barnett and D. Booth, eds. *Beyond the Sociology of Development: Economy and Society in Latin America and Africa* (London: Routledge, 1975); Edna Bonacich, 'A Theory of Ethnic Antagonism: The Split Labor Market'. *American Sociological Review* 37, no. 5 (1972): 547–559; Eduardo Bonilla-Silva, 'Rethinking racism: Toward a Structural Interpretation'. *American Sociological Review* 62 (1997): 465–480.

5 Max Weber, 'Class, Status, Party', *From Max Weber: Essays in Sociology* (Translated by H. H. Gerth and C. Wright Mills) (New York: Oxford University Press, 1946).

6 Daniel P. S. Goh, 'States of Ethnography: Colonialism, Resistance and Cultural Transcription in Malaya and the Philippines, 1890s–1930s'. *Comparative Studies in Society and History* 49, no. 1 (2007): 109–142.

7 Charles Hirschman, 'The Meaning and Measurement of Ethnicity in Malaysia: An Analysis of Census Classifications'. *Journal of Asian Studies* 46 (1987): 555–582.

8 Charles Hirschman, 'The Making of Race in Colonial Malaya: Political Economy and Racial Ideology'. *Sociological Forum* 1 (1986): 330–361.

9 David Brown, *The State and Ethnic Politics in South-East Asia* (London: Routledge, 1994).

10 Lily Zubaidah Rahim, *The Singapore Dilemma: The Political and Educational Marginality of the Malay Community* (Kuala Lumpur: Oxford University Press, 1998), p. 85; Garry Rodan, 'State–society Relations and Political Opposition in Singapore', in Garry Rodan, ed. *Political Oppositions in Industrialising Asia* (London: Routledge, 1996), p. 104.

11 David Brown, *The State and Ethnic Politics in South-East Asia*, p. 101; Garry Rodan, 'State–society Relations and Political Opposition in Singapore', p. 105.

12 Chih Hoong Sin, 'The Politics of Ethnic Integration in Singapore: Malay "Regrouping" as an Ideological Construct'. *International Journal of Urban and Regional Research* 27, no. 3 (2003): 527–544.

13 Lily Zubaidah Rahim, *The Singapore Dilemma*, pp. 75–80.

14 John Sydenham Furnivall, *Colonial Policy and Practice: A Comparative Study of Burma and Netherlands India* (Cambridge: Cambridge University Press, 1948), p. 304.

15 Lai Ah Eng, *Meanings of Multiethnicity: A Case-study of Ethnicity and Ethnic Relations in Singapore* (Kuala Lumpur: Oxford University Press, 1995), p. 191.

16 Maria R. Markus, 'Cultural Pluralism and the Subversion of the "Taken-for-Granted" World', in Philomena Essed and David Theo Goldberg, eds. *Race Critical Theories: Text and Context* (Oxford: Blackwell, 2002).

17 Chua Beng Huat and Kwok Kian Woon, 'Social Pluralism in Singapore', in *The Politics of Multiculturalism: Pluralism and Citizenship in Malaysia, Singapore and Indonesia* (Honolulu: University of Hawai'i Press, 2001), pp. 115–116.

18 Chua Beng Huat, 'Culture, Multiracialism, and National Identity in Singapore', in Kuan-Hsing Chen, eds. *Trajectories: Inter-Asia Cultural Studies* (London: Routledge, 1998).

19 John Sydenham Furnivall, *Colonial Policy and Practice*, pp. 307–311.

20 Chiew Seen Kong, 'The Socio-cultural Framework of Politics', in Jon S. T. Quah, Chan Heng Chee and Seah Chee Meow, eds. *Government and Politics of Singapore* (Singapore: Oxford University Press, 1985).

21 Geoffrey Benjamin, 'The Cultural Logic of Singapore's "Multiracialism"' in Riaz Hassan, ed. *Singapore: Society in Transition* (Kuala Lumpur: Oxford University Press, 1976), p. 30.
22 Chiew Seen Kong, 'The Socio-cultural Framework of Politics'; David Chan, *Attitudes on Race and Religion: Survey of Social Attitudes of Singaporeans 2001* (Singapore: Ministry of Community Development and Sports, 2002); Yolanda Chin and Norman Vasu, *The Ties that Bind and Blind: A Report on Inter-racial and Inter-religious Relations in Singapore* (Singapore: Centre of Excellence for National Security, S. Rajaratnam School of International Studies, Nanyang Technological University, 2007); Gillian Koh, 'Social Resilience and its Bases in Multicultural Singapore', in Norman Vasu, ed. *Social Resilience in Singapore: Reflections from the London Bombings* (Singapore: Select Publishing, 2007).
23 Lily Kong and Brenda S. A. Yeoh, *The Politics of Landscapes in Singapore: Constructions of 'Nation'* (Syracuse, NY: Syracuse University Press, 2003); Robbie B. H. Goh, *Contours of Culture: Space and Social Difference in Singapore* (Hong Kong: Hong Kong University Press, 2005).
24 Nirmala S. PuruShotam, *Negotiating Multiculturalism: Disciplining Difference in Singapore* (Berlin: Mouton de Gruyter, 2000).
25 Chua Beng Huat, 'The Cost of Membership in Ascribed Community', in Will Kymlicka and Baogang He, eds. *Multiculturalism in Asia* (Oxford: Oxford University Press, 2005), pp. 190–191.
26 Tania Li, *Malays in Singapore: Culture, Economy, and Ideology* (Singapore: Oxford University Press, 1989), pp. 108–111.
27 Chih Hoong Sin, 'Segregation and Marginalisation within Public Housing: The Disadvantaged in Bedok New Town, Singapore'. *Housing Studies* 17, no. 2 (2002a): 267–288.
28 Lily Zubaidah Rahim, *The Singapore Dilemma*, pp. 205–207; R. Quinn Moore, 'Multiracialism and Meritocracy: Singapore's Approach to Race and Inequality'. *Review of Social Economy* 58, no. 3 (2000): 339–360.
29 Michael D. Barr and Jevon Low, 'Assimilation as Multiracialism: The Case of Singapore's Malays'. *Asian Ethnicity* 6, no. 3 (2005): 161–182.
30 Chiew Seen Kong, 'The Socio-cultural Framework of Politics'; Yolanda Chin and Norman Vasu, *The Ties that Bind and Blind*.
31 Sharon Siddique, 'Singaporean Identity', in Kernial Singh Sandhu and Paul Wheatley, eds. *Management of Success: The Moulding of Modern Singapore* (Singapore: Institute of Southeast Asian Studies, 1989), p. 575.
32 David Brown, *The State and Ethnic Politics in South-East Asia*.
33 Michael Hill and Lian Kwen Fee, *The Politics of Nation Building and Citizenship in Singapore* (London: Routledge, 1995), pp. 107–112.
34 Raj Vasil, *Asianising Singapore: The PAP's Management of Ethnicity* (Singapore: Heinemann Asia, 1995).
35 Eugene K. B. Tan, '"We, the Citizens of Singapore…": Multiethnicity, its Evolution and its Aberrations', in Lai Ah Eng, ed. *Beyond Rituals and Riots: Ethnic Pluralism and Social Cohesion in Singapore* (Singapore: Institute of Policy Studies, 2004).
36 S. Rajaratnam, 'Our Cultural Heritage', in Kwa Chong Guan, ed. *S. Rajaratnam on Singapore: From Ideas to Reality* (Singapore: World Scientific, 2006).
37 Yaacob Ibrahim, 'Accomodating Differences: Building a Culture of Understanding and Peace', speech at the Wee Kim Wee Seminar on Cross-Cultural Understanding, 2 August 2003. Available at http://stars.nhb.gov.sg/stars/public/.
38 Emile Durkheim, *The Division of Labor in Society* (Translated by W. D. Halls) (New York: Macmillan, 1933 [1893]).
39 Daniel P. S. Goh, 'Multiculturalism and the Problem of Solidarity', in Terence Chong, ed. *The Management of Success: Singapore Revisited* (Singapore: Institute of Southeast Asian Studies, 2010).

40 Will Kymlicka, *Multicultural Odysseys: Negotiating the New International Politics of Diversity* (Oxford: Oxford University Press, 2007).
41 Charles R. Hale, 'Neoliberal Multiculturalism: The Remaking of Cultural Rights and Racial Dominance in Central America'. *PoLAR: Political and Legal Anthropology Review* 28, no. 1 (2005): 10–19; Park Yun-Joo and Patricia Richards, 'Negotiating Neoliberal Multiculturalism: Mapuche Workers in the Chilean State'. *Social Forces* 85, no. 3 (2007): 1319–1339; Nancy Postero, *Now We Are Citizens: Indigenous Politics in Postmulticultural Bolivia* (Stanford, CA: Stanford University Press, 2006).
42 Paul Gilroy, 'The End of Antiracism', in Philomena Essed and David Theo Goldberg, eds. *Race Critical Theories: Text and Context* (Oxford: Blackwell, 2002), p. 251.
43 Chua Beng Huat, 'Multiculturalism in Singapore: An Instrument of Social Control'. *Race and Class* 44, no. 3, (2003): 58–77; Brenda S. A. Yeoh, 'Migration, International Labour and Multicultural Policies in Singapore', Asia Research Institute Working Paper, no. 19, February 2004. Available at www.ari.nus.edu.sg/pub/wps.htm.
44 Tania Li, *Malays in Singapore*, pp. 166–183; Lily Zubaidah Rahim, *The Singapore Dilemma*, pp. 186–188.
45 Ministry of Community Development, Youth and Sports, Singapore Government, 'Progress of the Malay Community in Singapore since 1980', August 2007. Available at www.mcys.gov.sg/MCDSFiles/download/ProgressofMalayCommunity.pdf.
46 Yaacob Ibrahim, 'Accomodating Differences'.
47 Brian Walker, C. S. Holling, Stephen R. Carpenter and Ann Kinzig, 'Resilience, Adaptability and Transformability in Social-ecological Systems'. *Ecology and Society* 9, no. 2 (2004): 5 (emphasis mine).
48 Niklas Luhmann, *Social Systems* (Stanford, CA: Stanford University Press, 1995).
49 Chih Hoong Sin, 'The Quest for a Balanced Ethnic Mix: Singapore's Ethnic Quota Policy Examined'. *Urban Studies* 39, no. 8 (2002b): 1347–1374.
50 Douglas S. Massey and Nancy A. Denton, *American Apartheid: Segregation and Making of the Underclass* (Cambridge, MA: Harvard University Press, 1993).
51 Chua Beng Huat, 'The Cost of Membership in Ascribed Community'.

References

Barr, Michael D. and Jevon Low. 'Assimilation as Multiracialism: The Case of Singapore's Malays'. *Asian Ethnicity* 6, no. 3 (2005): 161–182.
Benjamin, Geoffrey. 'The Cultural Logic of Singapore's "Multiracialism"', in Riaz Hassan, ed. *Singapore: Society in Transition* (Kuala Lumpur: Oxford University Press, 1976).
Bonacich, Edna. 'A Theory of Ethnic Antagonism: The Split Labor Market'. *American Sociological Review* 37, no. 5 (1972): 547–559.
Bonilla-Silva, Eduardo. 'Rethinking Racism: Toward a Structural Interpretation'. *American Sociological Review* 62 (1997): 465–480.
Brown, David. *The State and Ethnic Politics in South-East Asia* (London: Routledge, 1994).
Chan, David. *Attitudes on Race and Religion: Survey of Social Attitudes of Singaporeans 2001* (Singapore: Ministry of Community Development and Sports, 2002).
Chiew Seen Kong. 'The Socio-cultural Framework of Politics', in Jon S. T. Quah, Chan Heng Chee and Seah Chee Meow, eds. *Government and Politics of Singapore* (Singapore: Oxford University Press, 1985).
Chih Hoong Sin. 'Segregation and Marginalisation within Public Housing: The Disadvantaged in Bedok New Town, Singapore'. *Housing Studies* 17, no. 2 (2002a): 267–288.

Chih Hoong Sin. 'The Quest for a Balanced Ethnic Mix: Singapore's Ethnic Quota Policy Examined'. *Urban Studies* 39, no. 8 (2002b): 1347–1374.

Chih Hoong Sin. 'The Politics of Ethnic Integration in Singapore: Malay "Regrouping" as an Ideological Construct'. *International Journal of Urban and Regional Research* 27, no. 3 (2003): 527–544.

Chin, Yolanda and Norman Vasu. *The Ties that Bind and Blind: A Report on Inter-racial and Inter-religious Relations in Singapore* (Singapore: Centre of Excellence for National Security, S. Rajaratnam School of International Studies, Nanyang Technological University, 2007).

Chua Beng Huat. 'Culture, Multiracialism, and National Identity in Singapore', in Kuan-Hsing Chen, ed. *Trajectories: Inter-Asia Cultural Studies* (London: Routledge, 1998).

Chua Beng Huat. 'Multiculturalism in Singapore: An Instrument of Social Control'. *Race and Class* 44, no. 3 (2003): 58–77.

Chua Beng Huat. 'The Cost of Membership in Ascribed Community', in Will Kymlicka and Baogang He, ed. *Multiculturalism in Asia* (Oxford: Oxford University Press, 2005).

Chua Beng Huat and Kwok Kian Woon. 'Social Pluralism in Singapore', in *The Politics of Multiculturalism: Pluralism and Citizenship in Malaysia, Singapore and Indonesia* (Honolulu: University of Hawai'i Press, 2001).

Durkheim, Emile. *The Division of Labor in Society* (Translated by W. D. Halls) (New York: Macmillan, 1933 [1893]).

Furnivall, John Sydenham. *Colonial Policy and Practice: A Comparative Study of Burma and Netherlands India* (Cambridge: Cambridge University Press, 1948).

Gilroy, Paul. 'The End of Antiracism', in Philomena Essed and David Theo Goldberg, eds. *Race Critical Theories: Text and Context* (Oxford: Blackwell, 2002).

Goh, Daniel P. S. 'States of Ethnography: Colonialism, Resistance and Cultural Transcription in Malaya and the Philippines, 1890s–1930s'. *Comparative Studies in Society and History* 49, no. 1 (2007): 109–142.

Goh, Daniel P. S. 'From Colonial Pluralism to Postcolonial Multiculturalism: Race, State Formation and the Question of Cultural Diversity in Malaysia and Singapore'. *Sociology Compass* 2, no. 1 (2008): 232–252.

Goh, Daniel P. S. 'Multiculturalism and the Problem of Solidarity', in Terence Chong, ed. *Management of Success: Singapore Revisited* (Singapore: Institute of Southeast Asian Studies, 2010).

Goh, Robbie B. H. *Contours of Culture: Space and Social Difference in Singapore* (Hong Kong: Hong Kong University Press, 2005).

Hale, Charles R. 'Neoliberal Multiculturalism: The Remaking of Cultural Rights and Racial Dominance in Central America'. *PoLAR: Political and Legal Anthropology Review* 28, no. 1 (2005): 10–19.

Hill, Michael and Lian Kwen Fee. *The Politics of Nation Building and Citizenship in Singapore* (London: Routledge, 1995).

Hirschman, Charles. 'The Making of Race in Colonial Malaya: Political Economy and Racial Ideology'. *Sociological Forum* 1 (1986): 330–361.

Hirschman, Charles. 'The Meaning and Measurement of Ethnicity in Malaysia: An Analysis of Census Classifications'. *Journal of Asian Studies* 46 (1987): 555–582.

Koh, Gillian. 'Social Resilience and its Bases in Multicultural Singapore', in Norman Vasu, ed. *Social Resilience in Singapore: Reflections from the London Bombings* (Singapore: Select Publishing, 2007).

Kong, Lily and Brenda S. A. Yeoh. *The Politics of Landscapes in Singapore: Construc-tions of 'Nation'* (Syracuse, NY: Syracuse University Press, 2003).

Kymlicka, Will. 'Multicultural Citizenship', in Gershon Shafir, ed. *The Citizenship Debates* (Minneapolis: University of Minnesota Press, 1998).

Kymlicka, Will. *Multicultural Odysseys: Negotiating the New International Politics of Diversity* (Oxford: Oxford University Press, 2007).

Lai Ah Eng. *Meanings of Multiethnicity: A Case-study of Ethnicity and Ethnic Relations in Singapore* (Kuala Lumpur: Oxford University Press, 1995).

Li, Tania. *Malays in Singapore: Culture, Economy, and Ideology* (Singapore: Oxford University Press, 1989).

Luhmann, Niklas. *Social Systems* (Stanford, CA: Stanford University Press, 1995).

Markus, Maria R. 'Cultural Pluralism and the Subversion of the "Taken-for-Granted" World', in Philomena Essed and David Theo Goldberg, eds. *Race Critical Theories: Text and Context* (Oxford: Blackwell, 2002).

Massey, Douglas S. and Nancy A. Denton. *American Apartheid: Segregation and Making of the Underclass* (Cambridge, MA: Harvard University Press, 1993).

Ministry of Community Development, Youth and Sports, Singapore Government. 'Pro-gress of the Malay Community in Singapore since 1980', August 2007. Available at www.mcys.gov.sg/MCDSFiles/download/ProgressofMalayCommunity.pdf.

Moore, R. Quinn. 'Multiracialism and Meritocracy: Singapore's Approach to Race and Inequality'. *Review of Social Economy* 58, no. 3 (2000): 339–360.

Park, Yun-Joo and Patricia Richards. 'Negotiating Neoliberal Multiculturalism: Mapuche Workers in the Chilean State'. *Social Forces* 85, no. 3 (2007): 1319–1339.

Postero, Nancy. *Now We Are Citizens: Indigenous Politics in Postmulticultural Bolivia* (Stanford, CA: Stanford University Press, 2006).

PuruShotam, Nirmala S. *Negotiating Multiculturalism: Disciplining Difference in Singa-pore* (Berlin: Mouton de Gruyter, 2000).

Rahim, Lily Zubaidah. *The Singapore Dilemma: The Political and Educational Margin-ality of the Malay Community* (Kuala Lumpur: Oxford University Press, 1998).

Rajaratnam, S. 'Our Cultural Heritage' (1960),in Kwa Chong Guan, ed. *S. Rajaratnam on Singapore: From Ideas to Reality* (Singapore: World Scientific, 2006).

Rodan, Garry. 'State–society Relations and Political Opposition in Singapore', in Garry Rodan, ed. *Political Oppositions in Industrialising Asia* (London: Routledge, 1996).

Siddique, Sharon. 'Singaporean Identity', in Kernial Singh Sandhu and Paul Wheatley, eds. *Management of Success: The Moulding of Modern Singapore* (Singapore: Institute of Southeast Asian Studies, 1989).

Tan, Eugene K. B. '"We, the Citizens of Singapore…": Multiethnicity, its Evolution and its Aberrations', in Lai Ah Eng, ed. *Beyond Rituals and Riots: Ethnic Pluralism and Social Cohesion in Singapore* (Singapore: Institute of Policy Studies, 2004).

Taylor, Charles. 'The Politics of Recognition', in Amy Gutmann, ed. *Multiculturalism: Examining the Politics of Recognition* (Princeton, NJ: Princeton University Press, 1994).

Vasil, Raj. *Asianising Singapore: The PAP's Management of Ethnicity* (Singapore: Hein-emann Asia, 1995).

Walker, Brian, C. S. Holling, Stephen R. Carpenter and Ann Kinzig. 'Resilience, Adapta-bility and Transformability in Social-ecological Systems'. *Ecology and Society* 9, no. 2 (2004): 5.

Weber, Max. 'Class, Status, Party'. *From Max Weber: Essays in Sociology* (Translated by H. H. Gerth and C. Wright Mills) (New York: Oxford University Press, 1946).

Wolpe, Harold. 'The Theory of Internal Colonialism: The South African Case', in I. Oxaal, T. Barnett and D. Booth, eds. *Beyond the Sociology of Development: Economy and Society in Latin America and Africa* (London: Routledge, 1975).

Yaacob Ibrahim. 'Accomodating Differences: Building a Culture of Understanding and Peace', Speech at the Wee Kim Wee Seminar on Cross-Cultural Understanding, 2 August 2003. Available at http://stars.nhb.gov.sg/stars/public/.

Yeoh, Brenda S. A. 'Migration, International Labour and Multicultural Policies in Singapore', Asia Research Institute Working Paper, no. 19, February 2004. Available at www.ari.nus.edu.sg/pub/wps.htm.

4   (Un)problematic multiculturalism

Challenges and opportunities for social cohesion in New Zealand

Allen Bartley

Introduction

On 15 October 2007, amidst sensationalized media speculation, squads of New Zealand police – many armed with automatic weapons – executed a number of search warrants on addresses around the country. Using for the first time powers granted to the police under the Terrorism Suppression Act 2002, they entered homes and businesses, and confiscated a wide range of evidence, including computers and other electronic equipment, clothing, rifles and ammunition, diaries and correspondence. As part of the raids, police descended on the small, rural settlement of Ruatoki North and, in an extraordinary show of force, blocked roads in and out of the town while armed officers identified and photographed the occupants of every vehicle stopped. By the end of the day, police had arrested 16 people, citing the Terrorism Suppression Act and the Arms Act. What will not be immediately apparent to many is that Ruatoki is a settlement at the gateway of the Urewera National Park, an area of dense and inhospitable bush, and is populated largely by the Maori. When news of the police raids broke, and it was revealed that one of those arrested was a prominent radical Maori activist, a disturbing fact became clear: the police were accusing Maori activists of being a terrorist group, and of running 'military-style training camps' in the Urewera. In the weeks following the raids, New Zealand's Solicitor-General ruled that a police case could not be made under the Terrorism Suppression Act and, as a result, firearms charges against some of those arrested would be dropped because the case against them relied on evidence that could not have been gained without the extraordinary powers granted under the terror laws. Under the Arms Act, most of those finally tried are likely to face only fines if found guilty.[1]

Despite the sensationalism and disquiet caused (albeit briefly) by the spectre of indigenous separatist terrorists, Maori political separatism is not a significant threat to social cohesion in New Zealand. On the contrary, New Zealand's indigenous populations are well integrated into the political and social policy frameworks across all levels of government. Nonetheless, many Maori – along with New Zealanders identified as Pacific Islanders – continue to be at the economic margins of New Zealand society. As a result, they are at risk of experiencing worrying levels of social exclusion, and are caught up in the constellation of negative and socially disruptive forces attendant with high concentrations of relative economic deprivation.

At the same time, new migrants from non-traditional source countries, granted New Zealand residency on the basis of high levels of economic or human capital – educational qualifications, professional experience, technical and professional skills, entrepreneurial success – have dramatically altered New Zealand's demographic, cultural and 'racial' landscape. They have met with an ambivalent reception in New Zealand, however, characterized by unsatisfactory labour market outcomes, widely assumed to be the result of discriminatory employment practices, and a general reluctance to include Asian New Zealanders in the 'national identity' discourse.[2] This has resulted in large numbers of new migrants being unemployed or underemployed, or disengaged altogether from the labour market and either living off savings and investment income, or maintaining employment and business interests overseas, and engaging in transnational family strategies.[3]

This chapter seeks to track these social faultlines and their impacts on the outlook for social cohesion in contemporary New Zealand society, and suggest indicators for measuring such impacts.

Maori

'Maori' is the general ethnic designation given to the indigenous people of New Zealand, though many individuals so designated choose to self-identify by tribal affiliation. The mechanism by which formal sovereignty over New Zealand was ceded to the British Crown was the Treaty of Waitangi, signed in 1840 by Governor William Hobson, representing Queen Victoria, and 500 leaders of *iwi* and *hapu*.[4] The treaty was intended to accomplish three objectives: the securing of sovereignty for the Crown; the protection of Maori interests; and the promotion of settler interests (through the acquisition – via the Crown – of land from Maori).[5] In 1877, after explosive growth of the settler population and the decimation of the Maori population through disease, intertribal conflict and dispossession resulting from colonial wars and confiscation,[6] the chief justice of the Supreme Court legitimized successive governments' ignoring of the treaty, by declaring it a 'simple nullity'.[7]

Thereafter, up until the mid-1980s, New Zealand social policy operated within a monocultural – and institutionally racist – framework. This monocultural disposition of the New Zealand state began to be challenged vigorously by Maori cultural and political activists from the 1970s, and official reports of state agencies in the 1980s.[8] Such developments eventually brought about a greater legal and political recognition of the aboriginal rights of the Maori as *tangata whenua*,[9] and of the Treaty of Waitangi as a founding constitutional document – a moral (though not in itself a *legal*) guarantor for Maori rights.[10] At that time, the president of the New Zealand Court of Appeal, Sir Robin Cooke (now Lord Cooke of Thorndon), likened the treaty relationship between Maori and the Crown to a 'partnership', which carried obligations of reciprocity and good faith, and bound the Crown to protect Maori interests actively.[11]

Since that time, a significant body of legislation, common law, policy and practice has accumulated that has reinforced the position of the Maori as both partner with, and client of, the state. Also reinforced has been the notion that *culture matters*. The association in New Zealand between socio-economic status and ethnicity has been – and continues to be – strong; so strong, in fact, that conventionally each has been thought to explain the other. 'Being Maori, for example, is often seen as a synonym for being poor and being poor is sometimes seen as the distinguishing characteristic of Maori and Pacific peoples.'[12] However, by the mid-1980s the socially and economically marginalized position of the Maori was being increasingly explained with reference to New Zealand's colonial past, and the continuing institutional racism inherent in most of the country's major institutions – particularly the agencies of the state. In response to such criticisms levelled at the Department of Social Welfare, in 1985 the then-Minister of Social Welfare commissioned an Advisory Committee to report on the operations of the department from a Maori perspective. The committee's report, entitled *Puao-te-Ata-Tu* (*Daybreak*), was unequivocal in its assessment:

> We comment on the institutional racism reflected in this Department and indeed in society itself. We have identified a number of problem areas – policy formation, service delivery, communication, racial imbalances in the staffing, appointment, promotion and training practices. We are in no doubt that changes are essential and must be made urgently...
>
> We have been disturbed at the extent to which Social Welfare institutions and indeed the courts, have a clientele which is predominantly Maori. We think that as a society we cannot survive much longer if we continue to ignore these facts and the situation which gives rise to them.
>
> Although we invited the people to talk to us about the operations of the Department of Social Welfare, discussions invariably brought out equally grave concerns about the operations of the other Government departments, particularly those working in the social area. There is no doubt that the young people who come to the attention of the Police and the Department of Social Welfare invariably bring with them histories of substandard housing, health deficiencies, abysmal education records, and an inability to break out of the ranks of the unemployed. It is no exaggeration to say, as we do in our report[,] that in many ways the picture we have received is one of crisis proportions. To redress the imbalances will require concerted action from all agencies involved – central and local government, the business community, Maoridom and the community at large. We make recommendations for a comprehensive approach accordingly. Our problems of cultural imperialism, deprivation and alienation mean that we cannot afford to wait longer. The problem is with us here and now.[13]

Carrying the imprimatur of a minister of the Crown, *Puao-te-Ata-Tu* marked a turning point in the New Zealand state's acknowledgement that state institutions tended to reflect the cultural imperatives of the dominant cultural group, and that arrangements based on 'universalist' principles (inevitably defined by the dominant population) could actively disadvantage minority groups – specifically the indigenous population.[14] The emergence of biculturalism was an official policy and institutional response to the challenges raised by such postcolonial critiques.[15] By 1988, the State Sector Act required chief executives of state agencies to acknowledge the aspirations of the Maori, and to act on the need for greater Maori involvement in the public service.[16] Biculturalism thereafter was enshrined in government policy, particularly in relation to education, social welfare and health. For example, reforms in the 1989 Education Act required all schools to draft a charter in which they would pledge, amongst other things, to uphold the principles of the Treaty of Waitangi; the Children, Young Persons and Their Families Act 1989 legislated nearly all of the relevant recommendations presented to the Department of Social Welfare in *Puao-Te-Ata-Tu*, particularly those relating to the involvement of *iwi*, *hapu* and *whanau*[17] in decisions regarding the care and placement of Maori children.

This bicultural relationship reflects what Soysal[18] describes as a corporatist model of membership, in which the state actively engages with the Maori through a variety of collective agencies, most notably *iwi*, *hapu* and pan-tribal authorities. By thus recognizing the Maori as *tangata whenua*, the state ascribed special status to the 'dominant minority' in New Zealand society, and confirmed that there were two sorts of citizenship in New Zealand. One of these embodies a set of rights and the protection afforded to individuals by a liberal-democratic state which are universally available, and which were guaranteed to the Maori under Article Three of the Treaty of Waitangi. The other contains those rights that are associated with being Maori, specifically as members of *iwi* and *hapu*, and the rights specified in Article Two of the treaty, relating to resources, including land, fisheries and forests, among other things.

That the political and constitutional position of the Maori has been rehabilitated significantly over the past 30 years is manifest across a range of initiatives, including Maori-specific policies (and the contracting of Maori providers) in health, education, justice and the provision of social services; the settlement of historic grievances, either through the recommendations of the Waitangi Tribunal and/or direct negotiations with the Crown via the Office of Treaty Settlements; the statutory role of *iwi* and *hapu* within local government structures, regarding matters of conservation and heritage; or the reservation for the Maori of a significant proportion of the commercial fisheries, under the Quota Management Scheme. However it must be acknowledged that such moves have often been made begrudgingly, and amidst contradictory measures which seem to deny a good faith partnership between the Maori and the Crown – as in the 2004 legislation to deny tribes the right to test in court any claims of customary title to parts of the New Zealand foreshore or seabed. Moreover, few of the initiatives cited here represent permanent or constitutional arrangements: the nature of the

Crown's relationship with Maori could be altered dramatically by a change of government, and the electoral success of various political parties that advocate diminished recognition of the Treaty of Waitangi or of Maori cultural aspirations more generally.

The state also maintains a corporatist regime similar to that with the Maori – though significantly less structured, and for quite different historical reasons – with the Pacific peoples in New Zealand. Unlike other migrant groups, the Pacific peoples have a constitutional relationship with the New Zealand state, stemming from the historical role New Zealand had in enforcing and extending the British Empire through the South Pacific from the early twentieth century onwards. Some – such as those from the Cook Islands, Nieue and Tokelau – have automatic rights to New Zealand citizenship. Also, unlike other migrants, the Pacific peoples in New Zealand tend to be concentrated geographically (Manukau City, in South Auckland, is billed as the world's largest Polynesian city), and thus in reasonably homogeneous communities. Ethnic institutions (the chief of which is the church) and status hierarchies (such as the Samoan *matai* structure) also facilitate the identification of community leaders and spokespeople. These have a high-level relationship with the state, through liaison officers working in many public sectors, such as health, education and local government, and through the Ministry of Pacific Island Affairs. The role of the ministry is to provide policy advice regarding (and representing the interests of) Pasifika communities in New Zealand to ministers, government officials and Pacific communities, and to monitor social policy outcomes for the Pacific peoples.[19]

Despite such high-level and corporatist engagement with the state, social outcomes for the Maori and Pacific peoples are comparatively poor. Given their historical socio-economic location as manual, semi- or unskilled labourers and recipients of high levels of social assistance, these populations were disproportionately affected by the economic 'structural adjustment' that occurred in New Zealand in the 1980s and 1990s. During that time, the domestic manufacturing sector was opened to deregulated competition from global markets, resulting in large-scale redundancies, and the government moved to cut spending on social welfare benefits. Combined, these developments rapidly thrust many Maori and Pasifika families into poverty.[20] Unemployment rates for both the Maori and Pacific peoples remain more than twice those for New Zealanders of European descent,[21] and a significantly higher proportion of Maori and Pasifika children are raised in single-parent households dependant on social assistance (the Domestic Purposes Benefit) for a basic income. The result is that they are far more likely to be living on less than 60 per cent of the average income.[22] Educational outcomes are similarly worrying: Maori and Pasifika young people leave secondary school without any qualifications at much higher rates than other ethnic groups, and are less likely than others to be enrolled in degree-level tertiary education courses.[23] As predictors of social exclusion – especially given the recent emphasis in New Zealand on transformation to a 'knowledge economy' – low levels of income and education tend to be reproduced generationally, and lead to what Waldegrave and Pole refer to as the growing 'knowledge divide'.[24]

'These disadvantages are very serious because they have the potential to substantially limit [Maori and Pacific peoples] from access to higher education and training and from active involvement in knowledge based economic activity...'[25]

An additional consequence of the social and economic position of Maori communities is reflected in New Zealand's crime and imprisonment statistics over the past 30 years: from a low in 1981, when individuals identified as Maori accounted for 12 per cent of all criminal convictions, the Maori now comprise 37 per cent of all convictions.[26] Imprisonment rates have always been higher for Maori than for non-Maori, and for the past 30 years have comprised half of all custodial sentences handed down by judges each year. While those who self-identify as Maori comprise only 14 per cent of the whole New Zealand population, they make up fully half of the country's prison population.[27] The growing levels of participation in, and violence stemming from, predominantly Polynesian urban youth gangs in Auckland suggest that the demographic distribution in the crime statistics is unlikely to change in the foreseeable future.[28]

'New' migration and migrant integration

It is ironic that, just as the bicultural relationship between the Maori and the Crown began to be formalized, and a number of agencies of the New Zealand state began struggling to build new models of biculturalism into policy and practice, the government moved to adopt 'multiculturalism' as an explicit value in an overhaul of New Zealand's immigration policies. In doing so, the government set aside more than a hundred years of discriminatory immigration policies based on limiting the numbers of non-British and non-Irish migrants, and almost completely excluding Asians. These changes were to produce in a dramatic fashion a cultural diversity of a sort that had been unknown previously in New Zealand. For example, in 1987, migrants from Asia comprised 18.7 per cent of permanent and long-term arrivals in New Zealand. By 1993, they constituted 48 per cent of all arrivals. At the time of the 2006 Census, those residents identifying themselves as Asian[29] comprised 9 per cent of the population, whereas in 1986 (just before the changes to immigration policy were introduced) the same group accounted for just 1.5 per cent of the New Zealand population. In Auckland, arguably New Zealand's only international city and where most migrants settle, the impact is even more pronounced: 18 per cent of the population in Auckland identify as Asian.[30]

Historically, little official attention was paid to the incorporation of new migrants into the bourgeoning settler society. The task had generally been unproblematic: the assimilation of migrants into New Zealand society was managed through limiting – or prohibiting altogether – any migrants not of British or Irish stock. Thus, by enforcing a British identity on settler society via restricted entry (and public discourse), the New Zealand state largely avoided the need to address itself to managing the settlement and adjustment of heterogeneous migrant populations.

This is not to say that non-British settlers had never before come to New Zealand, however. The first organized group of Chinese migrants arrived in New Zealand from Australia in 1866, invited by the Dunedin Chamber of Commerce to work as miners in the Otago goldfields.[31] By 1871 public criticism of the presence of Chinese migrants was sufficient to prompt the formation of a Parliamentary Select Committee on Chinese Immigration.[32] Though that committee determined there was no need for action to be taken to restrict Chinese immigration to New Zealand, within ten years the government had passed the Anti-Chinese Act, which imposed a £10 poll tax on each Chinese immigrant (roughly equivalent to a waterside worker's monthly income), and restricted their arrival numbers by specifying that no more than one Chinese would be accepted for every ten tons of weight on all arriving vessels. The New Zealand census conducted the same year showed that the Chinese comprised a mere 1.02 per cent of the total population.[33]

Those restrictions were maintained for the next 40 years. At various times they were made even more onerous, with the intention of prohibiting, rather than merely restricting, the migration of the Chinese to New Zealand. Of course the Chinese were not the only targets of discriminatory rhetoric and policy. In fact, the net was thrown even wider than to the 'Asiatics', which included all Asians, including Indians – variously referred to as 'Assyrians' and 'Hindus' – who migrated from Fiji after completing contracts as indentured labourers.[34] Southern Europeans, from Yugoslavia, Italy and Greece, were also targeted. The 1889 Kauri Gum Industry Act was specifically enacted to discourage 'Dalmatian' (Croatian) immigration, by reserving the gum fields 'for the exclusive use of naturalised British subjects'.[35] Then, in 1920, the Dominion government devised 'a splendid essay at legislation – achieving all the powers for the maintenance of a white New Zealand, without any ugly stigma of "racialism" being attached to it'.[36] The Immigration Restriction Amendment Act of 1920 stated that those people who were not of British or Irish parentage and birth could migrate only if they submitted a postal application to do so. Approval of such applications was at the sole discretion of the minister of customs, who was not required to offer an explanation for any rejected applications. The appearance of magnanimousness was supported by the repeal of both the 'Natal test' and the objectionable practice of thumbprinting only Chinese migrants, though the poll tax and shipping restrictions remained in force until 1934.[37]

The discriminatory approach taken by New Zealand was far more subtle than those adopted by other dominions such as Australia, Canada and South Africa. All these continued to employ the 'Natal test', which required prospective migrants to demonstrate aptitude in any European language.[38] To ensure the effectiveness of the policy, the New Zealand government had earlier been advised by the Colonial Secretary 'that the best results from a language test [as applied in Australia] could be obtained if Customs officers were empowered to demand a knowledge of any European language they chose, or all of them if necessary'.[39] The subtlety was required both to make the immigration restrictions acceptable to the imperial government, which faced complaints from India and elsewhere across the empire, and to deflect direct criticism from the increasingly indignant governments of China and Japan. Ironically, such criticism was attracted by Australia for its 'White Australia' policy, which in its acceptance of Southern and Eastern Europeans was actually more liberal than New Zealand's 'British only' preference. New Zealand was content to exploit the illusory difference between its immigration policies and those of its 'benighted' neighbour[40] well into the 1960s, however. Politicians and public officials would flatly deny that New Zealand's policy was discriminatory,[41] or go so far as to proclaim, as Prime Minister Fraser did in Ceylon in 1948, that there was no discrimination against Indians in New Zealand 'because no white policy on Australian lines operated there'.[42] Rather than the 'white' policy overtly expressed by Australia, New Zealand can be said to have had a shrewder, 'whiter than white' policy.[43]

The structure of New Zealand immigration remained stable well into the 1960s, based on the near-exclusive preference for Britons and Australians (of British descent), with an occasional influx from other 'white' migrants from the Commonwealth, Northern Europe and North America. However there was some periodic softening of attitudes towards Asians. For example, Chinese migrants were given a somewhat more favourable acceptance after the Second World War, given the collaboration of China in the war against Japan, and again after the communist takeover of China, when it was recognized that many Chinese might prefer to remain in New Zealand or be unable to return to China. This caused the New Zealand government in 1952 to restore to Chinese the right to seek naturalization in New Zealand, which had been denied to them 44 years earlier.[44] However, even into the 1970s, the entry of 'race-aliens' (that is, anyone not of European stock) into New Zealand essentially was limited to those who already had family ties there.[45] The 1976 New Zealand Census indicated that the Chinese population comprised 1,653 – just 0.053 per cent of the total population of over 3 million,[46] and a much smaller proportion than identified in the census a hundred years earlier.

Exceptional during this period was the labour migration from the Pacific Islands, predominantly from the New Zealand territories and former territories of Western Samoa, the Cook Islands, Niue and the Tokelau Islands.[47] As highlighted earlier, these migrants, along with the urban migration of the Maori,[48] supplied much of the semi-skilled and unskilled labour for New Zealand's burgeoning post-war industries. Between active recruitment of labour migrants, particularly for work in the manufacturing sector, and the process of chain migration,[49] the population of the Pacific peoples in New Zealand by 1976 was 65,694 – 2 per cent of the total New Zealand population, and 40 times greater than the Chinese population. However, during the severe economic downturn in the 1970s, caused by the dual blows of oil crises and the loss of protected export markets when Britain joined the EEC, the Pacific peoples were thrust into unemployment and racialized as a 'problem' – as gang members, 'overstayers' (that is, migrants who illegally overstay their residency permits) and 'violent people who broke the law and who took jobs away from "New Zealanders"'.[50]

In fact, Britain's severing of traditional ties of economic patronage in 1973 was one of the major factors that caused New Zealand to redirect its orientation away from the United Kingdom and Europe, and towards Asia. The need to improve relations with the promising emergent markets in Asia provided the impetus to restructure New Zealand's immigration policy. Those who advocated looking to Asia to bolster the economic prosperity of New Zealanders made the link to immigration explicit. Norman Kirk, prime minister from 1972 to 1974, was remarkably candid in his assessment – both of the economic realities and of New Zealand's historic approach to immigrant selection: 'New Zealand's future lay with Asia and the Pacific. It is vitally necessary to establish sincerity in the eyes of Asians. A fair and just immigration policy would be a way of showing good faith.'[51] Another pragmatic commentator noted that, 'if New Zealand wishes to expand her markets in South East Asia, it may be advisable to allow a good number of people from that region to come to New Zealand so that contacts with these countries can be safely built on knowledge and close relations'.[52]

The traditional country-of-origin preference and ministerial discretion remained intact until 1987. However, a shift was signalled the year before, with the release of a White Paper from the then-minister of immigration, Kerry Burke. The White Paper, a ministerial review of immigration policy, distanced the government from the long-practised country-of-origin preference[53] and instead presented as an objective:

> to enrich the multicultural social fabric of New Zealand society through the selection of new settlers principally on the strength of their personal contribution to the future well-being of New Zealand.[54]

Gone was the assumption that migrants from Britain were inherently more desirable than others. Also missing from the new policy was the explicit and overriding concern for migrants' ability to assimilate into the dominant culture – one reason for the earlier preference for the Dutch and Scandinavians as 'third-tier' European migrants. Instead, economic (investment) capital and human capital – in the form of educational qualifications and professional experience – were the most desirable traits. For the first time in New Zealand, as a result of the need for economic revitalization, multiculturalism became a normative feature of the social policy landscape.

Post-1987 New Zealand immigration

The significance of the 1986 Review and the 1987 Act is difficult to overstate. It was as though the desire, some 15 years prior, of the late Norman Kirk – prime minister of the third Labour government – for an economic alignment with Asia and a 'fair and just immigration policy' had finally prevailed. With this single piece of legislation, the fifth Labour government confirmed New Zealand's economic realignment away from Britain and towards the economies of East Asia and the Pacific. The Act also overturned 106 years of discriminatory immigration policies, and began to alter radically the structure of New Zealand immigration. Its effect on the ethnic composition of the New Zealand population was almost immediate: in 1991, just five years after the radical policy shift, the population of Chinese in New Zealand reached 44,793.[55] Though just 1.3 per cent of the total population, the growth in the 15 years since 1975 (from 1,653 – a more than 2,600 per cent increase) was phenomenal. While British migrants continued to gain the highest number of residency approvals of all nationalities most years, approvals for migrants from Taiwan, Korea, Japan, Hong Kong and India – and, since the mid-1990s, the People's Republic of China – quickly rose in number.[56] Taken together, the number of residency approvals for 'Asians' have supplanted approvals for Europeans every year since 1987. As a result, the demographic profile of New Zealand – and especially of Auckland, where the vast majority of migrants settle – has been altered dramatically, as Table 4.1 illustrates. While the category 'Asian' is unquestionably crude as an ethnic iden-tifier, it is useful in this case to illustrate the significant rise of a new and 'racially' distinct population.

The changes in the structure of New Zealand immigration follow similar, though not so dramatic, policy changes in Australia and Canada.[57]

Given the conspicuous shift in the ethnic profile of immigrants after 1987, and the factors that motivated this, perhaps it is not surprising that the policy changes were greeted with concern and resistance by various individuals and groups within the host society. Most of the effects of East Asian immigration have been seen in Auckland, where most of the 'new' migrants have chosen to settle. This has been readily apparent in the real estate boom, particularly in Auckland's eastern suburbs, where very large and expensive homes were built in developments catering to tastes and styles tested through market research in

Table 4.1 NZ ethnic groupings (Census 1996, 2001, 2006)

	1986 N	2001 N*	2006 N
European	2,650,845	2,868,009	3,039,018
	81.2%	80.0%	75.4%
Maori	404,775	526,281	565,329
	12.4%	14.7%	14%
Pacific Peoples	119,370	231,801	265,974
	3.7%	6.5%	6.6%
Asian	47,979	237,459	354,549
	1.5%	6.6%	8.8%
Other	40,314	24,924	36,234
	1.2%	0.7%	0.9%

Source: Statistics New Zealand.

Note
* From 2001 percentages add to more than 100 per cent due to separate coding when multiple ethnic categories were claimed.

Hong Kong and Taiwan, and influenced by *feng shui* consultants.[58] Suburbs such as Howick, one preferred destination of Asian migrants, developed derisively Asian-sounding nicknames such as 'Chowick', and 'The Far Eastern Suburbs'.[59]

Because the changes to immigration policy were just one element in the then Labour government's strategy to deregulate and internationalize the economy, it should be noted that, during the same period, the rules governing foreign investment were also liberalized. Commentators within the business and financial sectors were generally in favour of increased foreign investment, and did not seem troubled about where it would come from.[60] However, investment and immigration were often conflated in public debate, and the tenor of the resistance to the new Asian immigration (quickly dubbed 'The Asian Invasion') was most frequently alarmist. Asian immigration was represented as a threat, and stories in the print media emphasized this threat with sensationalist headlines that played on racialized types and heightened tensions. The Asian threat was represented on several fronts. First, the threat was to New Zealand's sovereignty, both economic (through greater foreign ownership of assets and shares in the New Zealand stock market, as well as being credited with driving up Auckland property prices and national interest rates), and cultural (as a result of greater numbers of residents whose language was not English, evidenced by the proliferation of foreign language shopfront signs).[61] However, Asians were characterized also as a threat to 'New Zealand culture' (and 'our way of life'), and to public order and safety, with sensationalized accounts of the threat of crime (and potential links, however tenuous or unfounded, with Asian organized crime syndicates) and anecdotes of the threat to public safety from the reputed poor driving habits of Asian migrants.[62]

While there is evidence that social attitudes towards Asian migrants have softened – especially in Auckland, where the majority of new migrants settle, and where more than a third of the population identify as being foreign-born – the ambivalence with which Asian migrants to New Zealand are received continues to be reflected in labour market outcomes. Despite qualifying for New Zealand residency on the basis of high levels of human capital (professional qualifications, employment experience and skills), the New Zealand labour market has tended not to recognize or value such forms of capital – especially when derived in non-Anglo source countries. Working-age East Asian migrants are more likely than most to be unemployed or underemployed, or disengaged from the New Zealand labour market altogether (37 per cent in 2006) – despite having higher average levels of education.[63] These migrants face formidable institutional and attitudinal barriers to gaining employment commensurate with their qualifications and experience.[64] Given the liberal incorporation regime for migrants in New Zealand, in which there are no 'state-sponsored formal structures through which new populations and their interests can be incorporated',[65] the labour market is the primary means by which adult migrants are incorporated. Exclusion from, or dissatisfaction with, the New Zealand labour market has led many East Asian migrants to (euphemistically) 'retire', or to engage in transnational strategies in order to continue their careers and provide acceptable incomes for their families.

Transnationalism

Given the unsatisfactory employment or investment outcomes for so many Asian migrants in New Zealand, some are prepared either to return, on-migrate or adopt the 'astronaut' lifestyle as a survival strategy.[66] In this last sense, according to Ip, the transnational characteristics and behaviour of many ethnic Chinese – and perhaps other – migrants in New Zealand may not be so much by design and intent, as they may be motivated by sheer necessity. Drawing on Skeldon's[67] characterization of emigrants from Hong Kong in the lead-up to that territory's return to China in 1997 as 'reluctant exiles', we may perhaps refer to these individuals as 'reluctant transmigrants'.

Ho also reinforces Ip's contention that the 'astronaut' phenomenon has been motivated largely by difficulties faced by migrants in establishing business ventures or gaining suitable employment in New Zealand. This argument is made even more forcefully by Beal and Sos,[68] whose study into Taiwanese transmigrants in New Zealand and Australia found that 'astronauts' felt a great sense of failure at not having achieved their business or employment aspirations in their destination countries. However, according to Beal and Sos,[69] given that these migrants were motivated by lifestyle aspirations as much as by economic factors, it was seen to be preferable to adopt the 'astronaut' strategy so that the rest of the family could benefit from the social, environmental and educational opportunities in New Zealand, while the breadwinner returned to Taiwan to continue earning the family income. Of course, the astronaut paradigm allows for the maintenance of economic security for the migrant family, but often at a cost of family cohesion and stability.[70]

These practices had an impact not only on migrant adults, but also – and perhaps more significantly – on their children, members of the 1.5 and second generations. This is a sizeable population: in the 2006 Census, a third of those overseas-born were under 30 years old.[71] As a result, there is a significant population of children who grow up embedded in social networks characterized by transnational (or, as Ho terms it, 'multi-local') family structures. Within the ethnic migrant networks of Auckland, conversations are dominated by talk about the difficulty of finding suitable employment in New Zealand, the plentiful opportunities at 'home' or elsewhere in the world and of those of its members who have left New Zealand – either to return or to on-migrate to Australia, the United States or other parts of Asia. Children raised in this environment, who occasionally take family holidays back in their countries of origin, are well versed in a transnationalist discourse and outlook. All 1.5-generation Asian New Zealanders know some families who have engaged the 'astronaut' strategy – many are children of 'astronauts' themselves. They may view the post-university 'overseas experience' not so much as a cultural rite of passage but as an economic necessity, believing that they will be as unlikely to gain employment in New Zealand as their parents' generation has been.[72] To many 1.5-generation young people, transnationalism is a normal and pragmatic response to the desire to fulfil both economic and lifestyle aspirations of experiencing the best the world can offer. This sort of globalized outlook is naturally unsettling for host nation states, for whom the reproduction of committed and economically active citizens is a central imperative of migration policy.[73] An actively transnational migrant population also poses significant challenges to the nation state's imperative to promote a shared set of fundamental civic values and universal commitment to – and participation in – the economic, social and political institutions of the society.[74]

Indicators of social cohesion in New Zealand

While nation states with diverse populations (such as the classic New World Countries of Immigration (NWCIs) – the United States of America, Canada, Australia and New Zealand) have long grappled with incorporating new members into their social and economic life, 'social cohesion' is a reasonably new policy concept used to describe the goal of social inclusion, participation and harmony. The concept has become increasingly prevalent in social policy work in the European Union, Canada and Australia, and only more latterly by theorists and policy experts in New Zealand. In *The Social Report 2007* the Ministry of Social Development explicitly acknowledged the implications for social cohesion of three distinct indicators: income inequality; participation in leisure and recreation activities (including involvement in cultural and arts activities); and the prevalence – and fear – of crime.[75] Such a selection of measures is ad hoc, however, and chosen largely on the basis that data for them are already available, rather than developed for this purpose.[76] The 2004 New Zealand Immigration Settlement Strategy suggested an aspirational outcome of social cohesion that enumerated five intermediate outcomes: social cohesion would be achieved when 'all groups have a sense of belonging, participation, inclusion, recognition and legitimacy'.[77] However, New Zealand social policy agencies have yet to develop a framework for measuring social cohesion as such, or to identify the set of agreed-upon indicators with which to advise government and social agencies of the existence of – and threats to – social cohesion in New Zealand society.

In response to the Immigration Settlement Strategy, an attempt was made to define those five conditions identified further, and to suggest some indicators by which to monitor and assess social outcomes for migrants to New Zealand.[78] Spoonley and his collaborators developed a framework in which they specified that some of the stated intermediate outcomes described elements of socially cohesive *behaviour* (belonging and participation), while other outcomes focused on *social conditions* conducive to social cohesion.[79] Their framework is built on the assumption that the socially cohesive behaviours of belonging (being part of a wider community, trusting in others, sharing a common respect for the rule of law and for civil and human rights) and participation (involvement in economic and social activities, including in the labour market, family and community settings, groups and organizations, and political and civil life) occur in a wider social context, in which conditions may or may not encourage and support such behaviours. As such, conditions conducive to social cohesion involve: inclusion (equity of opportunity in labour market participation and rewards, access to education and training, social benefits, housing and health services); recognition (the valuing of diversity and respecting of differences; protection from discrimination and harassment, a sense of safety); and legitimacy (confidence in public institutions). The authors suggest a range of both quantitative and qualitative data for each indicator, while pointing out that most data required are not currently available, either not collected at all or captured at levels of generality that resist analysis for this purpose.[80]

Utilizing quite a different conceptualization, recent Canadian research sought to develop both a framework of social cohesion indicators and an instrument with which to measure the social cohesion of specific geographical and ethnic communities within a wider society – in this case, communities of Inuit peoples living in the Canadian Arctic.[81] Like the New Zealand-based effort described earlier, the Canadian work includes indicators of social and economic inclusion and support, subjective well-being and quality of life measures to indicate social cohesion. Also, like the New Zealand work, Duhaime and his colleagues critique the strong economic focus of much work done on social cohesion, arguing that attempts to measure social cohesion in a given community must incorporate both material and symbolic/relational values – that is, 'access to making a living and access to meaningful life'.[82] In this conceptualization, material values include access to formal economic and government institutions and services (including education, public housing, health care, etc.), participation in the labour market and political activities; symbolic values involve social ties, such as participation in family and community networks that promote reciprocity, trust and physical, emotional and spiritual support. The authors argue that the model is necessarily complex because it must measure both material and symbolic values, as well as the relative weighting of both in a given community – a disequillibrium between material and symbolic values risks negative social outcomes as communities experience either too little or too much social cohesion.

The New Zealand and Canadian works cited demonstrate a high level of general agreement on the factors that indicate social cohesion: economic inclusion, social inclusion and civic participation. Duhaime and his colleagues include two additional factors: demographic stability and subjective assessments of the quality of life – both of one's own and of the wider community. While the instrument they develop is a stand-alone administered survey focusing on individual perceptions and experiences, they acknowledge the need to cross-reference other statistical data indicating additional features of social cohesion, such as crime rates – to which could also be added imprisonment and suicide rates as well. The Canadian focus on intracommunity dynamics contains an inherent critique of the normative aspect of much of the work on social cohesion, arguing that, while social cohesion at the community level is an asset for those who are well integrated, such communities can also exercise considerable degrees of social closure, leading to exclusionary and isolating practices.[83] Perversely, high levels of social cohesion at the community level may work against wider manifestations of cohesion at regional or national levels. In the New Zealand context, this warning is particularly apropos when examining outcomes across the various ethnic communities under discussion in this chapter.

The synthesis of the Canadian and New Zealand works suggests opportunities to develop indicators for measuring social cohesion outcomes across diverse New Zealand communities and the society as a whole, focusing as they do on the interplay of both structural and institutional conditions and processes outside the direct control of communities, but which impact on them, and on the activities, perceptions, experiences and networks of those in the given communities themselves. Particularly useful from the New Zealand material is the distinction made between those elements whose locus are individuals and communities and that indicate socially cohesive behaviour, and those whose locus is the wider society (often in structural or institutional arrangements) and that influence social conditions that make cohesion possible.

Building on those models – and with the caveat that much of the data suggested are not readily available – I suggest the framework in Table 4.2 for measuring and assessing social cohesion in New Zealand.

These indicators may be applied to assess social cohesion of communities, as well as in the wider population, incorporating both ethnic communities (whether migrant or indigenous) and the host society.

Conclusion: Opportunities and threats

Cultural diversity presents significant challenges to social cohesion in New Zealand society – primarily because of the ways in which ethnic differences are associated with unequal economic and social outcomes. The state, then, is confronted with the challenge of promoting forms of social cohesion that facilitate the incorporation of new (and newly visible) migrant populations, on the one hand, while also improving the economic, educational and social outcomes of the Maori and Pacific peoples, on the other.

Despite the dramatic demographic shift that has taken place since 1987, resulting in a highly diverse, multi-ethnic population, the New Zealand state has not embraced multiculturalism as a social policy principle. This is because the change in migration policy occurred as New Zealand embarked on the pathway of officially recognizing the indigenous status of the Maori, and the guarantee of a special relationship between the Maori and the Crown struck in the Treaty of Waitangi. This policy framework has been known in New Zealand as biculturalism – a term which, as a product of its time, reflected the previously monocultural nature of the New Zealand state. This assignation was not generally seen to be problematic at the time; now, however, as the relationships of migrants to the Treaty of Waitangi, and therefore between migrants and the Maori, have not been sufficiently formalized or articulated in policy, the notion of biculturalism raises the question of where in the treaty relationship New Zealand's non-Maori, non-European migrants are to be found. This causes persistent tension between biculturalism and multiculturalism as suitable social policy frameworks for New Zealand.

At least part of that tension stems from the tendency to view biculturalism and multiculturalism as mutually exclusive imperatives, resulting in the dilemma of having to choose either one or the other. Many commentators share the cynical view adopted by the Maori of some New Zealanders' latter-day rush to embrace multiculturalism. In this light, multiculturalism is seen as a 'dishonest' and 'reactionary' position that serves to deny the Maori status as a treaty partner

Table 4.2 Framework for measuring and assessing social cohesion in New Zealand

Structural/institutional conditions and processes (locus: wider society)

Economic inclusion	• Labour market participation rates
	• Unemployment rates
	• Labour market location
	• Household income
	• Recognition of qualifications and professional experience
	• Access to social assistance
	• Home ownership/quality of housing
	• Satisfaction with job opportunities
Social inclusion	• Access to affective social support (e.g. social networks)
	• Access to appropriate health and social services
	• Access to appropriate education
	• Political representation
	• Media representation
	• Own-language media
	• Experiences of racism and discrimination
	• Satisfaction with community amenities
	• Perception of personal safety
Demography	• Community stability (immigration/emigration)
	• Age distribution
	• Health statistics

Behaviours, perceptions and resources (locus: individuals/communities)

Social capital	• Participation in civic institutions (e.g. voting)
	• Satisfaction with civic institutions (government, police, justice)
	• Crime statistics: victimization/conviction/incarceration
	• Participation in voluntary associations
	• Participation in education (preschool, tertiary, adult)
	• Satisfaction with availability/delivery of health and social services
	• Satisfaction with educational opportunities
	• Reasons to remain in local community/New Zealand
	• Reasons to leave local community/New Zealand
Social inclusion	• Participation in social networks
	• Participation in cultural/leisure activities
	• Suicide rates
	• Current job satisfaction
	• Transnational/multi-local family practices
	• Subjective well-being measures
	• Origin-language use
	• English use/literacy
	• Access to technology (telephone, computer, the Internet)

and solidify Pakeha power.[84] The Maori have become just one more ethnic minority, whose interests must be balanced by the (Pakeha) state against the interests of all other ethnic minorities. Multiculturalism 'can also be used as a weapon to subvert the additional rights of indigenes who do not wish to be viewed in the same way as immigrant communities'.[85] This form of multiculturalism I call 'facile multiculturalism', as its proponents appear unwilling or unable to address the complex historical, cultural and constitutional challenges posed by Maori indigeneity:

> We are very fond of the term 'multi-culturalism' which sounds very good but is really a smokescreen under which the battleships of the Pakeha world maintain their hold on power and wealth. For the ordinary citizen the concept is ready made for diversionary questions such as: What about the Greeks? And how about the Vietnamese and Samoans? How about their languages? Most of these strategies of avoidance are aimed at creating distance between us and the issues of Maori–Pakeha relationships.[86]

However, as unsatisfactory as facile multiculturalism is, some commentators also view biculturalism as problematic. Pearson argues that, while the flaw of facile multiculturalism in New Zealand is its inability to cater for the Maori, the flaw of biculturalism is that it completely ignores all who are neither Maori nor Pakeha – all others are swept into 'a nonsensical residual category'.[87] Such a position denies status not only to the Pacific peoples, who have their own historic relationships with the New Zealand state, and claims to special status as a result, but also to the many non-European and non-Polynesian migrants to New Zealand. This has implications for the incorporation of such migrants, who tend to believe that the Treaty relationship, and biculturalism in general, excludes them, thus also precluding them from enjoying the status of recognition that could come from a policy of official multiculturalism, for instance.

The corporatist regime negotiated with the Maori (and, to a lesser extent, with the Pacific peoples) is in contrast with the liberal regime of incorporation that confronts new migrants. It is not surprising that migrants who, for assistance and engagement, must rely on personal networks and private and voluntary associations in the absence of state-sponsored collective entities, may look at the state's engagement with the Maori with some bemusement. Thus, biculturalism and multiculturalism have been seen – in migrant communities at least – as being irreconcilably opposed.[88] This is a reasonable enough interpretation because, since the late 1980s, successive New Zealand governments have found themselves in the invidious position of pursuing, on the one hand, normative biculturalism (as a guiding social policy principle) and, on the other, multiculturalism (via immigration), without effectively reconciling the two.

Attempts to reconcile such simplistic and stark conceptualizations of biculturalism and multiculturalism are few, however. Undertaken by those committed to the bicultural imperative, these tend to rely on two foundational principles: the first is a focus on the Treaty of Waitangi as New Zealand's founding constitutional document, and an insistence that the treaty was not between the Maori and Pakeha – the error that Pearson, and others, appear to make[89] – but rather between the Maori and the Crown.[90] The second principle is that, for meaningful dialogue to occur, the Maori must be recognized as having status as *tangata whenua*, the indigenous people of New Zealand. Recognition of the *tangata whenua* status of the Maori leads to an acceptance of the Maori – including their culture and custom – as a constitutional entity, even prior to parliamentary recognition.[91] As Durie insists, Maori custom 'is part of the law of the land because it always has been. It grew from out of this earth.'[92] Currently, the political will to tackle this vexed question seems to be lacking in New Zealand. However the tensions between biculturalism and multiculturalism will best be resolved when the two are not taken to be binary opposites[93] but, rather, when biculturalism is conceived *as the framework within which multiculturalism may be realized.* That is, migrant groups need to be engaged in meaningful relationships with both the Maori and the Crown, as envisaged in the Treaty of Waitangi.

In most countries of immigration, conferring citizenship on migrants is seen to be a means of facilitating migrant integration into the society, and thus promoting social cohesion.[94] In countries such as Canada, Australia and the United States, the granting of political rights that come from citizenship – the status which allows migrants to vote in federal elections, gain employment in some fields and hold elected office – is one of the primary factors motivating migrants to those countries to seek naturalization.[95] In multicultural Australia and Canada, for instance, migrants are fully incorporated on the basis of their rights *as Australians or Canadians.* New Zealand is exceptional in this regard. As a result of the largely homogeneous historical immigration stream into New Zealand, particularly prior to the labour migration from the Pacific Islands, the threshold for political or civic participation in New Zealand society is very low. Prior to the Citizenship Act 1977, Commonwealth citizens had full civil and political rights, undifferentiated from New Zealand citizens. Since 1977, permanent residents share virtually all the same rights as citizens, with only two major exceptions: only citizens may stand for Parliamentary office or travel on a New Zealand passport. Some provisions of the welfare state are available only after residency criteria are met (normally two or three years). Otherwise, non-citizen permanent residents in New Zealand have all the social, political and civil rights of citizens.[96]

Citizenship has not traditionally been a pivotal element of New Zealand identity. 'Becoming a New Zealander', in terms of citizenship, has not had the same weight in nationalist discourse as has 'becoming an American', for instance. There are a number of reasons for this. Primarily, New Zealanders were British subjects, without a separate citizenship regimen, until 1948. Given its history (briefly described above in relation to immigration), the emphasis of nationalist discourse in New Zealand has traditionally centred not around citizenship but around 'race'. Also, the similarity between the rights of citizens and residents in New Zealand has made it easy for non-citizens (historically almost indistinguishable, culturally and 'racially', from citizens) to participate in all aspects of social and civic life. In one sense, this ease of participation has made naturalization unnecessary for most non-citizen residents. However, it creates a dilemma for the contemporary state, which must establish the conditions for inclusion, participation and incorporation of migrants without the ability to enforce a citizenship regime as part of the social contract. The sustained growth of such forms of transnationalism further frustrates the efforts of nation states to reinforce physical and symbolic boundaries, as transmigrants' engagement in frequent cross-border activities tends to limit fealty to any single nation, and instead produces an instrumental and flexible approach to considerations of citizenship.[97]

Another factor working against the development of a strong discourse or regime of citizenship in New Zealand involves the perverse ambiguity of what New Zealand citizenship actually means for those wishing to be naturalized. In other NWCIs, the taking up of citizenship has important symbolic meaning both for the denizen and for the host society, as a declaration of intention, loyalty and commitment. However, because of the Closer Economic Relations (CER) agreement with Australia, and the existence of a single trans-Tasman labour market, New Zealand citizenship literally opens doors for migrants that would otherwise be closed to them, particularly the opportunity to on-migrate to Australia.[98] As a result, a declared intention to take up New Zealand citizenship *may* be a declaration of loyalty to one's chosen destination, and an intention to belong fully in one's new home, but it may also signal one's intention to depart imminently for Australia!

The social cohesion indicators suggested above will help to capture important data for assessing the strength of social cohesion by examining both the perceptions and behaviours of individuals in particular communities, and the social conditions resulting from structural and institutional arrangements and processes, which persist beyond the control of individuals and communities. They also provide a mechanism to signal the most pressing threats to social cohesion. As described above, these come from two primary sources. The first is the under-utilization of migrants in the labour market, and the subsequent transnational practices which undermine other aspects of the migrants' social inclusion. The second major threat to social cohesion involves the continued economic and social marginalization of New Zealand's Polynesian populations – that is, Pasifika migrants and their descendents, and the Maori, New Zealand's *tangata whenua*. It is the persistence and intergenerational reproduction of this social exclusion – and the constellation of negative outcomes that flow from it, including poor educational and health outcomes, and higher levels of crime, victimization and disruption of families and communities – which carries the greatest, and most immediate, threat to social cohesion in New Zealand.

Notes

1 Phil Taylor, 'War of Words and Ethical Agendas', *New Zealand Herald*, 17 November 2007, p. B5.
2 See, for instance, former Foreign Minister (2005–2008) Winston Peters' political speeches: Hon. Winston Peters, 'New Zealand First – A New Beginning', speech

delivered 18 July 1993, Alexandra Park, Auckland; 'Immigrants Fiddle while Kiwis Pay', speech delivered 15 July 2002, Rotorua Citizens Club; Manying Ip and Nigel Murphy, *Aliens at My Table: Asians in the Eyes of New Zealanders* (Auckland: Penguin Books, 2005).
3 Elsie Ho, 'Reluctant Exiles or Roaming Transnationals? The Hong Kong Chinese in New Zealand', in Manying Ip, ed. *Unfolding History, Evolving Identity: The Chinese in New Zealand* (Auckland: Auckland University Press, 2003); Ellie Hyun-Kyung Seo, 'Return Migrants or Transmigrants? Return Migration of 1.5 Generation Korean New Zealanders' (MA thesis, University of Auckland, 2007); Raymond Chi Fai Chui, 'Towards a Transnational Sociology of Migration: Chinese Migrants, Networks and Transnationalism in New Zealand and Beyond' (PhD thesis, University of Auckland, 2007).
4 That is, tribes and subtribes.
5 Mason Durie, *Te Mana, Te Kawanatanga: The Politics of Maori Self-Determination* (Auckland: Oxford University Press, 1998), p. 183.
6 Michael King, *The Penguin History of New Zealand* (Auckland: Penguin Books, 2003), pp. 150, 223.
7 Ranginui Walker, 'The Treaty of Waitangi in the Postcolonial Era', in Michael Belgrave, Merata Kawharu and David Williams, eds. *Waitangi Revisited: Perspectives on the Treaty of Waitangi* (Auckland: Oxford University Press, 2005).
8 New Zealand Human Rights Commission, *Report of the Human Rights Commission on Representations by the Auckland Committee on Racism and Discrimination: Children and Young Persons Homes Administered by the Dept. of Social Welfare* (Wellington: The Commission, 1982); Ministerial Advisory Committee on a Maori Perspective for the Department of Social Welfare, *Puao-Te-Ata-Tu (Daybreak)* (Wellington: The Committee, 1986).
9 Literally, 'people of the land', denoting the indigenous people of a given area imbued with customary authority.
10 Though references to the treaty have since been made in dozens of statutes, the actual treaty text has never been enacted in law.
11 Mason Durie, *Te Mana, Te Kawanatanga: The Politics of Maori Self-determination* (Auckland: Oxford University Press, 1998), p. 183.
12 Mason Durie, 'Race and Ethnicity in Public Policy: Does it Work?'. *Social Policy Journal of New Zealand* 24 (March 2005): 1–11.
13 Ministerial Advisory Committee on a Maori Perspective for the Department of Social Welfare, *Puao-Te-Ata-Tu*, pp. 7–8.
14 Emily Keddell, 'Cultural Identity and the Children, Young Persons and Their Families Act 1989: Ideology, Policy and Practice'. *Social Policy Journal of New Zealand* 32 (November 2007): 49–71.
15 Allen Bartley and Paul Spoonley, 'Constructing a Workable Multiculturalism in a Bicultural Society', in Michael Belgrave, Merata Kawharu and David Williams, eds. *Waitangi Revisited: Perspectives on the Treaty of Waitangi* (Auckland: Oxford University Press, 2005).
16 Jane Kelsey, 'From Flagpoles to Pine Trees: Tino Rangatiratanga and Treaty Policy Today', in Paul Spoonley, David Pearson and Cluny Macpherson, eds. *Nga Patai: Racism and Ethnic Relations in Aotearoa/New Zealand* (Palmerston North: Dunmore Press, 1996).
17 Or, 'tribe, sub-tribe and extended family'; in Maori society these are kin-based political as well as social structures.
18 Yasemin Nuhoğlu Soysal, *Limits of Citizenship: Migrants and Postnational Membership in Europe* (Chicago, IL: University of Chicago Press, 1994).
19 Ministry of Pacific Island Affairs, *Briefing for the Incoming Minister*. Available at www.minpac.govt.nz/docs/MPIA%20Bim%2012%20Nov%2007.pdf.

20 C. Waldegrave and Nicholas Pole, 'Taking Our Opportunities: Social Cohesion and the Knowledge Divide in Aotearoa, New Zealand', in 'The Proceedings of the Catching the Knowledge Wave Conference', 1–3 August 2001. Available at www.knowledgewave.org.nz/conference_2001/documents/Social%20Cohesion2.pdf.

21 Ministry of Social Development, *The Social Report 2007* (Wellington: Ministry of Social Development 2007), p. 45.

22 Ibid., p. 60.

23 Ibid., p. 39.

24 Waldegrave and Pole, 'Taking Our Opportunities', pp. 6–7.

25 Ibid., p. 6.

26 Ministry of Justice, *An Overview of Conviction and Sentencing Statistics, 1997–2006*. Available at www.justice.govt.nz/pubs/reports/2007/conviction-sentencing-1997–2006/index2.html.

27 Department of Corrections, *Census of Prison Inmates and Home Detainees* (Wellington: Department of Corrections, 2004), p. 19.

28 Tim Hume, 'Little Boys Lost', *Sunday Star Times*, 4 November 2007, pp. C1, C4–5; Dana Peterson Lynskey *et al.*, 'Linking Gender, Minority Group Status and Family Matters to Self-control Theory: A Multivariate Analysis of Key Self-control Concepts in a Youth-gang Context'. *Juvenile and Family Court Journal* 51, no. 3 (2000): 1–19.

29 The Statistics New Zealand definition of 'Asian' is very broad, incorporating more than 20 different national or ethnic identities. The significance of this statistic, however, is that these residents are 'racially' so different from the other major ethnic groups in New Zealand.

30 Statistics New Zealand, *2006 Census of Population and Dwellings*. Available at www.stats.govt.nz/census/2006-census-data/regional-summary-tables.htm.

31 Manying Ip, *Home Away from Home: Life Stories of Chinese Women in New Zealand* (Auckland: New Women's Press, 1990), p. 13.

32 Ibid., p. 14; P. S. O'Connor, 'Keeping New Zealand White, 1908–1920'. *New Zealand Journal of History* 2, no. 2 (1968): 41–65.

33 Ibid., p. 42.

34 P. S. O'Connor, 'Keeping New Zealand White', pp. 47–48. These restrictions were particularly galling for the Indians who were, after all, British subjects. O'Connor notes the resentment of the Indian Government – particularly on behalf of the Indian elite, 'that, while they can move freely in the best society of any European capital, they could not set foot in some of the dominions without undergoing vexatious catechisms from petty officials'. The Imperial government's threat – and occasionally the act – of withholding the royal assent from New Zealand legislation prevented the passage of exclusionary laws that London found especially problematic.

35 T. Brooking and R. Rabel, 'Neither British nor Polynesian: A Brief History of New Zealand's Other Immigrants', in Stuart William Greif, ed. *Immigration and National Identity in New Zealand: One People, Two Peoples, Many Peoples?* (Palmerston North: Dunmore Press, 1995), p. 28.

36 S. Brawley, *The White Peril: Foreign Relations and Asian Immigration to Australasia and North America, 1919–1978* (Sydney: University of New South Wales Press, 1995), p. 63.

37 Manying Ip, *Home Away from Home*, p. 177.

38 S. Brawley, *The White Peril*, p. 49.

39 P. S. O'Connor, 'Keeping New Zealand White', p. 50.

40 Ibid., p. 65.

41 S. Brawley, *The White Peril*, p. 270.

42 Quoted in S. Brawley, *The White Peril*, p. 264.

43 T. Brooking and R. Rabel, 'Neither British nor Polynesian', p. 39.

44 Manying Ip, *Home Away from Home*, p. 178; Malcolm McKinnon, *Immigrants and Citizens: New Zealanders and Asian Immigration in Historical Context* (Wellington: Institute of Policy Studies, Victoria University of Wellington, 1996), pp. 40–41.
45 Malcolm McKinnon, *Immigrants and Citizens*, pp. 42–43.
46 *New Zealand Official Yearbook [NZOYB] 1977* (Wellington: Government Printer, 1977), p. 82.
47 Cluny Macpherson, 'Pacific Islands Identity and Community', in Paul Spoonley, David Pearson and Cluny Macpherson, eds. *Nga Patai: Racism and Ethnic Relations in Aotearoa/New Zealand* (Palmerston North: Dunmore Press, 1996), pp. 124–125.
48 Peter Davis, 'Class, Ethnicity and Mortality: The Impact of Economic Change', in Paul Spoonley, Cluny Macpherson, David Pearson and Charles Sedgwick, eds. *Tauiwi: Racism and Ethnicity in New Zealand* (Palmerston North: Dunmore Press, 1984), pp. 142–155.
49 Cluny Macpherson, 'Pacific Islands Identity and Community', p. 125; Reginald Thomas Appleyard and Charles W. Stahl, *South Pacific Migration: New Zealand Experience and Implications for Australia* (Canberra: Australian Agency for International Development, 1995), pp. 16–18.
50 Reginald Thomas Appleyard and Charles W. Stahl, *South Pacific Migration*, p. 18; Paul Spoonley, 'Mahi Awatea? The Racialisation of Work in Aotearoa/New Zealand', in Paul Spoonley, David Pearson and Cluny Macpherson, eds. *Nga Patai: Racism and Ethnic Relations in Aotearoa/New Zealand* (Palmerston North: Dunmore Press, 1996), p. 64.
51 Quoted in S. Brawley, *The White Peril*, p. 321.
52 Ibid.
53 Hon. Kerry Burke, *Review of Immigration Policy, August 1986* (Wellington: Ministry of Immigration, 1986), p. 15.
54 Ibid., p. 10.
55 Statistics New Zealand, *2001 Census of Population and Dwellings*. Available at www.stats.govt.nz/census.htm.
56 Residency approvals do not necessarily translate directly into migrant arrivals, however. In the years before Hong Kong's return to China – and especially in the wake of the Tiananmen Square massacre – many who were understandably anxious about their future in Hong Kong applied for residency in the NWCIs (New World countries of immigration) as a form of insurance. However, many who gained residency elsewhere have chosen not to leave Hong Kong after all.
57 J. Atchison, 'Immigration in Two Federations: Canada and Australia'. *International Migration* 26, no. 1 (1988): 5–31.
58 R. Gordon and J. Reynolds, 'The Asian Invasion', *Metro (Auckland)* 8, no. 85 (1988): 150–163.
59 M. McLauchlan, 'Far Eastern Suburbs', *Metro (Auckland)*, 125 (November 1991): 114–124.
60 J. Irving, 'Foreign Gold on the Horizon?'. *Marketing Magazine* 8, no. 4 (1989): 14–21.
61 While my focus is specifically on the New Zealand response to the new Asian migration, this should not be read as suggesting that the New Zealand experience is unique in this regard. Wong briefly describes a similar, contemporary set of images attached to Chinese capitalist migrants in Canadian urban centres, as does Castles in the Australian context: L. L. Wong, 'Chinese Capitalist Migration to Canada: A Sociological Interpretation and its Effect on Canada'. *Asian and Pacific Migration Journal* 4, no. 4 (1995): 465–492; Stephen Castles, 'The "New" Migration and Australian Immigration Policy', in C. Inglis *et al.*, eds. *Asians in Australia: The Dynamics of Migration and Settlement* (Singapore: Institute of Southeast Asian Studies, 1992).

62 G. Wong, 'When East Meets West', *New Zealand Herald*, 22 February 1992, p. B3.
63 Ministry of Social Development, *The Social Report 2007*; Anne Henderson, 'Untapped Talents: The Employment and Settlement Experiences of Skilled Chinese in New Zealand', in Manying Ip, ed. *Unfolding History, Evolving Identity: The Chinese in New Zealand* (Auckland: Auckland University Press, 2003).
64 Andrew Butcher, Paul Spoonley and Andrew Trlin, *Being Accepted: The Experience of Discrimination and Social Exclusion by Immigrants and Refugees in New Zealand* (Palmerston North: Massey University, 2006).
65 Yasemin Nuhoğlu Soysal, *Limits of Citizenship*, p. 38.
66 Manying Ip, 'Beyond the "Settler" and "Astronaut" Paradigms: A New Approach to the Study of the New Chinese Immigrants to New Zealand', in Manying Ip, S. Kang and S. Page, eds. *Migration and Travel between Asia and New Zealand* (Auckland: Asia-Pacific Migration Research Network, 2000), p. 9.
67 Ray Skeldon, *Reluctant Exiles? Migration from Hong Kong and the New Overseas Chinese* (Hong Kong: Hong Kong University Press, 1994).
68 Tim Beal and Farib Sos, *Astronauts from Taiwan: Taiwanese Immigration to Australia and New Zealand and the Search for a New Life* (Wellington: Asia Pacific Research Institute & Steele Roberts, 1999), pp. 9–10.
69 Ibid., pp. 57–58.
70 David Ley, 'Seeking "Homo Economicus": The Canadian State and the Strange Story of the Business Immigration Program'. *Annals of the Association of American Geographers* 93, no. 2 (2003): 426–441; Raymond Chi Fai Chui, 'Towards a Transnational Sociology of Migration'.
71 Statistics New Zealand, *2006 Census*.
72 Ellie Hyun-Kyung Seo, 'Return Migrants or Transmigrants?'.
73 David Ley, 'Seeking "Homo Economicus"'.
74 Allen Bartley and Paul Spoonley, op. cit., 'Constructing a Workable Multiculturalism in a Bicultural Society'.
75 Ministry of Social Development, *The Social Report 2007*, pp. 59, 88, 89, 102.
76 Paul Spoonley *et al.*, 'Social Cohesion: A Policy and Indicator Framework for Assessing Immigrant and Host Outcomes'. *Social Policy Journal of New Zealand* 24 (March 2005): 85–110.
77 New Zealand Immigration Service, *A Future Together: The New Zealand Settlement Strategy in Outline* (Wellington: New Zealand Immigration Service, 2004).
78 Paul Spoonley *et al.*, 'Social Cohesion…'.
79 Ibid., pp. 102–103.
80 Ibid., p. 106.
81 Gérard Duhaime *et al.*, 'Social Cohesion and Living Conditions in the Canadian Arctic: From Theory to Measurement'. *Social Indicators Research* 66 (2004): 295–317.
82 Gérard Duhaime *et al.*, 'Social Cohesion and Living Conditions in the Canadian Arctic', p. 301.
83 Ibid., p. 312.
84 Raj Vasil and H. Yoon, *New Zealanders of Asian Origin* (Wellington: Institute of Policy Studies, Victoria University of Wellington, 2000), p. 35.
85 David Pearson, *A Dream Deferred: The Origins of Ethnic Conflict in New Zealand* (Wellington: Allen & Unwin, and Port Nicholson Press, 1990), p. 234.
86 H. M. Mead, quoted in Richard Mulgan, *Maori, Pakeha and Democracy* (Auckland: Oxford University Press, 1989), p. 8.
87 Pearson, *A Dream Deferred*, p. 239.
88 Pearson, *A Dream Deferred*; Kiri Wong, 'Immigration and Race Relations'. *Auckland University Law Review* 9, no. 1 (2000): 222–234.
89 R. Thakur, 'In Defense of Multiculturalism', in Stuart William Greif, ed. *Immigration and National Identity in New Zealand: One People, Two Peoples, Many Peoples?* (Palmerston North: Dunmore Press, 1995).

90 I. H. Kawharu, *Waitangi: Maori and Pakeha Perspectives of the Treaty of Waitangi* (Auckland: Oxford University Press, 1989), p. xiii.
91 Eddie T. Durie, 'Justice, Biculturalism and the Politics of Law', p. 34.
92 Ibid.
93 R. Thakur, 'In Defense of Multiculturalism', p. 271.
94 R. Rogers, 'The Transnational Nexus of Migration'. *Annals of the American Academy of Political and Social Science* 486 (May 1986): 34–50.
95 Phillip Q. Yang, 'Explaining Immigrant Naturalization'. *International Migration Review* 28, no. 3 (1994): 449–477.
96 Malcolm McKinnon, *Immigrants and Citizens*, pp. 42–45; Paul Spoonley, 'Aliens and Citizens in New Zealand', in A. Kondo, ed. *Citizenship in a Global World: Comparing Citizenship Rights for Aliens* (Basingstoke: Palgrave, 2001), p. 163.
97 David Ley, 'Seeking "Homo Economicus"'.
98 Jacqueline Lidgard *et al.*, *Immigrants from Korea, Taiwan and Hong Kong in New Zealand in the mid-1990s: Macro and Micro Perspectives*, Discussion Paper Number 29 (Hamilton: Population Studies Centre, University of Waikato, 1998), p. 37.

References

Appleyard, Reginald Thomas and Charles W. Stahl. *South Pacific Migration: New Zealand Experience and Implications for Australia* (Canberra: Australian Agency for International Development, 1995).

Atchison, J. 'Immigration in Two Federations: Canada and Australia'. *International Migration* 26, no. 1 (1988): 5–31.

Bartley, Allen and Paul Spoonley. 'Constructing a Workable Multiculturalism in a Bicultural Society', in Michael Belgrave, Merata Kawharu and David Williams, eds. *Waitangi Revisited: Perspectives on the Treaty of Waitangi* (Auckland: Oxford University Press, 2005).

Beal, Tim and Farib Sos. *Astronauts from Taiwan: Taiwanese Immigration to Australia and New Zealand and the Search for a New Life* (Wellington: Asia Pacific Research Institute & Steele Roberts, 1999).

Brawley, S. *The White Peril: Foreign Relations and Asian Immigration to Australasia and North America, 1919–1978* (Sydney: University of New South Wales Press, 1995).

Brooking, T. and R. Rabel. 'Neither British nor Polynesian: A Brief History of New Zealand's Other Immigrants', in Stuart William Greif, ed. *Immigration and National Identity in New Zealand: One People, Two Peoples, Many Peoples?* (Palmerston North: Dunmore Press, 1995).

Burke, Kerry (Hon.). *Review of Immigration Policy, August 1986* (Wellington: Ministry of Immigration, 1986).

Butcher, Andrew, Paul Spoonley and Andrew Trlin. *Being Accepted: The Experience of Discrimination and Social Exclusion by Immigrants and Refugees in New Zealand* (Palmerston North: Massey University, 2006).

Castles, Stephen. 'The "New" Migration and Australian Immigration Policy', in C. Inglis *et al.*, eds. *Asians in Australia: The Dynamics of Migration and Settlement* (Singapore: Institute of Southeast Asian Studies, 1992).

Chi, Raymond Fai Chui. 'Towards a Transnational Sociology of Migration: Chinese Migrants, Networks and Transnationalism in New Zealand and Beyond' (PhD thesis, University of Auckland, 2007).

Davis, Peter. 'Class, Ethnicity and Mortality: The Impact of Economic Change', in Paul Spoonley, Cluny Macpherson, David Pearson and Charles Sedgwick, eds. *Tauiwi: Racism and Ethnicity in New Zealand* (Palmerston North: Dunmore Press, 1984).

Department of Corrections. *Census of Prison Inmates and Home Detainees* (Wellington: Department of Corrections, 2004).

Duhaime, Gérard *et al.* 'Social Cohesion and Living Conditions in the Canadian Arctic: From Theory to Measurement'. *Social Indicators Research* 66 (2004): 295–317.

Durie, Eddie T. 'Justice, Biculturalism and the Politics of Law', in Margaret Wilson and Anna Yeatman, eds. *Justice and Identity: Antipodean Practices* (Wellington: Bridget Williams Books, 1995).

Durie, Mason. *Te Mana, Te Kawanatanga: The Politics of Maori Self-determination* (Auckland: Oxford University Press, 1998).

Durie, Mason. 'Race and Ethnicity in Public Policy: Does it Work?'. *Social Policy Journal of New Zealand* 24 (March 2005): 1–11.

Gordon, R. and J. Reynolds. 'The Asian Invasion'. *Metro (Auckland)* 8, no. 85 (1988): 150–163.

Henderson, Anne. 'Untapped Talents: The Employment and Settlement Experiences of Skilled Chinese in New Zealand', in Manying Ip, ed. *Unfolding History, Evolving Identity: The Chinese in New Zealand* (Auckland: Auckland University Press, 2003).

Ho, Elsie. 'Reluctant Exiles or Roaming Transnationals? The Hong Kong Chinese in New Zealand', in Manying Ip, ed. *Unfolding History, Evolving Identity: The Chinese in New Zealand* (Auckland: Auckland University Press, 2003).

Hume, Tim. 'Little Boys Lost', *Sunday Star Times*, 4 November 2007.

Ip, Manying. *Home Away from Home: Life Stories of Chinese Women in New Zealand* (Auckland: New Women's Press, 1990).

Ip, Manying. 'Beyond the "Settler" and "Astronaut" Paradigms: A New Approach to the Study of the New Chinese Immigrants to New Zealand', in Manying Ip, S. Kang and S. Page, eds. *Migration and Travel Between Asia and New Zealand* (Auckland: Asia-Pacific Migration Research Network, 2000).

Ip, Manying and Nigel Murphy. *Aliens at My Table: Asians in the Eyes of New Zealanders* (Auckland: Penguin Books, 2005).

Irving, J. 'Foreign Gold on the Horizon?'. *Marketing Magazine* 8, no. 4 (1989): 14–21.

Kawharu, I. H. *Waitangi: Maori and Pakeha Perspectives of the Treaty of Waitangi* (Auckland: Oxford University Press, 1989).

Keddell, Emily. 'Cultural Identity and the Children, Young Persons and Their Families Act 1989: Ideology, Policy and Practice'. *Social Policy Journal of New Zealand* 32 (November 2007): 49–71.

Kelsey, Jane. 'From Flagpoles to Pine Trees: Tino Rangatiratanga and Treaty Policy Today', in Paul Spoonley, David Pearson and Cluny Macpherson, eds. *Nga Patai: Racism and Ethnic Relations in Aotearoa/New Zealand* (Palmerston North: Dunmore Press, 1996).

King, Michael. *The Penguin History of New Zealand* (Auckland: Penguin Books, 2003).

Ley, David. 'Seeking "Homo Economicus": The Canadian State and the Strange Story of the Business Immigration Program'. *Annals of the Association of American Geographers* 93, no. 2 (2003): 426–441.

Lidgard, Jacqueline *et al. Immigrants from Korea, Taiwan and Hong Kong in New Zealand in the mid-1990s: Macro and Micro Perspectives*, Discussion Paper Number 29 (Hamilton: Population Studies Centre, University of Waikato, 1998).

Lynskey, Dana Peterson *et al.* 'Linking Gender, Minority Group Status and Family Matters to Self-control Theory: A Multivariate Analysis of Key Self-control Concepts in a Youth-gang Context'. *Juvenile and Family Court Journal* 51, no. 3 (2000): 1–19.

Macpherson, Cluny. 'Pacific Islands Identity and Community', in Paul Spoonley, David Pearson and Cluny Macpherson, eds. *Nga Patai: Racism and Ethnic Relations in Aotearoa/New Zealand* (Palmerston North: Dunmore Press, 1996).

McKinnon, Malcolm. *Immigrants and Citizens: New Zealanders and Asian Immigration in Historical Context* (Wellington: Institute of Policy Studies, Victoria University of Wellington, 1996).

McLauchlan, M. 'Far Eastern Suburbs'. *Metro (Auckland)* 125 (November 1991): 114–124.

Ministerial Advisory Committee on a Maori Perspective for the Department of Social Welfare. *Puao-Te-Ata-Tu (Daybreak)* (Wellington: The Committee, 1986).

Ministry of Justice. *An Overview of Conviction and Sentencing Statistics, 1997–2006.* Available at www.justice.govt.nz/pubs/reports/2007/conviction-sentencing-1997–2006/index2.html

Ministry of Pacific Island Affairs. *Briefing for the Incoming Minister.* Available at www.minpac.govt.nz/docs/MPIA% 20Bim%2012%20Nov%2007.pdf.

Ministry of Social Development. *The Social Report 2007* (Wellington: Ministry of Social Development, 2007).

Mulgan, Richard. *Maori, Pakeha and Democracy* (Auckland: Oxford University Press, 1989).

New Zealand Human Rights Commission. *Report of the Human Rights Commission on Representations by the Auckland Committee on Racism and Discrimination: Children and Young Persons Homes Administered by the Dept. of Social Welfare* (Wellington: The Commission, 1982).

New Zealand Immigration Service. *A Future Together: The New Zealand Settlement Strategy in Outline* (Wellington: New Zealand Immigration Service, 2004).

New Zealand Official Yearbook [NZOYB] 1977 (Wellington: Government Printer, 1977).

O'Connor, P. S. 'Keeping New Zealand White, 1908–1920'. *New Zealand Journal of History* 2, no. 2 (1968): 41–65.

Pearson, David. *A Dream Deferred: The Origins of Ethnic Conflict in New Zealand* (Wellington: Allen & Unwin, and Port Nicholson Press, 1990).

Peters, Winston. 'New Zealand First – A New Beginning', speech delivered 18 July 1993, Alexandra Park, Auckland.

Peters, Winston. 'Immigrants Fiddle while Kiwis Pay', speech delivered 15 July 2002, Rotorua Citizens Club.

Rogers, R. 'The Transnational Nexus of Migration'. *Annals of the American Academy of Political and Social Science* 486 (May 1986): 34–50.

Seo, Ellie Hyun-Kyung. 'Return Migrants or Transmigrants? Return Migration of 1.5 Generation Korean New Zealanders' (MA thesis, University of Auckland, 2007).

Skeldon, Ray. *Reluctant Exiles? Migration from Hong Kong and the New Overseas Chinese* (Hong Kong: Hong Kong University Press, 1994).

Soysal, Yasemin Nuhoğlu. *Limits of Citizenship: Migrants and Postnational Membership in Europe* (Chicago, IL: University of Chicago Press, 1994).

Spoonley, Paul. 'Aliens and Citizens in New Zealand', in A. Kondo, ed. *Citizenship in a Global World: Comparing Citizenship Rights for Aliens* (Basingstoke: Palgrave, 2001).

Spoonley, Paul *et al.* 'Mahi Awatea? The Racialisation of Work in Aotearoa/New Zealand', in Paul Spoonley, David Pearson and Cluny Macpherson, eds. *Nga Patai:*

Racism and Ethnic Relations in Aotearoa/New Zealand (Palmerston North: Dunmore Press, 1996).

Spoonley, Paul *et al.* 'Social Cohesion: A Policy and Indicator Framework for Assessing Immigrant and Host Outcomes'. *Social Policy Journal of New Zealand* 24 (March 2005): 85–110.

Statistics New Zealand. *2001 Census of Population and Dwellings.* Available at www.stats.govt.nz/census.htm.

Statistics New Zealand. *2006 Census of Population and Dwellings.* Available at www.stats.govt.nz/census/2006-census-data/regional-summary-tables.htm.

Taylor, Phil. 'War of Words and Ethical Agendas', *New Zealand Herald,* 17 November 2007.

Thakur, R. 'In Defense of Multiculturalism', in Stuart William Greif, ed. *Immigration and National Identity in New Zealand: One People, Two Peoples, Many Peoples?* (Palmerston North: Dunmore Press, 1995).

Vasil, Raj and H. Yoon. *New Zealanders of Asian Origin* (Wellington: Institute of Policy Studies, Victoria University of Wellington, 2000).

Waldegrave, C. and Nicholas Pole. 'Taking Our Opportunities: Social Cohesion and the Knowledge Divide in Aotearoa, New Zealand', in 'The Proceedings of the Catching the Knowledge Wave Conference', 1–3 August 2001. Available at www.knowledge-wave.org.nz/conference_2001/documents/Social%20Cohesion2.pdf.

Walker, Ranginui. 'The Treaty of Waitangi in the Postcolonial Era', in Michael Belgrave, Merata Kawharu and David Williams, eds. *Waitangi Revisited: Perspectives on the Treaty of Waitangi* (Auckland: Oxford University Press, 2005).

Wong, G. 'When East Meets West', *New Zealand Herald,* 22 February 1992.

Wong, Kiri. 'Immigration and Race Relations'. *Auckland University Law Review* 9, no. 1 (2000): 222–234.

Wong, L. L. 'Chinese Capitalist Migration to Canada: A Sociological Interpretation and its Effect on Canada'. *Asian and Pacific Migration Journal* 4, no. 4 (1995): 465–492.

Yang, Phillip Q. 'Explaining Immigrant Naturalization'. *International Migration Review* 28, no. 3 (1994): 449–477.

5 Colonialism, Sinicization and ethnic minorities in Hong Kong

Social exclusion and barely citizenship[1]

Kim-ming Lee and Kam-yee Law

Introduction

'We are Borg. You will be assimilated. You must comply. Resistance is futile.'

In *Star Trek: The Next Generation*, a popular US sci-fi TV series, there is a species called the Borg, which is militant, highly efficient, technologically sophisticated, emotionless and fearless. The Borg are organized as an interconnected collective headed by a queen and act as a homogenous and anonymous entity. There is no individuality and distinct personality within the Borg population, but a collective mind that makes them act as one. Despite their homogeneity, the Borg are actually a hybrid of multiple species. There is no procreation among the Borg; they expand through colonization. Colonization takes the form of forced assimilation through the injecting of nanoprobes which technologically transform the victim's body and mind. After assimilation, the 'invaded aliens' or drones, as labelled in the TV programme, internalize the single purpose of the Borg: to add the biological and technological distinctiveness of other species to their own, in pursuit of perfection. The drones are cybernetically connected to the whole. Although the drone can hear the thousands of other voices of the other drones, there is only one voice of consensus. When encountering other species, they exhibit no desire for negotiation or reason, only for assimilation. This attitude is often highlighted by one of their shibboleth: 'Negotiation is irrelevant.' They think they are superior to other species. However, when they perceive a species neither worth assimilating nor constituting an immediate threat, they simply ignore them.

In the real world, the closest thing to the Borg may be imperial powers such as Britain and China. With superior technology and weaponry, they colonized territories, and coerced and imposed their will on indigenous populations to serve their interests. In addition they resettled the colonized people away from their homes to help expand their empires.

Although the colonizers did not have the Borg's technology to assimilate and turn the colonized into conforming drones – far from it – they had weapons more destructive, in terms of unintended consequences, than those of the Borg: their soft power. Nye describes this as: 'the ability to get what you want by attracting and persuading others to adopt your goals'.[2]

This is, namely, colonialism or Gramsci's hegemonic power. In spite of the return of the territories to the indigenous population after decolonization, as postcolonial scholars argued, genuine independence, if possible, was far from being achieved.[3] The influences of colonialism and the related issues of assimilation never faded away (India is a good example). While the colonizers did not have the Borg nanoprobes to assimilate the colonized in a total and complete way, their cultural imperialism, albeit never complete and always ambivalent,[4] subtly framed the minds of the colonized, especially the elites, through education, official encounters, media and, above all, every kind of consumption practice (dining, reading, sports, clothing, lifestyle and so on). The colonial legacies crystallized at the deepest level of the once colonized society that could not be easily erased, because colonialism dispossessed the colonized of their own identities, traditions, pride and self-representation. The language, cultural practices, values and tastes, modes of perception, as well as representations of the colonizers, continuously haunt the colonized.

The detrimental legacy of colonialism manifests itself in two ways. In some cases, the colonized elites were assimilated by the colonizers' culture so that, when they took power, they still ruled in a way not so different from the colonizers. In other cases, when the colonized elites launched their resistance against the colonizers, nationalism in terms of similarity and unity was articulated to mobilize the masses that were heterogeneous and culturally different. The newly found state inevitably recruited certain groups of people selectively and strategically for its project of modernization and nation building, while some subaltern groups were consciously or unconsciously left out of the state project.[5] From a postcolonial perspective, both cases involve a dominating cultural discourse shaping the very identity of the subordinated through monopolizing their representation. In the former, the colonized elites, who had been civilized by the colonizers' education, administrative system, political socialization and lifestyle, continued to rule their people in a similar manner to their colonizers'. In other words, the colonized elites were merely in a body of the colonized but with a colonizer's mind. In the latter, on the one hand, the colonized elites were still intellectually struggling with the colonial, degenerate racial stereotypes of their people and culture by searching and building anti-colonial and anti-Eurocentric political knowledge and experiences in which nationalism and socialism were often employed as alternatives.[6] On the other hand, in pursuing a unitary *nation* as an anti-colonial strategy, the colonized elites were levelling the whole population, consciously or unconsciously ignoring class, gender, ethnic and cultural differences. Consequently, a new form of domination, or internal colonization if you like, was established. This new form of domination manifested itself in two ways: assimilating different subpopulations into the elites' culture; and marginalizing the unassimilated groups by misrepresenting their cultural values and ignoring their contributions to the *nation* in fighting against colonialism.[7]

In many ex-colonial countries, the above-mentioned postcolonial situation is still present in most, if not all, of them. For some newly industrializing economies, such as Singapore, Malaysia and Hong Kong, the colonial legacy is not only cultural but also demographic. As mentioned before, European colonization brought along with it both voluntary and involuntary migration of the colonized to other colonies for empire maintenance and expansion. As a result, besides white Europeans, people from other colonies of different races and ethnicities settled with the indigenous population of the host colony. This changed the rather homogenous ethnic demographic make-up of the host colony into a multi-ethnic one. During the struggles against colonialism, some of these migrated colonized groups might join the fight. After decolonization, native nationalism was always sought to unify diverse ethnic groups into a single nation state. This, however, only ended in the exacerbation of ethnic divisions, if the ethnic groups were numerically comparable, or with the marginalization of numerically small ethnic groups. Multiracial problems remain a major political issue in these ex-colonies.

The demographic composition of the ex-colonies becomes more complicated as a result of international migration alongside globalization. Although international migration is not a new phenomenon, the current trends and patterns of migration from globalization are different from those of the past.[8] Castles and Miller employ the term 'the age of migration' to denote these new trends and practices of transnational migration: more and more countries are affected by the growing volume of migratory movements, which take various forms, such as labour migration and refugee or permanent settlement.[9] Migratory chains, once started with one type of movement, often continue with other forms; migration movements are gendered and become more feminized; and migration has been politicized in many advanced countries. In all, migrants, both permanent and temporary, are increasingly integrated with the functioning of the global economy. But are the migrants integrated with their host countries? When globalization and transnational migration continue, more and more countries will have to face multiracial problems. A single-race *nation* will become a rarity.

Making things even more complicated is the neocolonialism associated with current trends of globalization. Neoliberal economic globalization, advocated by Western politicians, transnational corporations and Western-dominated international organizations, such as the International Monetary Fund (IMF) and World Trade Organization (WTO), establishes a new global economic order that perpetuates the old asymmetric, economic North–South relationships. In order to maintain competitiveness and attract Western capital, the indigenous elites and middle classes of the ex-colonies, just like their predecessors in the colonial period, mimic the Westerner, especially the American, in terms of language, business culture, policy and so on. Moreover, since the current form of globalization is basically Western-orientated, if not merely American-centred, former colonial stereotypes of the supreme white male and the degenerate, inferior non-white male are perpetuated and inscribed in the emerging global culture that affects not only the elites and middle classes of the ex-colonies but also the ordinary people. Consequently, the people of ex-colonies may increasingly appreciate Western values, admire the West's material progress, mimic Western cultural practices and pursue or aspire to a Western lifestyle, while at the same time demeaning their own as less civilized and less advanced. Even worse, they may internalize the white supremacy and negative stereotypes of other groups: pleasing Westerners but discriminating against others. Suffice it to say, this neo-colonial form of racism has become increasingly assimilating and pervasive.

In light of the above-mentioned prelude, we will examine the ethnic minorities in Hong Kong and see how colonialism, neocolonialism and Chinese neonationalism are combined differently to create two separate discriminatory and exclusionary mechanisms against two groups. By Hong Kong's ethnic minorities, we refer to new immigrants from Mainland China and non-Chinese inhabitants and immigrants from other countries.

Social exclusion of the Hong Kong ethnic minorities

After 155 years of colonization, the colonial discourse of white supremacy and degenerate others has deeply shaped the mindset of the Hong Kong people. People with darker skin are shown much less regard than white Westerners in Hong Kong. Indeed, race and ethnicity, mingled with class, play an important role in constituting a racist mentality. In the past, the Hong Kong government insisted that Hong Kong did not have any serious racial discrimination problems, and preferred educating the public to legislating the Racial Discrimination Ordinance (RDO hereafter). Indeed, the major reason for the government denying the existence of racial discrimination is its ignorance of the problem. Before 1999, the government did not collect information, even basic demographic profiles, on Hong Kong's ethnic minorities. In response to increasing pressure from local NGOs and international representatives from the UN Human Rights Committee, the UN Committee on Economic Social and Cultural Rights and the UN Committee on the Elimination of Racial Discrimination, the government conducted its first survey on ethnic minorities in 1999 and asked 'relevant' questions in its recent population census. In 2002, the government at last set up the Committee on the Promotion of Racial Harmony and the Race Relations Unit to deal with racial problems. In 2003, the government decided to legislate against racial discrimination and began to consult the public. However, it still insisted on not considering new Chinese immigrants an ethnic minority and excluded them from the protection against discrimination, despite numerous objections raised by NGOs and scholars.[10]

From the issue of the RDO, we can see that the notion of 'multicultural' can only be applied to Hong Kong as a descriptive term. It merely implies the existence of diverse ethnic groups. Multiculturalism in terms of mutual tolerance and recognition is absent in Hong Kong. Hong Kong ethnic minorities seldom receive the recognition they deserve. Instead, social exclusion, if not outright discrimination, is commonly experienced by them. According to Madanipour *et al.*, 'Social exclusion is defined as a multi-dimensional process, in which various forms of exclusion are combined ... [which] create acute forms of exclusion that find a spatial manifestation in particular neighbourhoods.'[11] In the following, we will show the social exclusion of the non-white ethnic minorities and attempt to explain this phenomenon through Sassen's social polarization thesis.[12]

Some ethnic minorities in Hong Kong do receive high praise. Hong Kong's ethnic minority population is bifurcated.[13] There is a small portion of highly paid migrants or inhabitants who mostly come from advanced countries such as the United States and Japan, and a large proportion of lowly paid migrant labour or inhabitants from developing areas such as Mainland China, the Philippines and Thailand. The distribution of ethnic groups and their median monthly income, according to their ethnicities, are presented in Table 5.1, which indicates that non-Chinese groups constitute 5.1 per cent of the total population. However, there are some difficulties in defining Chinese immigrants because Hong Kong is basically a Chinese society, which, because of historical reasons, has been separated from China for one and a half centuries. Currently, although Hong Kong has been returned to China, it has been allowed to maintain its borders under the 'one country, two systems' arrangement.

This is illustrated by the fact that the Hong Kong government has adopted a seven-year criterion to distinguish new Chinese immigrants from earlier ones because, under the Immigration Ordinance, one can become a permanent resident after living continuously in Hong Kong for at least seven years. Thus, new Chinese immigrants are defined as 'persons from the Mainland having resided in Hong Kong for less than seven years' (PMR hereafter). In 2001, PMRs constituted about 4.0 per cent of the total population.

Table 5.1 shows the income inequality among different ethnic groups. On the one hand, the median incomes of Filipino, Indonesian, Thai, Pakistani, Nepalese and new China Mainland immigrants are below those of the whole population. On the other hand, the median incomes of the ethnic groups from advanced countries, especially Westerners, are way beyond those of the whole population. Moreover, it should be noted that the Hong Kong Census and Statistics Department has made a questionable error by classifying blacks who are Europeans, Americans, Australians and New Zealanders as Others. This actually reflects how white supremacy has been shaping the mentality of Hong Kong government officials even after decolonization. The huge income difference reflects how class and ethnicity are mingled together: Westerners are mostly in the upper class, while South Asian and new immigrants are in the lower class. The income polarization among the ethnic groups can be attributed to the effects of Western-centred globalization.

Sassen uses the social polarization thesis to describe how poverty and social inequalities occur in economically advanced global cities.[14] According to the thesis, on the one hand, the traditional unionized working class and middle managers in the manufacturing sectors suffer job losses because of de-industrialization, deregulation and technological rationalization caused by economic restructuring. On the other hand, there is a huge demand for top administrative and professional talent for the booming financial and producer services. In order to serve the consumption needs of top administrators and professionals, a large pool of service workers who suffer from the casualization and informalization of employment relations, such as low pay and lack of mobility, is also created. In addition, the expansion of low-skilled and low-paid jobs

Table 5.1 Ethnic groups and median monthly income by ethnicity, 2006

Ethnicity	Number	Median monthly income from main employment (HK$)	Percentage	Proportion of each ethnic minority in the whole population (%)
Asian (other than Chinese)				
Filipino	112,453	3,370	32.9	1.6
Indonesian	87,840	3,320	25.7	1.3
Indian	20,444	15,000	6.0	0.3
Nepalese	15,950	8,000	4.7	0.2
Japanese	13,189	30,000	3.9	0.2
Thai	11,900	4,000	3.5	0.2
Pakistani	11,111	9,000	3.2	0.2
Korean	4,812	25,000	1.4	0.1
Other Asian	7,851	10,500	2.3	0.1
White	36,384	45,000	10.6	0.5
Mixed	18,092	9,500	5.3	0.3
Others*	2,172	16,000	0.6	0.03
Total	342,198	3,500	100.0	5.0
PMR (Chinese)**	217,103	6,000	100.0	3.2
Whole population	6,864,346	10,000		100.0

Sources: Hong Kong 2006 Population By-census Thematic Report – Ethnic Minorities, and Hong Kong 2006 Population By-census Thematic Report – Persons from the Mainland Having Resided in Hong Kong for Less Than Seven Years.

Notes
* The figures include 'Black', 'Latin American', etc.
** PMR is the short form for 'Persons from the Mainland having resided in Hong Kong for less than seven years'.

attracts a massive influx of migrant workers from less-developed areas. These processes create an hour-glass income and occupational structure.

Sassen further discusses two roles of immigration in the economic restructuring processes of global cities:[15] one, providing labour to both the expanding and declining economic sectors and, two, being active agents in 'rehabilitating' devastated neighbourhoods of the city. With regard to the first aspect, although there are some highly educated immigrants, most immigrants are lowly educated and are disproportionately concentrated in low-wage jobs and the casual labour markets. As for the second aspect, most low-income immigrants are spatially concentrated in deprived areas and form their own immigrant communities. As a global city develops, it will undergo spatial reorganization through urban redevelopment, infrastructure building and real estate development. In this spatial restructuring process, a number of areas and neighbourhoods, notably the traditional industrial zones, will be left out because of their lack of profitability, and will have a high proportion of abandoned housing and closed down stores as people with higher income leave to seek better living conditions. Since most immigrants cannot afford expensive goods and housing in gentrified or redeveloped areas with luxury housing estates and high-priced shopping arcades, they have to seek living quarters in the 'abandoned' areas. Consequently, these areas are kept 'alive' by poor immigrants who create low-cost, immigrant-run businesses within the neighbourhoods in order to fulfil their own needs.

Now let us take a closer look to see whether the non-white ethnic minorities are really concentrated in the low-skilled job sectors (labour market exclusion, that is, denied upward mobility chances) and spatially in the devastated areas (residential segregation). With regard to employment, Chiu and Lui effectively demonstrate that one of the reasons for the serious income inequality in Hong Kong is the over-representation of migrant workers in low-paid elementary occupations, particularly as domestic helpers.[16] In fact, according to their estimation, foreign domestic helpers (FDHs hereafter) alone account for at least 55 per cent of the lowest income deciles. In his research on Hong Kong's Thai migrant workers, Hewison reports that 78 per cent of his informants were domestic workers, and the rest had other working-class occupations in shops (19 per cent), restaurants (8 per cent) and cleaning stores (4 per cent).[17] The highest-paid workers were employed in restaurants with monthly incomes of between $9,000 and $10,000. Aside from FDHs, it was found that quite a number of Nepalese work in the construction sector. In his survey of Nepalese construction workers, Frost discovered that 24 per cent of them earn less than $9,001 per month, about 9 per cent earn above $15,000, and most of them earn between $9,000 and $15,000.[18] At first glance, their income level seems comparable to the Hong Kong Chinese. However, nearly 62 per cent of them have to work for more than 60 hours per week, and most of them are casual labourers paid on a daily basis. In their survey of Hong Kong Pakistanis, Ku *et al.* predictably found that, among their respondents who were employed full time, 75.2 per cent of them were engaged in an elementary occupation, with 57 per cent as construction workers and 13.2 per cent as security guards. Shockingly, many Pakistani workers are overworked: about 34.2 per cent of them work more than 69 hours per week, and 32.5per cent earn less than $10,000 per month. In addition, most of the surveyed Pakistanis (81.9 per cent) regard employment as the most serious problem they have while living in Hong Kong, and 19.0 per cent of them are unemployed.[19]

The situation involving Hong Kong's non-Chinese immigrants and inhabitants does not tell the whole story of income inequality and occupational segregation because the largest ethnic minority population comes from Mainland China. Indeed, Hong Kong was an immigrant society until those from the second generation of earlier immigrants grew up. Since a massive influx of Mainland Chinese would produce a serious social and political problem, in 1950 the colonial government implemented a quota system to restrict the entry of Chinese citizens. This quota system has continued to the current day.[20] According to Law and Lee, new Chinese immigrants or new arrival families constitute a major proportion of Hong Kong's impoverished group since new arrival families earn much less than the average Hong Kong family. As well as lower family income, the educational level of the new arrivals is also, on average, lower than that of the overall Hong Kong population. With regard to employment, new arrivals are mainly concentrated in either the sunset industries (manufacturing) or the low-paid and low-skilled service sector (wholesale, retail, import/export trades, restaurants and hotels).[21]

As Siu observes, the disadvantaged labour market position of new arrivals results from local people's prejudice against their educational attainments and pre-migration working experiences.[22] This observation is confirmed by Lam and Liu.[23] They put forward the assumption that the widening earnings gap between Mainland immigrants and natives is the result of the widening differential in the rate of return to schooling, and working experience. They further suggest that, since Mainland immigrants acquire most of their schooling and part of their work experience in China, their education and experience are priced increasingly lower as Hong Kong turns into an economy that demands high value-added and knowledge-based skills. Chiu *et al.* also highlight that the labour market situation of Mainland immigrants is deteriorating because of deindustrialization.[24] Because many better-paid services require language skills, local knowledge and cultural capital that the new arrivals usually lack, the only channel for them to get a better job is in the manufacturing sector. Unfortunately, deindustrialization reduces their chances.

With regard to residential segregation, immigrants at first sight seem to be scattered all over Hong Kong (see Tables 5.2a and 5.2b) without any significant indication of spatial segregation. However, on closer look, one can still find signs of the concentration of disadvantaged, ethnic minority immigrants and inhabitants in poor areas. In 2006, of the 18 district council districts, Wan Chai had the largest non-Chinese population (16.1 per cent), followed by Central and Western (14.4 per cent). As shown in Table 5.3, both of the districts are high-income districts. In contrast, Sham Shui Po had the greatest proportion of Chinese immigrants (5.7 per cent), which is the lowest-income district. There are higher proportions of non-Chinese immigrants in high-income areas because most of the non-Chinese immigrants are live-in domestic helpers. Thus, it is not surprising to find them residing in high-income districts.

Table 5.2a Proportion of ethnic minorities in the whole population by district, 2006

District	Proportion of ethnic minorities (%)	District	Proportion of ethnic minorities (%)	District	Proportion of ethnic minorities (%)
Wan Chai	16.1	Eastern	5.8	Tai Po	3.5
Central and Western	14.4	Sai Kung	4.8	Kwun Tong	2.6
Islands	11.6	Tsuen Wan	4.2	Tuen Mun	2.4
Yau Tsim Mong	9.8	Yuen Long	3.6	North	2.3
Southern	9.3	Sham Shui Po	3.6	Kwai Tsing	2.3
Kowloon City	7.7	Sha Tin	3.5	Wong Tai Sin	2.0

Source: Hong Kong 2006 Population By-census Thematic Report – Ethnic Minorities.

Table 5.2b Proportion of PMRs in the whole population by district, 2006

District	Proportion of PMRs (%)	District	Proportion of PMRs (%)	District	Proportion of PMRs (%)
Sham Shui Po	5.7	North	3.4	Central and Western	2.4
Islands	5.0	Tuen Mun	2.9	Sha Tin	2.1
Yau Tsim Mong	4.5	Wong Tai Sin	2.9	Wan Chai	1.9
Kwun Tong	4.4	Kowloon City	2.8	Southern	1.9
Yuen Long	4.3	Tsuen Wan	2.6	Tai Po	1.9
Kwai Tsing	4.0	Sai Kung	2.5	Eastern	1.8

Source: Hong Kong 2006 Population By-census Thematic Report – Persons from the Mainland Having Resided in Hong Kong for Less Than Seven Years.

Apart from the live-in domestic helpers who are mainly women from the Philippines, Indonesia and Thailand, other Southeast and South Asian ethnic groups have different residential patterns. In 2001, more than one-third of the Nepalese were living in Yuen Long, and another third lived in Yau Tsim Mong. The reason most Nepalese live there is that many Nepalese soldiers, known as Gurkhas, were recruited by the British colonial government and thus resided in the military camps located there. The Pakistani community mainly resides in three poorer districts of Hong Kong: Yau Tsim Mong (13.2 per cent), Kwun Tong (11.6 per cent) and Kwai Tsing (10.8 per cent). Meanwhile, the residential pattern for Indians is interesting, with 19.1 per cent in Kowloon City and 18.8 per cent in Yau Tsim Mong, but 15.5 per cent in Central and Western, a rich district.[25] The Indian residential pattern reflects the income inequality within the group. Another piece of information that reflects the spatial segregation of Hong Kong's ethnic minorities is their trend of internal migration or home moving, especially away from the poor districts. In 2001, only 17.9 per cent moved out of their homes, whilst most stayed put.[26]

Table 5.3 Monthly median domestic household income (HK$) by district, 2006

District	Median household income	District	Median household income	District	Median household income
Wan Chai	27,500	Kowloon City	20,000	Tuen Mun	15,000
Central and Western	26,250	Sha Tin	19,320	Yuen Long	14,810
Eastern	21,705	Tai Po	18,000	Kwai Tsing	14,500
Southern	21,000	Yau Tsim Mong	17,500	Wong Tai Sin	14,250
Sai Kung	21,000	Islands	16,263	Kwun Tong	14,050
Tsuen Wan	20,000	North	16,000	Sham Shui Po	13,500

Source: Main Tables of the 2006 Population By-census.

Note
The monthly median domestic household income of Hong Kong was $17,250 in 2006.

In 1991, almost one-third of Chinese immigrants lived in Kowloon City (12.2 per cent), Eastern (11.6 per cent) or Kwun Tong (9.9 per cent), with the first two districts having better living conditions than Kwun Tong. However, in 2001, more than a quarter of Chinese migrants resided in the poorest districts: Kwun Tong (10.1 per cent), Sham Shui Po (9.7 per cent) and Yau Tsim Mong (8.4 per cent).[27] Remember that those considered Chinese migrants in 1991 were no longer classified as PMRs in 2001 by the government's definition because they had lived for more than seven years in Hong Kong. Hence, in a broader sense, the poorest districts should have more Chinese migrants than the figures reflect. To summarize, spatial segregation, though not as serious as that in New York, London[28] and Chicago,[29] does occur in Hong Kong. Notably, the Nepalese, Pakistani and new Chinese immigrants are concentrated in the poorest districts of Yau Tsim Mong, Sham Shui Po, Yuen Long and Kwun Tong.

As mentioned earlier, social exclusion is a multidimensional concept. So far we have seen how ethnicity, race and class are combined to create labour market and spatial exclusions of ethnic minority groups in Hong Kong. This is not the end of the story. The non-white, Hong Kong ethnic minority groups also experience tremendous cultural exclusion. Despite Hong Kong being a 'global city', the Hong Kong ethnic Chinese are culturally insensitive to non-Western cultures. As reported by Ho, the Hong Kong Hospital Authority served pork to its Muslim patients![30] Ku also demonstrates that Pakistani women encounter great pressures to conform to the dress norms in Hong Kong because ethnic Chinese always look at them strangely and avoid interacting with them when they wear their traditional clothes.[31] Moreover, very few schools allow ethnic minority children to wear their traditional dress, and most of them require children from ethnic minorities to wear the standard school uniform. Instead of considering this as being simply culturally insensitive, Ku argues that it is outright discrimination: 'Pakistani women's traditional dress, in local Hongkongers' eyes, signifies something "backward" and "uncivilized".'[32]

Culture and language are inseparable. The cultural exclusion of ethnic minorities is primarily manifested in the language barrier they encounter when accessing Hong Kong's public services. Many of them, especially the women, find it difficult to communicate in English or Cantonese and are deprived of basic public services. For example, there is a lack of translators available for members of ethnic minorities being treated in public hospitals, the result of which is delayed or inappropriate treatments.[33] Another prominent example is education. When the parents of children from an ethnic minority try to find primary schools for their children, they have difficulty accessing relevant information because most of it is in Chinese.[34] The same situation occurs in continuing education because most government-funded vocational programmes are taught mainly in Chinese. As a result, a vicious circle may be formed: lacking opportunities in formal and continuing education, 'many of these ethnic minorities can only pick up the lowest positions in the job market, as most of their parents already do'.[35]

Bogardus creates a social distance scale to measure the willingness of respondents to accept other races. The scale represents a continuum – from close family relationships to complete physical and geographical separation – within which respondents may place a particular race group to indicate their social distance towards the race group. On this scale, the highest acceptance level is represented by whether the respondent would marry a person of that particular race.[36] In other words, inter-ethnic marriage can be used as an indicator of acceptance of other ethnic groups. Table 5.4 shows that the percentages of inter-ethnic marriage with the Chinese for Indians, Nepalese and Pakistanis are very low. Most of them have a spouse of the same ethnicity. However, the rates of inter-ethnic marriage with the Chinese for Indonesians and Thais are quite high, and for Filipinos it reaches 27.8 per cent. Do these figures suggest ethnic Hong Kong Chinese find them more acceptable?

Let us take a look at the Filipino figures first. Among the Filipino population, only 48.6 per cent are married. Among the married Filipinos, the majority of them (87.1 per cent) do not live with their spouse in Hong Kong. Of the 12.9 per cent Filipinos living with their spouses in Hong Kong, slightly more than one-quarter of them are married to a Chinese person. In other words, the actual number of inter-ethnic marriages with the Chinese for Filipinos is not high. The same situation applies to Indonesians, of whom only 46.7 per cent are married. Among the married Indonesians, the majority of them (84.2 per cent) do not live with their spouse in Hong Kong. However, of the 15.8 per cent of Indonesians living with their spouses in Hong Kong, the majority of them have a Chinese partner. One possibility for this could be that most of these Indonesians are Chinese Indonesians. We also suspect that 83.3 per cent of the Thais who have a

Table 5.4 Proportion of now-married population living with spouse in the same household in Hong Kong (%), 2001

Ethnicity	Ethnicity of Spouse			Total
	Same Ethnicity	Different Ethnicity		
		Chinese	Other than Chinese	
Asian (other than Chinese)				
Filipino	54.9	27.8	17.3	100
Indonesian	14.1	81.7	4.2	100
Indian	92.7	3.5	3.8	100
Nepalese	97.1	1.7	1.1	100
Japanese	78.5	17	4.6	100
Thai	12.2	83.3	4.5	100
Pakistani	87.3	4.6	8.1	100
Korean	74.3	19.7	6.1	100
White-British	55.9	18.5	25.7	100
White-American/Canadian	60.2	21	18.7	100
White-Australian/New Zealander	65.4	14.4	20.3	100
Total	64	25.1	10.9	100
Whole Population	98.5	0.6	1	100

Source: Hong Kong 2001 Population Census Thematic Report – Ethnic Minorities.

Chinese spouse living in Hong Kong are Sino-Thais. In contrast, about 87 per cent to 94 per cent of the married whites are living with their spouses in Hong Kong. More significantly, among them, the rates of inter-ethnic marriage between whites and Chinese range from 14.4 to 21 per cent. Again, the evidence suggests that Hong Kong ethnic Chinese accept the whites more than the non-whites.

Social exclusion is only part of the story of the non-white ethnic minorities in Hong Kong. Since the beginning of the new millennium, numerous studies have shown that ethnic minorities in Hong Kong face various forms of racial discrimination on a daily basis,[37] including for employment,[38] housing,[39] education[40] and the receipt of social services. In addition to the problems encountered in their search for employment, housing and education, they are prime targets of harassment by the police who subject them to ID checks at will, and they also face rudeness and discriminatory attitudes in their dealings with government departments. The unfair or outright biased treatment of Hong Kong ethnic minorities by the police and government agencies may be the result of racial profiling, which refers to a law enforcement agent relying on race and ethnicity in selecting individuals for routine or spontaneous investigatory activities.[41]

The new Chinese immigrants' situation is no better than that for non-white, non-Chinese ethnic minorities. A survey conducted by the Hong Kong Psychological Society in 1997 reveals that Hong Kong people consider new migrants from China ignorant, rude, dirty and greedy, and believe they are introducing evil ways from the Mainland. The newcomers are also seen as aggravating the territory's social problems by increasing competition for jobs, houses and welfare benefits. Hong Kong people showed little sympathy for the Mainlanders' plight, felt that the new immigrants deserved the hardships they experienced and would not make much progress even if given more government assistance.[42] As Hong Kong's economic recession deepened, the Hong Kong people's negative perception of new arrivals further deteriorated; a 2002 survey showed that, since 2000, the percentage of respondents agreeing that new arrivals were selfish, emotional, greedy, cowardly, annoying, arrogant, isolated and uncivilized had increased, and these increases applied equally to all respondents, ranging from school students to adults.[43] According to a SoCO's survey, 82 per cent of new, adult, Mainland immigrant respondents believe they are racially discriminated against by Hong Kong people, and are denounced as 'parasites' (78.5 per cent).[44]

Colonialism and Sinicization

From the above empirical evidence, it suffices to say that genuine multiculturalism has never existed in Hong Kong. Instead, racism and social exclusion pervade Hong Kong society. Non-whites and Mainland Chinese are both being racially discriminated against and socially excluded. However, the mechanisms that engender racism and social exclusion against the two groups are quite different. In this section, we attempt to analyse how colonialism and Chinese neonationalism or Sinicization are combined differently to create two separate discriminatory and exclusionary mechanisms against the two groups.

The cultural assimilation of the colonized

Similar to those in other European colonies, the Hong Kong elite was basically assimilated by British culture. McLeod remarks that:

> British Empire did not rule by military and physical force alone. It endured by getting both *colonising* and *colonised people* to see their world and themselves in a particular way, internalising the language of Empire as representing the natural, true order of life [original emphases].[45]

As Carroll and Hui demonstrate, the British ruling of Hong Kong not only depended on military strength, but also on the collaboration of the Chinese elite who provided support and trading networks to enable the British to penetrate the Asian markets.[46] In return, the colonized elite enjoyed the blessings of the colonizers: material rewards, status and privileges.

The more the colonized elite worked on behalf of the colonizers in controlling other colonized subjects, the more the colonized elite started to mimic the British. As Carroll argues, Hong Kong, once established as a British colony, had attained a special status as a cultural-historical place, a part of a global British empire, with its distinctive class of colonized bicultural elite.[47] The assimilation of the colonized elite into the colonizers' culture started in the early 1900s. In 1901, the colonized elite petitioned the colonizers for 'a suitable English School for the education of the children – both boys and girls – of the upper classes of the Chinese resident'. They argued that the majority of the Chinese elite had 'failed to assimilate to any extent English sympathies and ideas, and are ever backward in responding to the call of public duties'. They further argued that the new school would 'not only endow our young men and women with more open minds and greater public spirit' but would also 'result in the more cordial co-operation of the British and Chinese nations and closer intercourse between them'.[48] In addition to learning English and mimicking British living styles, the Hong Kong colonized elite actively participated in activities (such as contributing to imperial war funds, organizing ceremonies for visiting British royalty and attending imperial trade exhibitions) and helped to construct the Hong Kong economic success story so as to legitimize the colonial rule.[49]

After the War, Hong Kong experienced rapid industrialization with the help of a mass influx of Chinese refugees and the whole set of structural conditions of colonial Hong Kong changed. It was doubtful if merely relying on the assimilated colonized elite would handle the emerging problems. The cultural assimilation of the general Hong Kong people, especially the middle classes, into the British culture started after the 1966 and 1967 riots, which 'showed that colonialism failed to provide the new generation a framework for their quest for identity'.[50] In the 1970s, numerous social movements with various political demands challenged the colonial rule. These movements precipitated a series of state building projects aimed at constructing a society that would enhance the colonial state's legitimacy.

> To accommodate the growing demands ... the colonial administration recruited the emerging young professionals and executives into the major decision-making bodies to replace the old elites ... by increasing the state's responsiveness to local demands, fighting corruption, broadening the scope of social services, and improving administrative efficiency.[51]

By extending its hegemonic power to the general colonized, the colonizers not only successfully transformed the mindset of the ethnic Chinese into a Western-like one, but also turned them from challenging into confirming their colonial rule.

The culturally assimilated colonized Hongkongers internalize colonialism's representations and values. The colonial representation of races categorizes people into a hierarchy of superiority and inferiority, based on skin colour. At the top of the hierarchy are the white. The whites are represented as civilized, advanced, elegant, intelligent and rational, while people of colour are taken to be savage, backward, vulgar, stupid and irrational (Rwanda is another good example of where this is so). In 2000, an incident aroused public concern about the racism in Hong Kong. The wife of British writer Martin Jacques, Harinder Veriah, an Indian-Malaysian working in a Hong Kong law firm, died at Rutton-jee Hospital as the result of a lack of medical attention. According to Jacques, his wife died because she was a person of colour.[52] Although after a series of investigations, the authority decided that Veriah died of natural causes and made no reference to the racism claim, the incident spawned intense campaigns against racial discrimination and sparked urgent calls for a law to protect ethnic minorities.[53] The incident effectively demonstrates how deeply colonial ethnic representations had been implanted in the colonized Hong Kong Chinese, and shows that racism has been so intensely ingrained into Hong Kong's culture. Later, as Jacques remarks, the Hong Kong ethnic Chinese 'consider themselves to be number two in the pecking order and look down upon all other races as inferior'.[54]

The subaltern ethnic groups in Hong Kong

British colonialism not only culturally assimilated the Hong Kong Chinese, but also brought along a subaltern class of ethnic minority groups to Hong Kong. The non-white Hong Kong ethnic minorities are a subaltern class because their voices were never heard, not until the moment before the 1997 handover, and after the Veriah incident. Their contributions to the Hong Kong economy are never recognized in any Hong Kong success stories. As mentioned before, the Hong Kong government did not bother to find out how many ethnic minorities there were in Hong Kong until it was condemned by international organizations and domestic NGOs. Not long ago, the Hong Kong government still claimed that racism was not an issue. To put it bluntly, non-white ethnic minorities were basically invisible before the mid-1990s.

Despite their invisibility during the 155 years of Hong Kong's colonial history, non-white ethnic minorities came to Hong Kong at the exact moment the British colonized Hong Kong, and have contributed a great deal to Hong Kong society. Indians, as the colonized, came on the coat-tails of the British, as sailors, traders and soldiers. Living in a predominately Chinese society, they found a niche mainly in security-related occupations, including the military, the police and other guard services, while others built successful careers in business and the professions.[55] In today's Hong Kong, the Indian community largely engages in business activities, mainly trading. Most of them look on Hong Kong as their home and do not see themselves as foreigners.[56] Ho also notes, 'One distinctive feature of ethnic minority Muslims in Hong Kong is that most of them have been living in Hong Kong for several generations and have acquired the local culture and dialect.'[57] The Nepalese, like the Indians, also came with the British army, and have served Hong Kong for near 50 years as British Gurkha soldiers.[58] After the handover, most of the ex-Gurkhas went into the private security sector.

Besides these ethnic minorities who have been living in Hong Kong for generations, the non-white ethnic minority workers also contribute a lot to the Hong Kong economy by taking up low-paid jobs. A good example is provided by the foreign domestic helpers (FDHs). From the mid-1970s onwards, Hong Kong's manufacturing industry was developing rapidly, and the service economy began to grow. More and more women were participating in the labour market because of their elevated education level and career aspirations.[59] In particular, the female labour participation rate rose from 47.5 per cent in 1982 to 51.9 per cent in 2004. The total number of working women was up to about 897,800 in 1982, and rose to 1,566,300 in 2004, an increase of 74.5 per cent.[60] As more and more women, especially the middle classes, were able and eager to work, their household duties needed to be delegated. Thus, in the late 1970s and early 1980s, it was very common for young couples, after having children, to have their mothers live with them to serve as caregivers for their children. However, this was not a viable long-term strategy. The importation of FDHs helped Hong Kong women resolve this dilemma and released them from their domestic responsibilities so that they could pursue their careers. As a result, the proportion of FDHs in the total labour market rose from 1 per cent in 1982 to 7 per cent in 2001. Moreover, in 2001, it was found that 61 per cent of FDH–employer households have two economically active members (likely to be dual-working households) as opposed to 32 per cent for non-FDH–employer households.[61] However, it is not surprising to find that some public housing households also hire FDHs. One may wonder whether or not these public housing households belong to the middle class. Indeed, it is not uncommon for traditional, male-breadwinner families to employ FDHs, so that the mother can be released from most of the housework and concentrate instead on building up the children's human, social and cultural capital. In summation, FDHs help improve the quality of life of ethnic Chinese Hong Kong families in certain aspects and increase Hong Kong's productivity by releasing capable women into the labour market.

If Hong Kong's ethnic minorities contribute so much to Hong Kong, why are they never mentioned, let alone celebrated in Hong Kong's public discourses? As mentioned previously, the colonial ethnic representations are implanted in the mind of the colonized Hong Kong Chinese. If the Chinese recognize the contribution of the ethnic minorities, how could they demonstrate their superiority towards them? Indeed, within the colonialism discourse, it is *incomprehensible* to think of the role of the ethnic minorities; all the credit for turning Hong Kong from a fishing village, first into an industrialized city, and then an Asian world city, would have to be attributed first to colonial rule, then to the hardship and flexibility of the Hong Kong Chinese. In the mindset of the Hong Kong Chinese, Hong Kong, as a modern, cosmopolitan and urban society exposed to Western acculturation, is much better than the home countries of Hong Kong's ethnic minorities. If Filipinos, Indonesians, Indians, Nepalese, Thais and Pakistanis cannot make their own countries as wealthy as Hong Kong, the Hong Kong Chinese may ask, how could they contribute to Hong Kong's prosperity? From a Foucauldian perspective, the discourse of the Hong Kong success story, co-constructed by the colonial authority and the colonized Hong Kong elite, makes the question about the contribution of Hong Kong ethnic minorities 'unimaginable' and 'non-existent'. This is the reason Hong Kong ethnic minorities have remained invisible for such a long time.

Not only is the contribution of minorities 'unimaginable' and 'non-existent', so is racism against them, hence it was hitherto undiscoverable and undetected. Wong and Wan's survey finds that less than 10 per cent of Hong Kong people feel that disharmony exists in daily interaction between different ethnicities, 60 per cent cannot differentiate which ethnic groups' daily habits and thoughts are different to those of ordinary Hong Kong people and cannot differentiate which ethnic group's standard of living is lower than ordinary ones.[62] Such 'innocence' coexists with the fact that 67 per cent of South Asian minorities find that they are discriminated against by the local Chinese in various aspects of daily life;[63] a quarter of FDHs have been assaulted by their employers;[64] 65 per cent of local employers acknowledged that new Chinese immigrants were employed mainly as a result of their lower pay in comparison with locals';[65] and 89 per cent of new Chinese immigrants believe they are racially discriminated against by the general public.[66]

The ideology of liberalism prevails in Hong Kong society in the people's minds: people generally believe that one's success or failure is generated under fair competition, and race or ethnicity does not matter.[67] Hong Kong people increasingly prefer to let the market mechanism distribute wealth and resources, even after the severe setbacks resulting from the Asian Economic Crisis in 1997.[68] The government has been jealously guarding this image of its liberalism and fair competition for decades – if not actually being the socializing agent for it. It takes great pride in having been placed at the top for more than a decade in the Global League Table of Economic Freedom produced by the Heritage Foundation, and ranked the world's freest economy for the past 35 years by the Cato Institute. Having branded itself 'Asia's world city', the government is much concerned about its image and reputation in the outside world, and sometimes seems to verge on paranoia.[69] Redistributing resources or offering social welfare social services on the ground of ethnicities is unthinkable from the government's perspective. For so many years, ethnic minorities have never been a subcategory of 'disadvantaged groups' in the financial secretary's annual budget speech or the chief executive's annual policy address. Yet up to one-fifth of Hong Kong people grumble that 'favouritism' is shown to ethnic minorities in recent years.[70]

When colonialism is combined with Sinicization

One may well ask, if Hong Kong ethnic minorities had not been receiving proper recognition and respect from the ethnic Chinese, why was Hong Kong able to maintain ethnic harmony for so long before the handover. First, Hong Kong ethnic minorities are numerically small and highly heterogeneous. It is difficult for them to become a united force against the majority Hong Kong Chinese. However, this does not mean that no protests, grievances and conflicts ever surfaced, especially with the Filipino FDHs. Indeed, ethnic harmony is a question of degree. Second, the colonial government adopted an accommodation-cum-segregation strategy to deal with the ethnic minorities who came with the British Army, that is, the Indians and Nepalese. The Nepalese concentrated and settled in Gurkha bases located in the rural New Territories during the colonial period. Their contacts with the Chinese were minimal. The Indians were mostly assigned jobs in the disciplinary forces (mainly police, military and correctional services). Because of their small numbers, actual contact with the Chinese was minimal. Moreover, as British colonized subjects, the colonial government provided sufficient resources for them to fulfil their needs. For example, as the number of Muslims increased in Hong Kong, the colonial government allocated land to them to build mosques and cemeteries, as well as provided Islamic education services. As a result, the ethnic minority Hong Kong residents were quite satisfied with the colonial government. Third, in dealing with the FDHs, the colonial government adopted strict immigration controls to silence potential troublemakers. Although by law people who live and work in Hong Kong for seven years can attain permanent residence, this rule does not apply to FDHs. Moreover, they have to abide by the two-week rule: once they lose their jobs, they only have two weeks to find a new job or they must return home. Consequently, if FDHs make trouble and are fired, they have to leave Hong Kong after two weeks. This constitutes a great barrier to FDHs voicing any grievances.

The 1997 handover marked the end of colonial rule as well as the beginning of the Sinicization process. Ma and Fung argue that sovereignty revision involves a process of mediated resinicization and nationalization of the Hong Kong identity. By resinicization, they refer to 'the recollection, reinvention and rediscovery of historical and cultural ties between Hong Kong and China'.[71]

Similarly, Lo uses the term 'Mainlandization' to refer to the policy changes after the handover. 'Mainlandization' comprises 'the policies of the Hong Kong government to make Hong Kong more politically dependent on Beijing, economically more reliant on the Mainland's support, socially more patriotic toward the motherland and legally more reliant on the interpretation of the Basic Law by China's National People's Congress', and put the interest of 'one country' ahead of the interest of 'two systems'.[72] In essence a very Borg-like approach.

Putting it in a wider context, Callahan argues that the Chinese Communist Party authority under-renewed its interest in promoting nationalism in the 1990s so as to confront political and economic crises both domestically, with the Tiananmen massacre, and globally, with the fall of the Soviet Union.[73] Chinese neonationalism employs the discourse of 'National Humiliation' to address the problem of imperialism to make Chinese people believe that a strong state is needed to save the nation from evil imperialists. This discourse uses modern Chinese history to reassert the connection between nation and state through essentializing Chineseness. This Chinese neonationalism was aimed not only at domestic Mainland Chinese but also at overseas Chinese. The overseas Chinese are drawn into the narrative of 'National Humiliation' and portrayed not only as victims of the failures of past Chinese states to counter the invasion of Western imperialism but also as patriots. 'Chinese identity thus expands, via National Humiliation, from being defined according to citizenship and territoriality to a wider transnational view of the Chinese race.' 'Diasporic Chinese are therefore not simply a financial resource for China ... [but are also] used as a symbolic resource for producing Chinese national identity.'[74] Putting Hong Kong in Callahan's framework makes more sense, for us at least, in explaining why Hong Kong needs to be Sinicized. The re-absorption of Hong Kong is not only to help China globalize but also to facilitate the spread of Chinese neonationalism. As Callahan observes, 'Official National Humiliation texts are increasingly co-published in Hong Kong in traditional Chinese characters for overseas distribution.'[75]

With regard to the Hong Kong ethnic minorities, Chinese neonationalism creates a problem: how can they be recruited into the narrative of National Humiliation? According to China's nationality laws, China does not recognize ethnic minorities as nationals, though they can continue living in Hong Kong. However, if they cannot obtain Chinese nationality, which is a prerequisite for qualifying for an HKSAR passport, some of them may have trouble travelling to other countries, not to mention being stateless, as Britain has been shrinking the scope of the right of abode.[76] The Chinese authorities have softened their attitude and allowed ethnic minorities to apply for Chinese nationality. But the government officer re-emphasizes that '[n]aturalization is not a right, but is subject to approval'.[77] In other words, Chinese Nationality Law *may* not confer nationality on all Hong Kong-born ethnic minorities.

Apart from the possible exclusion from gaining citizenship and nationality, Sinicization may reverse the previous colonial accommodation policy on ethnic minorities. As Ho discovers, the Muslim ethnic minorities 'felt betrayed by the rule of the Chinese when the British regime left. Many affirmative policies for the ethnic minority have gone after the rule of the Chinese-based SAR government,[78] As mentioned before, the colonial government allocated land to the Muslims to build mosques. However, the SAR government requires the Muslim community to pay HK$10 million for building a mosque in Sheung Shui, while the Heung Yee Kuk, a pro-Beijing organization which represents native Chinese clans in the New Territories, had its land granted for a nominal HK$1,000. These 'double standards' make Muslim minorities feel that they are being discriminated against.[79]

Another negative impact of Sinicization on Hong Kong ethnic minorities is the implementation of mother-tongue (that is, Chinese/Cantonese) teaching in Hong Kong secondary schools. During the colonial period, English was the major medium of instruction. However, in 1998, there was a major policy shift in order to reassert the Chineseness and decolonize the minds of the Hong Kong Chinese. The mother-tongue teaching policy significantly reduces the number of possible secondary schools which poor non-Chinese children can attend. Even worse, most ethnic minority students are always relegated to a handful of low-quality schools.[80] To sum up, Sinicization does not remove the colonial biases against ethnic minorities even though a rebuttal of imperialism is its major theme. Nor does it genuinely recognize and respect them. Instead, it removes the previous colonial accommodating policy. For the ordinary masses in this ex-British colony, the discourse of 'National Humiliation' has not yet appealed to them effectively. A local political scientist believes that the patriotism of Hong Kong Chinese to the Chinese nation is revealed through the sharing of national glory only – such as the advancement in aeronautic technology in recent years and the success of the Beijing Olympics in 2008 – but is still far 'beyond' the neonationalism engineered by the Chinese Communist Party.[81] Rather, Hong Kong people still prioritize some core (or 'egocentric') values, which were nurtured during the colonial age, over nationalism, such as a free economy and material well-being. Ironically, although these core values are not compatible with the state initiated neonationalism, ethnic minorities are still the common casualties of this odd-couple – their citizenship in the city is excluded as a result of the latter, and their sociocultural aspects are excluded because of the former.

Empire/colonialism strikes back: New Chinese immigrants as the casualties

According to Ma, the colonial government consciously adopted 'a double alienation policy' in which Hong Kong Chinese 'were discouraged from identifying themselves as national subjects of either China or the British Empire'.[82] However, the discourse of colonialism created a new hybrid identity, first for the colonized elite, later for the middle classes and ultimately for the ordinary Hong Kong Chinese. This hybrid identity comprises partially British, through mimicry, and partially Chinese, derived from indigenous Chinese cultures (plural because there is no single, unitary Chinese culture and Hong Kong is an immigrant society). As the Hong Kong society experiences economic take-off, industrialization, post-industrialization and finally establishes itself as a global city that plays an important part in Western-centred globalization, the hybrid identity becomes more Western and less Chinese as the temptation to be advanced, civilized and materially well off is too irresistible. Moreover, as Hong Kong-born Chinese grow up, they are immersed in a colonial setting, as well as an affluent economic environment. An indigenous Westernized cultural identity emerges. This identity emerges against a backward, authoritarian and underdeveloped Mainland China. Thus, this peculiar Hong Kong Chinese identity is established with an ambivalent and contradictory relationship towards the Mainland. As Ma and Fung remark, 'Hong Kong people identify with traditional Chinese culture in an abstract and detached sense, but, on the other hand, they discriminate against the particular cultural practices which are affiliated with the Communist regime in the mainland.'[83]

Suffice it to say, the indigenous Hong Kong identity is created through the differences vis-à-vis the colonizers (in the context of globalization, not only British but also white Westerners, especially white Americans) and the Mainland Chinese. This peculiar identity is partially engendered from mimicking the colonizers. However, as Bhabha states, 'mimicry emerges as the representation of a difference that is itself a process of disavowal'.[84] In other words, the Hong Kong Chinese can never become white Westerners, though they repeatedly learn and practise Western culture. This is very frustrating because Hong Kong has attained the socio-economic status of Western countries, yet its people still feel inferior to their colonizers. Fortunately, there are other Others, besides themselves, to be compared to and contrasted with. The non-white Hong Kong ethnic groups are one of these Others, the other being the Mainland Chinese. By highlighting the differences and similarities between the Hong Kong Chinese and Mainland Chinese, their second rank within the global hierarchy of race can be reaffirmed.[85] As a result, on the one hand, Ma and Fung find that: 'Hong Kong people have a historical Chinese identity which is past-oriented and feeds on the pride associated with the "great tradition" of Chinese civilization.'[86] On the other hand, they notice that 'in mass media, mainlanders were stigmatized as "uncivilized" outsiders and a ready-made cultural contrast against which modern, cosmopolitan Hongkongers could define themselves'.[87] The Chineseness of the Hong Kong hybrid identity is merely based on past glory shared with Mainland Chinese (that is, the similarities); the differences reproduce and reaffirm the superior Westernized side of the hybrid identity so as to compensate for the recurring process of disavowal embedded within mimicry. Against this ambivalent and compensatory Hong Kong Chinese identity, it is not surprising that the new Mainland Chinese immigrants are being socially excluded and discriminated against in Hong Kong.

Globalization, legitimacy and Sinicization

After the handover, the HKSAR government became the agent for carrying out Sinicization. Nonetheless, the government also needed to ensure the global economic status of Hong Kong and its domestic legitimacy. These three forces are not compatible and their conflicts cannot easily be resolved by the government. According to Ma, 'There is a popular collective desire to "save" Hong Kong from "down grading" to just one of the many Chinese cities within the nation', which will involve the loss of Hong Kong's autonomy and the failure of maintaining Hong Kong's global city status.[88] As a result, a general resentment against Sinicization pervades the Hong Kong Chinese, especially the middle classes. This will lead to a legitimation crisis. For example, when the government launched the mother-tongue teaching policy, lots of parents objected strongly, fearing that this will lower the English level of their children. More significantly, their command of English signifies the similarities between the Hong Kong Chinese and their colonizers, as well as demarcates the differences between them and the Mainland Chinese.[89] Moreover, this policy will also hamper Hong Kong's maintenance of its global city status. As a result, the legitimacy of the government has been eroded.

In order to maintain global city status, Hong Kong requires highly-skilled labour rather than lowly-skilled immigrants. An opinion pervades that the government deliberately manufactures the new Mainland Chinese immigrants as Others, and channels the frustration against the government's Sinicization efforts towards the manufactured scapegoat.[90] This strategy is silently approved by the Chinese authorities, as reflected by their successfully helping the HKSAR government to block the immediate entry of Mainland-born children of Hong Kong citizens.

According to the Basic Law (Hong Kong's constitutional document), Article 24, para 2(3), children of permanent Hong Kong residents have the right of abode (ROA) in the Special Administrative Region. Just after the handover ceremony, a number of children of permanent Hong Kong residents who had 'illegally' stayed in Hong Kong went to the Immigration office to claim their ROA. As a result, on 9 July 1997, the Provisional Legislative Council quickly amended the Immigration Ordinance so that Mainlanders are required to hold One-way Permits, which are issued by the Chinese authorities, before they can exercise their right of abode in Hong Kong. As for children born on the Mainland to the people of Hong Kong, one of their parents must be a Hong Kong permanent resident at the time of the birth. The amendment made many ROA claimants who had 'illegally' reunited with their families confront the fate of repatriation.

After numerous ROA court cases, on 29 January 1999, the Court of Final Appeal (CFA) issued a landmark judgement that these Mainland claimants were eligible for ROA. Nevertheless, the government immediately released an estimated and exaggerated figure of 1.67 million people in China who were eligible for entry and threatened that, if the CFA ruling were to be implemented, it would have great negative impacts on Hong Kong's overall economy, employment and various social services and facilities, such as housing, education, medical and health, and welfare services. 'In the process of making Mainlanders threatening "Others", they were portrayed as lazy, unemployable, welfare scrounging parasites feeding on societal resources and a menace to law and order.'[91] As a result, support and sympathy for the claimants of their right of abode collapsed almost overnight. In May 1999, the SAR government requested an interpretation of certain provisions of the Hong Kong Basic Law from China's National People's Congress in order to prevent a flood of mainland children born to Hong Kong people. The ROA issue indicates state-sponsored social exclusion and discrimination against new Mainland immigrants.

Conclusion: Who cares about protective multiculturalism?

According to Heller, there are two kinds of multiculturalism – protective and offensive. The government should adopt protective multiculturalism, which 'defends each culture against discrimination' by the state or society, 'protects the right of all groups to self-articulation and public assembly' and 'defends cultures against assimilation pressures'. In contrast, offensive multiculturalism asserts strong cultural rights and emphasizes the 'we-ness' and solidarity of the members of a cultural group. Heller warns that when offensive multiculturalism is carried out to the extreme, it becomes self-contradictory and leads to segregation and separatism. It becomes self-contradictory 'whenever it requires that members of a cultural community absolutely identify with that community'. Nonetheless, Heller adds that sometimes the boundary between protective and offensive multiculturalism is blurred because 'protective multiculturalism can also become offensive if its protective function so requires'.[92]

The HKSAR government has already begun integrating multiculturalism into Hong Kong's social policy; for example, the attempt to promulgate the RDO and the setting up of the Race Relations Unit. On the surface, it seems to be a kind of protective multiculturalism. But the question is whether the protective functions of the current policies are sufficient to deter social exclusion of ethnic minorities. Before the government decided to legislate the RDO in 2003, the setting up of the Committee on the Promotion of Racial Harmony and the Race Relations Unit was a kind of 'compromise' on the part of the government in order to resist NGOs' pressure to legalize the RDO. Cyd Ho, a legislative councillor, criticizes the fact that there are no representatives from the Department of Justice or legal profession as founding members of the committee, which clearly reveals the government's reservation and reluctance to advance legal protection to defend ethnic minorities against discrimination, and leaves the committee as a 'decoration' only.[93] The United Nations' and NGOs' persistence in advocating legal protection to ethnic minorities caused the government's reconsideration of the RDO as one of the possibilities of protective multiculturalism, but the principal and necessary blessing that the government sought before examining its realization was commercial leaders' non-oppositional attitude.[94] During the several years of consultation for drafting the RDO since 2003, no matter how the United Nations, NGOs and members of the Committee on the Promotion of Racial Harmony criticized them,[95] and in spite of the fact that more than one-third of the complaints received by the Race Relations Unit were cases against the government and public agencies, the government and public agencies have been granted immunity by the draft of the RDO. The priority of multiculturalism in the government's agenda is revealed yet again.

Hence, the Committee on the Promotion of Racial Harmony and the Race Relations Unit are left mainly to organize activities to enhance harmonious multiculturalism at the community level. This is one of the approaches that is in line with the advocacy of local NGOs and academics,[96] but not completely. Empowering ethnic minorities in various aspects of social life to defend themselves against social exclusion, such as in employment and education, is also important.[97] Some of the extraordinarily huge amount of surplus taxes collected by the government, as highlighted in the Budget Speech 2008–09, has been allocated to establish district support service centres and educational support for ethnic minorities. These measures are ground-breaking. However, by reviewing the agenda from 2004 to 2007, one would find that the committee has not been seriously consulted. In order to have adequate protective multiculturalism, some offensive elements may have to be added; organizers and mobilizers will, however, have to strike a balance so as not to tilt the movement towards segregation and separatism.

In descriptive terms, Hong Kong is a multicultural society in which different ethnic groups exist. But in normative terms, Hong Kong is a racist society in which non-white ethnic minorities and new Mainland immigrants are being socially excluded and discriminated against. Despite the various campaigns against ethnic discrimination, the government fails to cultivate genuinely a truly multicultural environment. Given that the Hong Kong Chinese have deeply internalized the colonial representations of the inferiority of ethnic minorities, and the HKSAR government deliberately manufactures the new Mainland immigrants as Others, we suspect it is unlikely that multiculturalism can be established in the near future. Moreover, our pessimistic view is also based on the fact that Hong Kong ethnic minorities are either small in number or lack bargaining power.

Notes

1 The authors' thanks go to the Research Grant Council for financial support of this project (No. GRF-HKIEd841609).
2 Joseph Nye, *Soft Power: The Means to Success in World Politics* (New York: Public Affairs, 2004).
3 Frantz Fanon, *Black Skin, White Masks* (New York: Grove Press, 1967); Edward W. Said, *Orientalism* (New York: Pantheon Books, 1978).
4 H. K. Bhabba, *The Location of Culture* (London: Routledge, 1994).
5 Ranajit Guha and Gayatri Chakravorty Spivak, *Selected Subaltern Studies* (Oxford: Oxford University Press, 1988).
6 Edward Said, *Orientalism*.
7 Ranajit Guha and Gayatri Chakravorty Spivak, *Selected Subaltern Studies*.
8 L. Pries, ed. *Migration and Transnational Social Spaces* (Aldershot: Ashgate, 1999); A. Portes, 'Conclusion: Theoretical Convergencies and Empirical Evidence in the Study of Immigrant Transnationalism'. *International Migration Review* 37 (2003): 874–892; P. Levitt, 'Transnational Migration: Taking Stock and Future Directions'. *Global Networks* 1, no. 3 (2001): 195–216.
9 Stephen Castles and Mark J. Miller, *The Age of Migration* (New York: Guilford Press, 2003), pp. 7–9.

10 *South China Morning Post* (*SCMP*), 11 February 2005.
11 A. Madanipour, G. Cars and J. Allen, 'Social Exclusion in European Cities', in A. Madanipour, G. Cars and J. Allen, eds. *Social Exclusion in European Cities: Processes, Experiences and Responses* (London: Stationery Office, 1998), p. 22.
12 Saskia Sassen, *The Global City: New York, London, Tokyo* (Princeton, NJ: Princeton University Press, 2001); Lee Kim Ming, Wong Hung and LawKam-yee, 'Social Polarisation and Poverty in the Global City: The Case of Hong Kong'. *China Report* 43, no. 1 (2007): 1–30.
13 Stephen W. K. Chiu and Lui Tai-lok, 'Testing the Global City–social Polarisation Thesis: Hong Kong since the 1990s'. *Urban Studies* 41, no. 10 (2004): 1863–1888.
14 Saskia Sassen, *The Global City*.
15 Ibid., p. 321.
16 Stephen W. K. Chiu and Lui Tai-lok, 'Testing the Global City–social Polarisation Thesis': 1876–1884.
17 Kevin Hewison, 'Thai Migrant Workers in Hong Kong'. *Journal of Contemporary Asia* 34, no. 3 (2004): 328.
18 Stephen Frost, 'Building Hong Kong: Nepalese Labour in the Construction Sector'. *Journal of Contemporary Asia* 34, no. 3 (2004): 373.
19 Ku Hok Bun *et al.*, *A Research Report on the Life Experiences of Pakistanis in Hong Kong* (Hong Kong: Centre for Social Policy Studies, Hong Kong Polytechnic University, 2003).
20 Lam Kit-chun and Liu Pak-wai, *Immigration and the Economy of Hong Kong* (Hong Kong: City University of Hong Kong Press, 1998), p. 9.
21 Law Kam-yee and Lee Kim-ming, 'Citizenship, Economy and Social Exclusion of Mainland Chinese Immigrants in Hong Kong'. *Journal of Contemporary Asia* 36, no. 2 (2006): 217–242.
22 Siu Yat-ming, 'Population and Immigration: With a Special Account on Chinese Immigrants', in Nyaw Mee-kau and Li Si-ming, eds. *The Other Hong Kong Report 1996* (Hong Kong: Chinese University Press, 1996), p. 220.
23 Lam Kit-chun and Liu Pak-wai, *Immigration and the Economy of Hong Kong*, pp. 104–110.
24 Stephen W. K. Chiu, Susanne Y. P. Choi, and Kwok-fai Ting, 'Getting Ahead in the Capitalist Paradise: Migration from China and Socio-economic Attachment in Colonial Hong Kong'. *International Migration Review* 39, no. 1 (2005): 203–227.
25 Census and Statistics Department, *2001 Population Census Thematic Report – Ethnic Minorities* (Hong Kong: Hong Kong SAR Government, 2002a).
26 Ibid.
27 Census and Statistics Department, *2001 Population Census Thematic Report – Persons from the Mainland Having Resided in Hong Kong for Less Than 7 Years* (Hong Kong: Hong Kong SAR Government, 2002b).
28 Saskia Sassen, *The Global City*.
29 William Julius Wilson, *The Truly Disadvantaged: The Inner City, the Underclass and Public Policy* (Chicago, IL: University of Chicago Press, 1987).
30 Ho Wai-yip, 'Historical Analysis of Islamic Community Development in Hong Kong: Struggle for Recognition in the Post-colonial Era'. *Journal of Muslim Minority Affairs* 21, no. 1 (2001): 68.
31 Ku Hok Bun, 'Body, Dress and Cultural Exclusion: Experiences of Pakistani Women in "Global" Hong Kong'. *Asian Ethnicity* 7, no. 3 (2006): 285–302.
32 Ibid.: 295.
33 *SCMP*, 4 March 2007.
34 Kelley Loper, 'Cultivating a Multicultural Society and Combating Racial Discrimination in Hong Kong' (Hong Kong: Civic Exchange, 2001), p. 8. Available at www.civic-exchange.org/publications/2001/racismpolicy.pdf.
35 *SCMP*, 25 June 2005.

36 Emory S. Bogardus, 'Measuring Social Distances'. *Journal of Applied Sociology* 9 (1925): 299–308.
37 Kelley Loper, 'Cultivating a Multicultural Society and Combating Racial Discrimination in Hong Kong'; Neetu Sakhrani, *A Relationship Denied: Foreign Domestic Helpers and Human Rights in Hong Kong*, 2002. Available at www.civic-exchange. org/publications/Intern/neetu.doc.; Yang Memorial Methodist Social Service, *A Study on Outlets of the South Asian Ethnic Youth in Hong Kong* (Hong Kong: Yang Memorial Methodist Social Services, Yau Tsim Mong Integrated Centre for Youth Development, 2002); Ku Hok Bun *et al.*, *A Research Report on the Life Experiences of Pakistanis in Hong Kong*; Hong Kong Christian Service, *Opinion Survey on Racial Discrimination of Minorities.* Available at www.hkcs.org/news/press/2005press/press20050207.htm; Social Work Department, Chinese University of Hong Kong, *Survey Results on Racial Discrimination in Hong Kong*, 2005. Available at www. cuhk.edu.hk/ipro/pressrelease/051028e.htm.
38 Stephen Frost, 'Building Hong Kong'; Kevin Hewison, 'Thai Migrant Workers in Hong Kong'; Annie Lin, 'Racial Discrimination at Work in Hong Kong', available at www.amrc.org.hk/5301.htm; Kam Ping-kwong and Wong Wai-fun, 'Social Exclusion of Ethnic Minorities: Employment Discrimination of the Hong Kong South Asian Minority Groups', in May Tam, Ku Hok-bun and Travis Kong, eds. *Rethinking and Recasting Citizenship: Social Exclusion and Marginality in Chinese Societies* (Hong Kong: Hong Kong Polytechnic University, 2005); Department of Applied Social Studies, CityU of Hong Kong, *Research Report on the Employment Situation of South Asian People in Hong Kong* (Hong Kong: City University of Hong Kong and Unison Hong Kong, 2003); Department of Applied Social Studies, CityU of Hong Kong, *Research Report of the Protection of Labour Rights among South Asian People in Hong Kong* (Hong Kong: City University of Hong Kong, 2004).
39 Chan Kam-wah and Ku Hok-bun, 'Exclusion of Minority Groups: The Housing Experiences of Hong Kong Pakistanis', in May Tam, Ku Hok-bun and Travis Kong, ed. *Rethinking and Recasting Citizenship: Social Exclusion and Marginality in Chinese Societies* (Hong Kong: Hong Kong Polytechnic University, 2005).
40 Kelley Loper, 'Cultivating a Multicultural Society and Combating Racial Discrimination in Hong Kong'.
41 Hong Kong Human Rights Monitor and Oxfam Hong Kong, 'Backgrounder on Enacting a Racial Discrimination Legislation for Hong Kong'. Available at www.hkhrm. org.hk/0905seminar/backgrounder.pdf.
42 Cited in *SCMP*, 10 March 1997.
43 Hong Kong Council of Social Services, 'The Cross Cultural Perception and Acceptance between Local Residents and New Arrivals, Research Report 2003'. Available at www.hkcss.org.hk/fs/er/Reference/NA03Full.pdf.
44 Society for Community Organization (SoCO), *Hong Kong Racial Discrimination, Study Series I: New Immigrants from Mainland China*, Executive Report, 2001, pp. 10–11. Available at www.soco.org.hk/publication/publication_index.htm.
45 John McLeod, *Beginning Postcolonialism* (Manchester: Manchester University Press, 2000), p. 19.
46 John M. Carroll, 'Chinese Collaboration in the Making of British Hong Kong', in Ngo Tak-wing, ed. *Hong Kong's History: State and Society under Colonial Rule* (London: Routledge, 1999); Hui Po-keung, 'Comprador Politics and Middleman Capitalism', in Ngo Tak-wing, ed. *Hong Kong's History: State and Society under Colonial Rule* (London: Routledge, 1999).
47 John M. Carroll, 'Colonial Hong Kong as a Cultural-historical Place'. *Modern Asian Studies* 40, no. 2 (2004): 517–543.
48 Ibid.: 521–522.
49 Ibid.
50 Lui Tai-lok and Stephen W. K. Chiu, 'Social Movements and Public Discourse on

Politics', in Ngo Tak-wing, ed. *Hong Kong's History: State and Society under Colonial Rule* (London: Routledge, 1999), p. 106.

51 Ibid., p. 110.

52 Martin Jacques, 'Racism in Hong Kong – In Memory of Harinder Veriah', *SCMP*, 6 March 2001.

53 *SCMP*, 10 July 2003.

54 Martin Jacques, 'The Global Hierarchy of Race', *Guardian*, 20 September 2003.

55 Barbara-Sue White, *Turbans and Traders: Hong Kong Indian Communities* (Oxford: Oxford University Press, 1994).

56 *SCMP*, 16 December 1996.

57 Ho Wai-yip, 'Historical Analysis of Islamic Community Development in Hong Kong': 64.

58 FEONA (Far East Overseas Nepalese Association), *Some Facts and Figures of Racial Discrimination in Hong Kong (Promulgation of Nepalese Community)*, paper presented at LegCo Panel on Home Affairs, 10 January 2000.

59 B. Leung, 'Women and Social Change: The Impact of Industrialization on Women in Hong Kong', in Veronica Pearson and Benjamin K. P. Leung, eds. *Women in Hong Kong* (Hong Kong: Oxford University Press, 1995).

60 www.info.gov.hk/censtatd/eng/hkstat/fas/labour/ghs/labour2.xls.

61 Census and Statistics Department, *General Household Survey, Third Quarter, 2003* (Hong Kong: Hong Kong SAR Government, 2003), p. 26.

62 Wong Ka-ying and Wan Po-san, 'The Condition of Ethnic Identity in Hong Kong', in Lau Siu-kai *et al.*, eds. *Social Transformation and Cultural Change in Chinese Societies* (Hong Kong: Chinese University of Hong Kong, 2001), p. 446.

63 *Wen Hui Po*, 29 October 2005.

64 W. K. Chiu and C. L. Lee. 'A Survey on the Working Conditions of FDHs in Hong Kong', pp. 266–268.

65 *Ming Pao*, 29 September 1998.

66 Society for Community Organization (SoCO), *Hong Kong Racial Discrimination, Study Series I: New Immigrants from Mainland China*, pp. 10–11.

67 Timothy Ka-ying Wong, 'The Ethnic and National Identities of the Hong Kong People: A Liberal Explanation'. *Issues & Studies* 32, no. 8 (1996): 105–130.

68 Lau Siu-kai, 'Hong Kong People's Confidence in the Capitalist Society', in Lau Siu-kai *et al.*, eds. *Social Transformation and Cultural Change in Chinese Societies* (Hong Kong: Chinese University of Hong Kong, 2001), p. 156.

69 Tony Latter, *Hands On or Hands Off? The Nature and Process of Economic Policy in Hong Kong* (Hong Kong: Hong Kong University Press, 2007), p. 13.

70 Wong Ka-ying and Wan Po-san, 'The Condition of Ethnic Identity in Hong Kong', p. 450.

71 Eric K. W. Ma and Anthony Y. H. Fung, 'Re-sinicization, Nationalism and the Hong Kong Identity', in Clement So and Joseph Chan, eds. *Press and Politics in Hong Kong: Case Studies from 1967 to 1997* (Hong Kong: Hong Kong Institute for Asia-Pacific Studies, 1999), pp. 500–501.

72 Sonny Lo, 'The Mainlandization and Recolonization of Hong Kong: A Triumph of Convergence over Divergence with Mainland China', in Joseph Y. S. Cheng, ed. *The Hong Kong Special Administrative Region in Its First Decade* (Hong Kong: City University of Hong Kong Press, 2007).

73 William A. Callahan, 'Beyond Cosmopolitanism and Nationalism: Diasporic Chinese and Neo-nationalism in China and Thailand'. *International Organization* 57 (2003): 481–517.

74 Ibid.: 493.

75 Ibid.: 492.

76 *SCMP*, 9 December 1996.

77 *SCMP*, 15 December 2002.

78 Ho Wai-yip, 'Historical Analysis of Islamic Community Development in Hong Kong': 72.
79 *SCMP*, 4 August 2001.
80 Kelley Loper, 'Cultivating a Multicultural Society and Combating Racial Discrimination in Hong Kong'.
81 *Hong Kong Economic Journal*, 3 May 2008.
82 Eric K. W. Ma, 'Renationalization and Me: My Hong Kong Story after 1997'. *Inter-Asia Cultural Studies* 1, no. 1 (2000): 175.
83 Eric K. W. Ma and Anthony Y. H. Fung, 'Re-sinicization, Nationalism and the Hong Kong Identity', p. 500.
84 H. K. Bhabba, *The Location of Culture*, p. 122.
85 Martin Jacques, 'The Global Hierarchy of Race'.
86 Eric K. W. Ma and Anthony Y. H. Fung, 'Re-sinicization, Nationalism and the Hong Kong Identity', p. 523.
87 Ibid., p. 500.
88 Eric K. W. Ma, 'Renationalization and Me'.
89 Elaine Chan, 'Beyond Pedagogy: Language and Identity in Post-colonial Hong Kong'. *British Journal of Sociology of Education* 23, no. 2 (2002): 271–285.
90 Law Kam-yee and Lee Kim-ming, 'Citizenship, Economy and Social Exclusion of Mainland Chinese Immigrants in Hong Kong': 238–239.
91 Elaine Chan, 'Defining Fellow Compatriots as "Others" – National Identity in Hong Kong'. *Government and Opposition* 34, no. 3 (1999): 352–371.
92 Agnes Heller, 'The Many Faces of Multiculturalism', in Rainer Baubock, Agnes Heller and Aristide R. Zolberg, eds. *The Challenge of Diversity* (Aldershot: Avebury, 1996), pp. 37–38.
93 *Hong Kong Economic Journal*, 21 June 2002.
94 www.legco.gov.hk/yr01–02/chinese/panels/ha/papers/ha0410cb2–1548–1c.pdf.
95 *Hong Kong Economic Journal*, 10 January 2008.
96 Kam Ping-kwong and Wong Wai-fun, 'Social Exclusion of Ethnic Minorities', p. 86; Ku Hok Bun, 'Body, Dress and Cultural Exclusion': 300.
97 Kam Ping-kwong and Wong Wai-fun, 'Social Exclusion of Ethnic Minorities', pp. 86–89; Ku Hok Bun *et al.*, *A Research Report on the Life Experiences of Pakistanis in Hong Kong*, pp. 236–237.

References

Bhabba, H. K. *The Location of Culture* (London: Routledge, 1994).
Bogardus, Emory S. 'Measuring Social Distances'. *Journal of Applied Sociology* 9 (1925): 299–308.
Callahan, William A. 'Beyond Cosmopolitanism and Nationalism: Diasporic Chinese and Neo-nationalism in China and Thailand'. *International Organization* 57 (2003): 481–517.
Carroll, John M. 'Chinese Collaboration in the Making of British Hong Kong', in Ngo Tak-wing, ed. *Hong Kong's History: State and Society under Colonial Rule* (London: Routledge, 1999).
Carroll, John M. 'Colonial Hong Kong as a Cultural-historical Place'. *Modern Asian Studies* 40, no. 2 (2004): 517–543.
Castles, Stephen and Mark J. Miller. *The Age of Migration* New York: Guilford Press, 2003).Census and Statistics Department. *2001 Population Census Thematic Report – Ethnic Minorities* (Hong Kong: Hong Kong SAR Government, 2002a).
Census and Statistics Department. *2001 Population Census Thematic Report – Persons from the Mainland Having Resided in Hong Kong for Less Than 7 Years* (Hong Kong: Hong Kong SAR Government, 2002b).

Census and Statistics Department. *General Household Survey, Third Quarter, 2003* (Hong Kong: Hong Kong SAR Government, 2003).

Chan, Elaine. 'Beyond Pedagogy: Language and Identity in Post-colonial Hong Kong'. *British Journal of Sociology of Education* 23, no. 2 (2002): 271–285.

Chan, Elaine. 'Defining Fellow Compatriots as "Others" – National Identity in Hong Kong'. *Government and Opposition* 34, no. 3 (1999): 352–371.

Chan, Kam-wah and Ku Hok-bun. 'Exclusion of Minority Groups: The Housing Experiences of Hong Kong Pakistanis', in May Tam, Ku Hok-bun and Travis Kong, eds. *Rethinking and Recasting Citizenship: Social Exclusion and Marginality in Chinese Societies* (Hong Kong: Hong Kong Polytechnic University, 2005).

Chiu, Stephen W. K. and Lui Tai-lok. 'Testing the Global City–social Polarisation Thesis: Hong Kong since the 1990s'. *Urban Studies* 41, no. 10 (2004): 1863–1888.

Chiu, Stephen W. K., Susanne Y. P. Choi and Kwok-fai Ting. 'Getting Ahead in the Capitalist Paradise: Migration from China and Socio-economic Attachment in Colonial Hong Kong'. *International Migration Review* 39, no. 1 (2005): 203–227.

Chiu, W. K. and C. L. Lee. 'A Survey on the Working Conditions of FDHs in Hong Kong', in Lau Siu-kai *et al.*, eds. *The Trends and Challenges to Social Development: Experiences in Hong Kong and Taiwan* (Hong Kong: Chinese University of Hong Kong, 2006).

Department of Applied Social Studies, CityU of Hong Kong. *Research Report on the Employment Situation of South Asian People in Hong Kong* (Hong Kong: City University of Hong Kong and Unison Hong Kong, 2003).

Department of Applied Social Studies, CityU of Hong Kong. *Research Report of the Protection of Labour Rights among South Asian People in Hong Kong* (Hong Kong: City University of Hong Kong, 2004).

Fanon, Frantz. *Black Skin, White Masks* (New York: Grove Press, 1967).

FEONA (Far East Overseas Nepalese Association). *Some Facts and Figures of Racial Discrimination in Hong Kong (Promulgation of Nepalese Community)*. Paper presented at LegCo Panel on Home Affairs, 10 January 2000.

Frost, Stephen. 'Building Hong Kong: Nepalese Labour in the Construction Sector'. *Journal of Contemporary Asia* 34, no. 3 (2004): 364–376.

Guha, Ranajit and Gayatri Chakravorty Spivak. *Selected Subaltern Studies* (Oxford: Oxford University Press, 1988).

Heller, Agnes. 'The Many Faces of Multiculturalism', in Rainer Baubock, Agnes Heller and Aristide R. Zolberg *The Challenge of Diversity* (Aldershot: Avebury, 1996).

Hewison, Kevin. 'Thai Migrant Workers in Hong Kong'. *Journal of Contemporary Asia* 34, no. 3 (2004): 318–335.

Ho, Wai-yip. 'Historical Analysis of Islamic Community Development in Hong Kong: Struggle for Recognition in the Post-colonial Era'. *Journal of Muslim Minority Affairs* 21, no. 1 (2001): 63–77.

Hong Kong Christian Service. *Opinion Survey on Racial Discrimination of Minorities*. Available at www.hkcs.org/news/press/2005press/press20050207.htm.

Hong Kong Council of Social Services. 'The Cross Cultural Perception and Acceptance between Local Residents and New Arrivals, Research Report 2003'. Available at www.hkcss.org.hk/fs/er/Reference/NA03Full.pdf.

Hong Kong Human Rights Monitor and Oxfam Hong Kong. 'Backgrounder on Enacting a Racial Discrimination Legislation for Hong Kong'. Available at www.hkhrm.org.hk/0905seminar/backgrounder.pdf.

Hui, Po-keung. 'Comprador Politics and Middleman Capitalism', in Ngo Tak-wing, ed.

Hong Kong's History: State and Society under Colonial Rule (London: Routledge, 1999).

Jacques, Martin. 'Racism in Hong Kong – In Memory of Harinder Veriah', *SCMP*, 6 March 2001.

Jacques, Martin. 'The Global Hierarchy of Race', *Guardian*, 20 September 2003.

Kam, Ping-kwong and Wong Wai-fun. 'Social Exclusion of Ethnic Minorities: Employment Discrimination of the Hong Kong South Asian Minority Groups', in May Tam, Ku Hok-bun and Travis Kong, eds. *Rethinking and Recasting Citizenship: Social Exclusion and Marginality in Chinese Societies* (Hong Kong: Hong Kong Polytechnic University, 2005).

Ku, Hok Bun. 'Body, Dress and Cultural Exclusion: Experiences of Pakistani Women in "Global" Hong Kong'. *Asian Ethnicity* 7, no. 3 (2006): 285–302.

Ku, Hok Bun. 'An Analysis of South Asian Ethnic Minorities' Job and Employment Conditions', in Lau Siu-kai *et al.*, eds. *New Faces of Chinese Societies in the New Century: Analysis of Social Indicators* (Hong Kong: Chinese University of Hong Kong, 2008).

Ku, Hok Bun *et al. A Research Report on the Life Experiences of Pakistanis in Hong Kong* (Hong Kong: Centre for Social Policy Studies, Hong Kong Polytechnic University, 2003).

Lam, Kit-chun and Liu Pak-wai. *Immigration and the Economy of Hong Kong* (Hong Kong: City University of Hong Kong Press, 1998).

Latter, Tony. *Hands On or Hands Off? The Nature and Process of Economic Policy in Hong Kong* (Hong Kong: Hong Kong University Press, 2007).

Lau, Siu-kai. *Society and Politics in Hong Kong* (Hong Kong: Chinese University Press, 1982).

Lau, Siu-kai. 'Hong Kong People's Confidence in the Capitalist Society', in Lau Siu-kai *et al.*, eds. *Social Transformation and Cultural Change in Chinese Societies* (Hong Kong: Chinese University of Hong Kong, 2001).

Law, Kam-yee and Lee Kim-ming. 'Citizenship, Economy and Social Exclusion of Mainland Chinese Immigrants in Hong Kong'. *Journal of Contemporary Asia* 36, no. 2 (2006): 217–242.

Lee, Kim Ming and Hung Wong. 'Marginalised Workers in Postindustrial Hong Kong'. *Journal of Comparative Asian Development* 3, no. 2 (2004): 249–280.

Lee, Kim Ming and Kam-yee Law. 'Social Polarisation and Poverty in the Global City: The Case of Hong Kong.' *China Report* 43, no. 1 (2007): 1–30.

Leung, B. 'Women and Social Change: The Impact of Industrialization on Women in Hong Kong', in Veronica Pearson and Benjamin K. P. Leung, eds. *Women in Hong Kong* (Hong Kong: Oxford University Press, 1995).

Levitt, P. 'Transnational Migration: Taking Stock and Future Directions'. *Global Networks* 1, no. 3 (2001): 195–216.

Lin, Annie. 'Racial Discrimination at Work in Hong Kong'. Available at www.amrc.org.hk/5301.htm.

Lo, Sonny. 'The Mainlandization and Recolonization of Hong Kong: A Triumph of Convergence over Divergence with Mainland China', in Joseph Y. S. Cheng, ed. *The Hong Kong Special Administrative Region in Its First Decade* (Hong Kong: City University of Hong Kong Press, 2007).

Loper, Kelley. 'Cultivating a Multicultural Society and Combating Racial Discrimination in Hong Kong' (Hong Kong: Civic Exchange, 2001). Available at www.civic-exchange.org/publications/2001/racismpolicy.pdf.

Loper, Kelley. 'Race and Equality: A Study of Ethnic Minorities in Hong Kong's Education System', Occasional Paper 12 (Centre for Comparative and Public Law, University of Hong Kong, 2004).

Lui, Tai-lok and Stephen W. K. Chiu. 'Social Movements and Public Discourse on Politics', in Ngo Tak-wing, ed. *Hong Kong's History: State and Society under Colonial Rule* (London: Routledge, 1999).

Ma, Eric K. W. 'Renationalization and Me: My Hong Kong Story after 1997'. *Inter-Asia Cultural Studies* 1, no. 1 (2000): 173–179.

Ma, Eric K. W. and Anthony Y. H. Fung. 'Re-sinicization, Nationalism and the Hong Kong Identity', in Clement So and Joseph Chan, eds. *Press and Politics in Hong Kong: Case Studies from 1967 to 1997* (Hong Kong: Hong Kong Institute for Asia-Pacific Studies, 1999).

Madanipour, A., G. Cars and J. Allen. 'Social Exclusion in European Cities', in A. Madanipour, G. Cars and J. Allen, eds. *Social Exclusion in European Cities: Processes, Experiences and Responses* (London: Stationery Office, 1998).

McLeod, John. *Beginning Postcolonialism* (Manchester: Manchester University Press, 2000).

Nye, Joseph. *Soft Power: The Means to Success in World Politics* (New York: Public Affairs, 2004).

Portes, A. 'Conclusion: Theoretical Convergencies and Empirical Evidence in the Study of Immigrant Transnationalism'. *International Migration Review* 37 (2003): 874–892.

Pries, L., ed. *Migration and Transnational Social Spaces* (Aldershot: Ashgate, 1999).

Said, Edward W. *Orientalism* (New York: Pantheon Books, 1978).

Sakhrani, Neetu. *A Relationship Denied: Foreign Domestic Helpers and Human Rights in Hong Kong*, 2002. Available at www.civic-exchange.org/publications/Intern/neetu.doc.

Sassen, Saskia. *The Global City: New York, London, Tokyo* (Princeton, NJ: Princeton University Press, 2001).

Siu, Yat-ming. 'Population and Immigration: With a Special Account on Chinese Immigrants', in Nyaw Mee-kau and Li Si-ming, eds. *The Other Hong Kong Report 1996* (Hong Kong: Chinese University Press, 1996).

Social Work Department, Chinese University of Hong Kong. *Survey Results on Racial Discrimination in Hong Kong*, 2005. Available at www.cuhk.edu.hk/ipro/pressrelease/051028e.htm.

Society for Community Organization (SoCO). *Hong Kong Racial Discrimination, Study Series I: New Immigrants from Mainland China*, Executive Report, 2001. Available at www.soco.org.hk/publication/publication_index.htm.

White, Barbara-Sue. *Turbans and Traders: Hong Kong Indian Communities* (Oxford: Oxford University Press, 1994).

Wilson, William Julius. *The Truly Disadvantaged: The Inner City, the Underclass and Public Policy* (Chicago, IL: University of Chicago Press, 1987).

Wong, Timothy Ka-ying. 'The Ethnic and National Identities of the Hong Kong People: A Liberal Explanation'. *Issues & Studies* 32, no. 8 (1996): 105–130.

Wong, Timothy Ka-ying and Wan Po-san. 'The Condition of Ethnic Identity in Hong Kong', in Lau Siu-kai *et al.*, eds. *Social Transformation and Cultural Change in Chinese Societies* (Hong Kong: Chinese University of Hong Kong, 2001).

Yang Memorial Methodist Social Service. *A Study on Outlets of the South Asian Ethnic Youth in Hong Kong* (Hong Kong: Yang Memorial Methodist Social Services, Yau Tsim Mong Integrated Centre for Youth Development, 2002).

6 Migrants, immigrants and multicultural society in South Korea

Multiculturalism and national identity

Inchoon Kim

Introduction

South Koreans (henceforth Koreans) have traditionally considered themselves as a homogeneous nation bound together by a common bloodline and culture. They did not and, in fact, could not endorse any immigrants and political refugees until the 1980s. Very limited numbers of old ethnic minorities, such as resident Chinese and 'mixed-blood' people were objects of exclusion during the last century. Recently, however, Koreans have been seeing a lot of foreign residents as a result of rapidly increasing numbers of international marriages and migrant workers since the mid-1990s. The number of foreign residents is about 1.4 million (Ministry of Justice, 2011), comprising 3 per cent of the total population, and is expected to reach 5 per cent in 2020. This phenomenon of rapidly increasing numbers of foreign residents has not only been changing the composition of the population, but has also made Korean society more ethnically and culturally diverse.

As a consequence, the notion of multiculturalism has become popular with academics as well as the media, in a country with a long history of monoculturalism. Korea is facing up to the multicultural challenges to its exiting homogeneous national identity, though, as Korean people have begun discussing multicultural societies, and debates on multiculturalism and multicultural societies have been provoking wide interest as well as acute controversy. The Korean government, media and NGOs, as well as academia, are joining their voices together to make Korea a friendlier place for foreign residents to live in. The Korean government has introduced plans to relax immigration and naturalization rules to open the country up to more foreigners and to sharpen global competitiveness with foreign human resources. It has also introduced various multicultural policies to promote social integration among foreign residents. As foreign residents have now become part of the fabric of Korean society, the central as well as local governments' policies towards foreign residents have taken on increasing significance in Korea.

Migration is primarily an economic phenomenon, shaped by economic incentives, such as huge income and wage differentials between countries. Historically, migration and free trade have been closely connected. Modern imperialism integrated Asia into the international economy, which resulted in free trade and migration in the region since the second half of the nineteenth century. In the aftermath of the Second World War, decolonization, and the rise of nation states and Asian nationalism, the situation changed and migration became increasingly restricted. Since the 1980s, the global redistribution of production has led to the resumption of migration in Asia. Japan was the first country to accept low-cost migrant worker inflows, beginning in the 1980s, and then Singapore, Hong Kong and Korea followed suit to supplement their domestic workforces, just like in developed Western countries. The increasing demand for highly-skilled as well as less-skilled migrants and the creation of sub-regional labour markets are all manifestations of global economic change. This has been linking economies and societies in that the migrants are being absorbed into societies that are themselves being transformed economically and culturally.[1]

In fact, Korea was a country from which migrants departed in large numbers until the 1970s. It then experienced the transition to receiving rapidly growing inflows of migrants from the 1990s onwards as its economic development objective became increasingly dependent on foreign labour. Key factors for this are industrial restructuring, labour shortages resulting from demographic changes and structural changes in labour supply. The demand for low-cost labour in services, as well as manufacturing industries, cannot be resolved by overseas investment and the adoption of labour-saving technologies.[2] Industrial restructuring in Korea has made several industries, such as agriculture, fishery and less-skilled manufacturing, much less competitive and lowered the social and economic status of people, especially young men, in these industries. This is the background of the phenomenon of international marriages between migrant brides from Southeast Asia or China and Korean men. The Korean government has become preoccupied with migration matters as migrants' multicultural practices have raised new questions of national identity, social integration and cultural diversity.

This chapter critically assesses recent debate on multiculturalism and multicultural policies in Korea in comparative perspective. For this, I will address the developments of the migration and immigration phenomenon and the impact of multicultural debates on cultural diversity and social integration. The chapter will also examine the reconciliation between the official state rhetoric regarding the multicultural society and understanding of cultural diversity with that of the public, since Korea's national identity, cultural patriotism and immigration policy are still significantly affecting the perceptions of, and attitudes of Korean people to, foreign residents. Finally, this chapter will critically consider Koreans' nationalist beliefs and pride that have produced unilateral assimilation and social exclusion of foreign residents, especially from developing countries.

Debates on multiculturalism in Korea

Multiculturalism: its proponents and critics

Multiculturalism refers to the doctrine that cultural diversity should be recognized as a permanent and valuable part of political societies and, thus, it requires that cultural rights should be supported by specific public policies.[3] The attempt to make democratic processes more inclusive for ethnic, as well as national, minorities has led to the notion of multiculturalism. It is based on a new principle that 'all voices should be heard' and 'equal respect' to every ethnicity has become the irreducible core of the liberal state. Multiculturalism is supposed to create a progressive society where the tolerance of cultural identity provides equality and opportunity for all.

However, there are intense academic and political debates on multiculturalism, from arguments concerning different framings of multiculturalism to claims of multiculturalism as 'a failed experiment'. According to the politics of recognition, a major theory of multiculturalism, cultural communities deserve protection because they provide their members with the basis of their identity.[4] The theory argues that liberal societies should protect minority communities because their continued existence is a necessary condition for the autonomy of their individual members. For them, banning wearing the traditional Muslim headscarf is considered an encroachment of civil and religious rights. Okin's framing of multiculturalism argues that minority cultures should be protected by special group rights or privileges.[5] It also reflects an essentialist and static understanding of culture and ethnicity that interprets culture as the cause of the problem and thus tends to neglect the influence of social structures or institutions. Cohen *et al.* present another framing of multiculturalism that supports claims for equal rights and equal worth for all individuals and social groups and, therefore, makes little of the conflicts between individual rights and group rights.[6] Parekh develops the theory subtly, arguing that a community's identity is not a substance, but a cluster of interrelated and relatively open-ended tendencies and impulses.[7]

Though the politics of recognition aims at including cultural groups within the political society, it may inevitably have exclusive effects of its own by segregating such groups. Exclusive characteristics of cultural identities cast doubt on the possibility of a general, inclusive theory of multiculturalism. Kymlicka's liberal multiculturalism tries to answer this question of non-exclusive politics of recognition. Liberal multiculturalism is such that liberal policies of multiculturalism, minority rights and indigenous rights are adapted, regardless of the wide perception that liberalism is individualistic and multiculturalism has 'communitarian' values. Kymlicka affirms the need for states to accommodate ethnocultural diversity, but within the framework of an underlying commitment to human rights and liberal democratic constitutionalism. His theory of multiculturalism holds that individuals are entitled to live in a culture of liberal society, and deals with how minority rights fit into broader issues in liberal-democratic theory. He argues for a deepening of citizenship and democracy within the nation state by extending minority rights as the solution to demands for recognition, and points out that there have been ongoing practices of liberal multiculturalism in many liberal-democratic countries in Western Europe.[8]

However, liberal multiculturalism has limitations since minority groups are often prohibited, in the name of liberalism, from engaging in the very activities that constitute their cultural identity. This 'repressive liberalism' or 'illiberal pressures'[9] becomes common when Western European states, where the 'strange death of multiculturalism'[10] has been witnessed, seek to justify anti-immigrant policies. The states no longer invoke national identities, but rather invoke universal liberal values, and argue that immigrants are a threat to these universal values and call for tougher immigration laws. France forbids Muslim girls from wearing the *hijab* in public schools and Denmark limits the freedom of immigrants to marry spouses from foreign countries. Definitive citizenship tests and parliamentary passport information control in the Netherlands, and enabling school authorities to ban forms of religious dress in Britain are also new phenomena.

It is believed that the liberal state has no obligation to preserve ethnic cultures, unless this is necessary for their equal integration and participation in the national culture. Religious symbols are considered a violation of the separation between the state and religion. Discontents of multiculturalism argue that the influence of Islam and, in particular, of very conservative religious groups who reject any form of integration in Western European society, undermine democracy and civil liberties, as well as 'national virtues'. In fact, many Western democracies, especially countries with national minorities, have moved away from older models of the unitary nation state, and repudiated older ideologies of 'one nation and one culture'. With their codes of political correctness, the multiculturism of Western European countries has been designed to promote harmonious coexistence, especially for their former colonial ethnic minorities.

However, after decades of the multicultural experiment, ethnic inequality is still evident and culturally divided communities are creating radicals, violence and animosity within the indigenous peoples. Questioning the wisdom of culturally divided communities, more people argue for greater integration and equality and an end to the counterproductive excesses of multiculturalism. Newly immigrated ethnic groups can obtain their rights to a societal culture by integrating as much as possible into the national culture of the host country. Many liberal states are adapting policies of assimilation or exclusion to a more 'multicultural' approach that recognizes and accommodates diversity and opposes illiberal practices of ethnic minority cultures. Homogenization of national culture is not only an unavoidable but also a legitimate state objective for the unity and collective prosperity of a nation state.

These developments produce critics of multiculturalism who argue that multiculturalism and liberal democracy are fundamentally incompatible and multiculturalism is thus a 'failure'. By encouraging 'differences' among ethnic subgroups, they argue, multiculturalism ends up turning these groups into targets of resentment and thereby ensuring their rejection by the majority national culture.[11] To critics, multiculturalism is functioning for immigrants being marginalized, isolated and excluded by racism and systematic discrimination. Therefore, cultural diversity or the politics of collective identity, rather than cultural assimilation or struggles for inclusion, will be socially, politically and economically dangerous. The multicultural status quo, far from being a successful model for harmonious coexistence, is in fact creating a gulf of separation between communities. Many host societies, having double standards, have never viewed themselves as equal partners in the multicultural mosaic even though they have defined themselves as egalitarians and champions of multiculturalism.

This is the background against which Fraser emphasizes the importance of social justice and distribution in the age of identity politics. Fraser argues that the struggle for recognition was fast becoming the paradigmatic form of political conflict, with group identity supplanting class interest, and a new language of identity and recognition replacing an earlier vocabulary of interest and redistribution. Insisting that justice requires both redistribution and recognition, Fraser redefines recognition struggles as struggles for citizen inclusion and political voice.[12] It is not a matter of choice between pursuing the 'recognition' objectives that require us to consolidate collective identities, or the 'redistribution' objectives that depend on reducing the salience of group differences. Fraser differentiates between the identity and status models of recognition, and recasts recognition struggles, not as claims about collective identities, but as seeking to establish the subordinated individuals as full partners in social life. The dynamic interplay between claims for respect and claims for social justice is important.[13]

Furthermore, many experts debating the problem argue with multiculturalism itself. First of all, there exists no uniform meaning or definition of multiculturalism and no consensus about the principles of multiculturalism. One of the main issues is about whether one type of rights should prevail over other rights, that is, religious freedom, socio-economic equality, human rights and so on. Defenders of Enlightenment values that are critical to ethnic identities, such as Muslim orthodoxy, have not given importance to religion and cultural beliefs, and have turned away from multiculturalism. Insofar as struggles for recognition propound 'authentic' collective identities, such struggles serve less to foster interaction across differences than to enforce separatism and intolerance.[14] Repressive forms of communitarianism will come into sharp conflict with the universal rights and autonomy of individuals, and can lead to a paralysed relativism that puts sensitivity to cultural difference over the rights or needs of individuals.

Korean national identity and multiculturalism

Historically, the national identity of Korea is stronger and even more exclusive than that of the East Asian countries of Japan and China, which are considered to have strong national identities, mainly as a result of their historical and cultural legacies.[15] In its 5,000 years of history, the country of Korea was repeatedly invaded by neighbouring countries, and thus placing emphasis on the 'pure Korean bloodline' was crucial for the survival of Koreans. The Koreans' 'collective memories' of various hardships, such as colonialism and national division, have not only underpinned the ideology of statehood and the sociocultural dynamics of contemporary Korea, but also fostered exclusive and resistant nationalist minds. School textbooks describe Korea as a 'nation unified by one bloodline'. As a consequence, Korea has not experienced harmonious coexistence with different ethnic people and, therefore, no ethnic minority group has rooted itself in the land of Korea. This may mean that Korea is lacking certain prerequisite conditions for multiculturalism.

Nevertheless, recently many discourses and debates are taking place concerning multiculturalism as the 'multiculturalism boom' has suddenly descended on Korea. How and why could this happen in Korea, a country with no ethnic minorities and no historical responsibility unlike many European countries that have huge numbers of immigrants from their ex-colonies? There may be many reasons and backgrounds. First, there has been growing academic interest in culture, minorities, cultural studies and area studies in Korea since the 1990s. Second, Korea has achieved a kind of 'sub-imperialist' status, a sort of expansionary nationalism, in Asia, which has enabled Koreans, since the 1990s, to also have 'Others', probably for the first time in its history. This 'sub-imperialist' status has been represented culturally in the 'Korean wave', *Hallu*, and economically in global corporations such as Samsung, Hyundai and LG. Third, there have been rapidly increasing numbers of foreign residents since the 1990s. Inflows of foreigners have facilitated multicultural rhetoric in Korea, but have also fostered expansionary nationalist thinking and cultural patriotism in the era of globalization.[16] Finally, Korea's extended democratization and the demands of civil society have played a significant role in developing multiculturalism rhetoric.

In a sense, the sudden mushrooming debates on multiculturalism or multicultural society in Korea reflect the superior but complex sentiments of Koreans who are covertly enjoying their status of cultural and economic superiority in Asia. At the same time, Koreans, as a majority, have minorities of darker-skinned ethnic groups from Southeast and South Asia. They are the 'Others'; objects and minorities to exclude, assimilate or integrate. Therefore, multiculturalism in Korea may have unintended racist and sub-imperialist implications, and may be advocated only rhetorically and used to express quite different framing of ideas and norms. Discriminatory and biased perceptions and practices against minorities usually stem from race, ethnicity, and social and economic status. This explains why there has been little debate on cultural differences, that is, the cultures of ethnic minorities that form the core of multiculturalism. This also explains why there is little prejudice in Korea towards white foreign residents from developed countries.[17]

The Korean national identity involves many elements but is mainly formed by those of the same blood, language and culture. This national identity has been effectively embedded in Korean society, particularly during the period when it consolidated itself as a unitary, homogenizing and strong nation state after its liberation from Japan in 1945. Since then, nationhood, sovereignty, cultural patriotism and supremacy, and patriotic citizens' education have fortified Korea's monocultural and exclusive national identity. This sense of national identity still exists today, even though the absolute supremacy of the nation state has been attenuated significantly since the democratization of Korea in the late

1980s.[18] According to a survey in 2003, Koreans hold negative attitudes toward the inflow of foreign immigrants and multiculturalism and they think it is impossible for people from different cultures to be fully incorporated into Korean society. They still have a strong ethnic and exclusive sense of national identity.[19]

Nevertheless, political rhetoric on the subject of multiculturalism is growing unprecedentedly strong in Korea and international norms of cultural diversity have been playing a role in reconfiguring the national identity of Korea. This trend has been followed by strong but uncertain anxiety and resistance from Koreans, which has also ignited debates on multiculturalism among conservative as well as radical nationalist groups.[20] The sudden presence of new ethnic minorities since the 1990s has been challenging to the 'one-blood unitary nation-state' and many Koreans are worried about huge numbers of migrant people from Southeast and South Asia and China becoming immigrants. They prefer an assimilation policy to protect the Korean national culture, and argue that the policy could be compatible with a multicultural policy when it secures proper rights for minorities.

However the related issues of assimilation could have different effects. Its premise of cultural domination can frame the minds of minorities through education and training, resulting in the dispossession of these groups' own identities, pride and self-representation. Multiculturalism is a multidimensional concept that may refer both to demands for the protection of minorities, and to demands for equal rights and anti-discrimination policies. The debate about multiculturalism refers both to empirical facts on increasing multi-ethnic societies connected to migration, and to multicultural policies, as well as to normative principles of social justice. The term, multicultural, covers many different forms of cultural pluralism. The key point is that the multicultural paradigm is not universal but contextual and situated.[21]

Whether or not a multicultural society is going to exist, whether or not multiculturalism is imminent, and what form of cultural pluralism we need, are some of the key questions we need to address in Korea. Some have argued that Korea is far from being a multicultural society since foreign residents comprise just over 2 per cent of the total population, compared with more than 5 per cent in most multicultural societies. Furthermore, most of the foreign residents are migrant workers who will leave Korea. Also, until now, the Korean government has not repressed minorities' cultures. Migrant workers who are dominant in numbers are more interested in social and economic rights and opportunities than in cultural recognition. Minorities in Korea have not been actively demanding the protection of their identities and their cultural differences. This has allowed Koreans to willingly embrace nationalism to keep their national identity and the majority culture of Korea intact, and to formulate multicultural policy in the form of social integration and cultural assimilation. Many Koreans believe or want to believe that multiculturalism is not a pressing matter yet, regardless of the rapidly growing numbers of ethnic groups in Korea.

Government policy on multicultural society and immigration

Foreign residents and immigration policy

Together with short-term foreign residents, the number of foreigners living in Korea reached 1.15 million in 2008, as shown in Table 6.1. They account for just over 2 per cent of the total population. This figure is projected to jump to 2.9 million by 2020, making up more than 5 per cent of the total population.

As Table 6.2 shows, the number of Chinese, including 267,000 Korean Chinese, is 442,000, comprising 44 per cent of the total number of foreign residents in Korea. Next are the Americans, numbering 118,000 and comprising 12 per cent, followed by the Vietnamese (65,000), Filipinos (53,000) and Thais (43,000).

Foreign residents can be classified roughly into five major groups, based on their purpose of migration, except for Group 1, as shown in Table 6.3. This first group comprises Chinese nationals of Korean descent and North Korean refugees. Most of the Korean Chinese are migrant workers or migrant brides. North Korean refugees who are granted citizenship are diverse in their occupations. The second group is made up of foreign nationals married to Koreans, who are mostly female and from Southeast Asia and China. The third group is composed of migrant workers from many countries – Nepal, India, Bangladesh, Pakistan, Vietnam, the Philippines, Russia and former Soviet satellite countries and are mostly less skilled and male. Then there is a fourth group comprising highly-skilled migrant residents from developed countries, such as the United States, Japan and those in Western Europe, among others. Finally, there is a group of college and graduate students from many countries.

Table 6.1 The number of foreign residents in South Korea

Year	1995	2001	2005	2008	2020*	2050*
Number	269,000	567,000	747,000	1,150,000	2,900,000	4,091,000
%**	0.6	1.2	1.6	2.1	5.1	9.2

Source: Korea Immigration Service, 2008.

Notes
* Projected.
** Of total population.

Table 6.2 Foreign residents in South Korea by country (2007)

Country	China	USA	Vietnam	The Philippines	Thailand	Others
Number	442,000	118,000	65,000	53,000	43,000	290,000
%*	44	12	6	5	4	29

Source: Ministry of Justice.

Note
* Of total number of foreign residents.

Table 6.3 Five groups of foreign residents in South Korea

(Approx. numbers)	Peoples	Main characteristics
Group 1 (270,000)	North Koreans and Korean Chinese	Welcomed and subject to assimilation policy; mostly less-skilled women and men; ethnic Korean minority problem
Group 2 (110,000)	Foreign spouses	Welcomed and subject to assimilation policy; mostly women from Southeast Asia and China; family dissolution problem
Group 3 (700,000)	Migrant workers	Needed, but expected to leave; mostly less-skilled men from Southeast and South Asia; illegal migrants problem
Group 4 (40,000)	Professionals and investors	Most welcomed and encouraged to stay; highly-skilled and mostly from developed countries
Group 5 (50,000)	Students	Welcomed college and graduate students from many countries

The Korean government accepts North Koreans as refugees, provides for them with various measures and supports them in settling down safely in South Korea. They are still Koreans even if they are from the communist country of North Korea, and are subjected to a complete assimilation policy. However, many Koreans have negative attitudes toward North Korean refugees. North Koreans and Korean Chinese are sometimes regarded as second-class Koreans or as ethnic Korean minorities. Migrant brides from Southeast Asia and China are also subjected to an assimilation policy since they are married to Korean men and many have the children of Korean nationals. About 110,000 foreign spouses receive much attention and support from the central and local governments, the media and civil society. But there is a family dissolution problem, as will be explained below.

Meanwhile, most of the migrant workers are from the developing countries of Southeast Asia, South Asia, Central Asia and China. Less-skilled migrant workers from Southeast and South Asia and China are, in fact, excluded people since they are ethnic minority guest workers, who are believed to leave Korea after completing their work contracts. But the problem is that a lot of guest workers are not willing to leave and are staying on in Korea as illegal immigrants. Multicultural policies and immigration measures in Korea are mostly directed at ethnic Koreans, migrant brides and highly-skilled foreigners. Most minorities, except migrant residents from developed countries, have been experiencing discrimination and prejudice, and a lack of adequate social rights and economic opportunities. Migrant residents from developed countries are mostly professionals and investors entering at the high end of the labour market and are considered a privileged group, with most of them having their own residential and cultural communities. Some 40,000 highly-skilled foreign residents out of the 1.15 million foreign residents are the most welcomed foreigners in Korea.

Many laws, measures and new changes in immigration administration have been introduced in the last several years that were unprecedented in the previous five decades in Korea, as shown in Table 6.4. Against the background of huge inflows of foreigners since the mid-1990s, the Ministry of Justice established the Committee on Immigration Administration and Research in September 2004 to develop agendas and mobilize experts' knowledge on immigration. The committee runs the Immigration Policy Forum to build consensus and share public opinions on immigration issues through hosting conferences and workshops. In 2005, a multiculturalism-orientated immigration policy was introduced for the first time. The rapid increase of international marriages has greatly contributed to the institutionalization of inclusion rhetoric in Korea's immigration policy.

The Industrial Trainees Programme, bringing about the first group-immigration of foreign labour, was started in 1993 to supplement the domestic labour force shortage in small and medium-sized manufacturing factories. The Employment Permit System, an advance immigration policy for foreign labour, was introduced in 2004 to supplement the existing Industrial Trainees Programme, and replaced it in January 2007 to secure major labour rights for all foreign workers, and to institutionalize foreign labour policy.[22] The Working Visit Policy was also introduced in 2007 for Korean-Chinese and Korean-Russians, including those from former members of the Soviet Union.

The Ministry of Justice enacted in July 2007 the Basic Laws on Treatment of Resident Foreigners, the nation's first law aimed at guaranteeing better treatment for foreigners in Korea. It also established the Korea Immigration Service (KIS) in May 2007 to deal effectively with social integration, immigration and naturalization affairs. The Korea Immigration Service implements systematic immigration policies and services that protect foreigners' human rights, attract qualified foreign workers and embrace overseas Koreans. Through these, KIS aims to enhance Korea's national competitiveness by making continuous efforts to ensure co-prosperity for and the coexistence of all.[23] The Korean government believes that opening the door more widely to immigrants is vital because they can bring significant social and economic benefits to Korea.

Table 6.4 Major developments in immigration policy in South Korea

Year	Major developments
1993	• Introduction of the Industrial Trainees Programme
1999	• Enactment of the Law on Immigration Control and Legal l Status for Overseas Koreans
2003	• Enactment of the Law on Foreign Workforce Employment
2004	• Implementation of the Employment Permit System (EPS)
2007	• Launch of the Korea Immigration Service
	• Enactment of Basic Laws on Treatment of Resident Foreigners
	• Introduction of the Working Visit Policy

It is noteworthy that permanent residency rules were eased in 2008. The Ministry of Justice relaxed permanent resident requirements for foreign investors, with revised enforcement ordinances of the Korea Immigration Law which took effect in August 2008, to help foreign nationals attain permanent resident status more easily in Korea.[24] Beneficiaries of the new rules also include Korean-Chinese people who are born in Korea and overseas Koreans with foreign nationalities who have been in Korea for at least two years, or who qualify for Korean nationality under the Korean Nationality Law.[25] According to the Ministry of Justice, measures will be taken to relax the rules further, including the granting of dual citizenship. Under the new rules, when people who meet naturalization requirements attain permanent residency, they will be allowed to invite their less immediate family to Korea. The Ministry of Justice says that receiving the same treatment as Korean nationals will enable overseas Koreans with foreign nationalities and Korean-Chinese people born in Korea to be better integrated into Korean society.[26]

The Korean government expects to see many effects as easier access to permanent residency is granted to foreign investors, as well as to overseas Koreans with well-paying jobs, including pension benefits. The government expects that foreign investment will be promoted, human capital flight prevented and therefore national competitiveness improved. As a result, for the last several years the Korean government has developed policies aimed at the expansion of immigration.[27]

However we can witness the discriminatory nature of the immigration policies, which tend to favour those who are highly educated and skilled, wealthy or ethnic Koreans. Historically, this kind of selectivity has been common in most nation states as these are inclined to select migrants according to either their origins or the host country's needs. However, a shift towards less discriminatory immigration policy needs to be developed as the majority of foreign residents in Korea are migrant workers and brides. But this kind of non-discriminatory immigration policy will provoke controversy since Korea's immigration policy has primarily focused on those who will stay permanently in Korea, thereby excluding migrant workers. More than 600,000 less-skilled migrant workers, including illegal workers, are not allowed to reside permanently in Korea. Encouraging all migrant workers to seek citizenship would be unrealistic, but a wholesale ban on their permanent residence goes against the trend in the era of globalization, as well as the characteristics of Korea's democratic polity.

Despite the Korean government's slogan of 'foreigner friendly', most of its policies appear to favour only selected groups of investors – highly-skilled professionals and ethnic Koreans to whom the government is granting dual citizenship or permanent residency.[28] Excessive favour towards those mostly from developed countries will bring about unintended consequences since it discriminates against migrant workers and brides from developing countries. This may reflect the Koreans' racist and biased perception of darker-skinned ethnic foreigners from developing countries. Moreover, even highly-skilled migrants are not shielded from this kind of discrimination.[29]

Multicultural and social integration policies

Most foreign residents in Korea are experiencing language problems, discrimination and lack of access to administrative services. As a greater number of foreigners come to live in Korea every year, the support measures have become an important step in the government's attempt to make Korea more open and welcoming to foreigners. The Korean government, as well as many NGOs, have paid a great deal of attention to the issue of social integration of foreign residents, especially foreign wives, as their numbers have surged in recent years.

But there are differences in the difficulties both among and within policy responses towards the groups of foreigners in Korea. The Korean government's multicultural policies have primarily focused on those who stay permanently in Korea, thereby excluding migrant workers. The policies are rather selective for different minorities, even though most of them are newly migrated people responding to the demands of globalization. Also, there is no differentiation between multicultural policies and integration policies. Multicultural policies are conceived primarily as a way of meeting a group's legitimate claims for cultural recognition and are deemed necessary to address the unequal treatment of minority cultural groups. There is a multicultural policy, in name, but the integration policy covers the multicultural one, in practice.

Various measures to promote social integration for foreign residents have reflected the Korean government's 'inclusion-orientated' immigration policy since 2003, when the new, rather progressive, government was in power. Programmes offering counselling services and Korean language lessons for immigrants are the most popular. Many ministries, such as the Ministry of Justice, the Ministry of Culture, the Ministry of Health, Welfare and Family Affairs, among others, are operating various programmes to address social integration, such as the Korean language and culture education programmes.[30] Also, the Ministry of Justice has been running a social integration programme for Koreans to understand people of different races and ethnicities since 2009 and the Ministry of Education has introduced education for a multicultural society in schools.

Policies for multicultural families

The number of immigrants from international marriages is rapidly increasing, and exceeded more than 140,000 people in 2007, when international marriages accounted for about 13 per cent of the total number of marriages, according to the Ministry of Public Administration and Security. Seven out of ten immigrants from international marriages resided in the nation's metropolitan areas and 88.4 per cent of them were women. In 2007, about 40 per cent of Korean men working in agriculture, forestry and fishery industries married foreign wives, mostly from Southeast Asian countries and China. Most migrant brides in rural areas have been socially excluded and have confronted many economic, cultural, educational and linguistic difficulties.[31] Against this background, in September 2008 a law was introduced to support multicultural families, which saw the transformation of 80 existing branches of Transnational Marriage and Family Support Centers nationwide into Multicultural Support Centers.[32] Multicultural Support Centers are required to maintain consultation centres and educational facilities, and its personnel are required to have professional skills. These centres are community-based service facilities, offering mainly cultural and linguistic programmes.

The naturalization process for foreign wives has been slow and they have to wait about four to five years on average to obtain Korean citizenship. They must live in Korea for at least two years, while most other foreign residents must reside for at least five years to be eligible to apply for citizenship. Foreign wives do not have proper civil rights since they are believed to be 'migrant' brides who may run away. The number of foreign spouses applying for citizenship in Korea jumped from 2,796 in 2002 to 13,908 in 2007, according to the Korea Immigration Services, but the numbers of foreign spouses granted citizenship were 2,126 in 2002, 7,075 in 2005 and 4,190 in 2007.

The Korean government's policies for multicultural families are mostly for foreign spouses from developing countries and orientated towards rather unilateral integration and assimilation. Most of the programmes assume that migrant minorities, as 'subjects to be educated', need help and are treated as passive recipients of services. Some NGOs are developing bilateral educational and cultural programmes such as teaching languages and cultures of migrant brides to their spouses and children.

The well-being of children from multicultural families has emerged as an urgent task to be addressed by the Korean government. Children, especially of Korean men with spouses from Southeast Asian countries, are said to be falling behind their classmates and experiencing isolation from or bullying by their peers. This is mainly the result of their mothers' unfamiliarity with the Korean culture and language, as well as their families' difficult economic situation. A worse situation is that more children from multicultural families are being left without mothers because of increasing numbers of failed marriages. The Korean government is pursuing significant efforts in educational support for children of multicultural families since these children could help build a multicultural society. These youths, who are the first to learn and master the language and habits of Korean society, will play a key role as cultural mediators in their families and communities in achieving integration. For this, they need resources to express their talents, forge an identity and realize their full potential. Therefore, the efforts of the Korean government, as well as civil society, to support children of multicultural families need to be focused on this.

Meanwhile, current law states that a foreign wife cannot bring her family to Korea unless her Korean husband approves. In the case of divorce or death of the husband, the women's children cannot become Korean citizens or receive welfare benefits, a law reflecting deep-rooted conservative values regarding the family. This is state-sponsored social exclusion and discrimination against the 'mixed-race' minorities. The current policies are not sufficient to deter social exclusion of ethnic minorities.

Policies on migrant workers and illegal migrant workers

Ansan is a city famous for various ethnic migrant workers in Korea. In the 1990s, the Korean government developed an industrial complex of small and medium-sized factories in Ansan, near to the Seoul metropolitan area which needed workers. But because of the shortage of domestic workers for '3D' jobs – meaning difficult, dangerous and dirty – the companies asked for the government's help to bring foreign workers in to work in these jobs as 'industrial trainees', the first type of migrant workers. This is the beginning of the history of migrant workers in Korea. Though they have been invited in to meet the country's needs to make up for its lack of manual workers, they have often been exploited and abused, and human rights conditions for them, though gradually improving, remain a challenge. They are predominantly less-skilled male workers recruited as guest workers from South and Southeast Asia to work in manufacturing and construction.

In recent years, many Koreans understand that Korean industries need migrant workers, and the arrangement mutually benefits Korea and the migrant workers. Nevertheless, many Koreans still do not accept them since the role of economic interests in political attitudes that Koreans hold in relation to immigrants is limited[33] and social integration policies are mostly centred on foreign spouses and ethnic Koreans. The government prevents them from staying long term in Korea, by limiting their stay to a maximum of three years. They are also prohibited from bringing with them their spouses and children. Basically, those who stay in Korea for five consecutive years are eligible to apply for citizenship, but migrant workers do not have this right. The Korean government plans to increase the maximum employment period from the current three years to five years to offer more job security and help local businesses grow. But, migrant workers will not be allowed to stay for five consecutive years and will be required to leave and re-enter after a maximum of three years. Korea cannot grant permanent residence for all migrant workers. But if the country continues to be negligent in integrating them into Korean society, the number of illegal workers will increase, and this will create some kind of xenophobia among the Koreans, lead to an increase in crime and result in ethnic isolation for the illegal workers. Migrant workers get jobs in Korea under the Employment Permit System. Many workers have left their workplaces for various reasons, including delays in salary payments and poor working conditions. Current law forbids foreign workers from switching jobs without employer agreement, thus forcing many foreign workers to remain in their jobs despite low pay and poor working conditions.

The illegal migrants issue is becoming a pressing one since illegal foreigners comprise about 20 per cent of the total number of foreign residents in Korea, compared with 10–15 per cent in most developed countries. Also, illegal migrant workers make up 40–50 per cent of all illegal foreigners in the country. Illegal migrant workers are believed to degrade the local labour market in certain industries by breaking the standard wage system, and are often associated in the public

mind with criminal activities. The Ministry of Justice periodically launches campaigns to eradicate the employment of illegal immigrants and plans to reduce
illegal immigrants to 10 per cent by 2013 by guiding or forcing them to leave
Korea.

The problem of undocumented children of illegal immigrants is another issue.
They are in need of immediate government assistance since they are jeopardized
by their marginal or excluded position for education and social services. Currently, any foreign child between the ages of seven and twelve, regardless of
their legal status, can register with a nearby elementary school. However admis-
sion to middle and high schools depends on each school's regulations. To avoid
urban ghettos of poor ethnic minorities, Korea needs to step up its integration
efforts, including social measures to enable these minorities to work and go to
school. NGOs, such as the Migrant Workers' House, the Borderless Village, as
well as Ansan city, are among those that actively protect the rights of migrant
workers and support them.

To reduce the number of illegal workers the government has to analyse the
need for migrant workers in the domestic labour market. It will not be good for
Korean manufacturing, and ultimately the Korean economy, if Korean companies do not increase their labour productivity to make them more competitive,
and if they earn their profits by hiring low-cost migrant workers. In order to
make the Korean economy more competitive, Korea requires a highly-skilled
labour force that includes foreign labour.

Nationalism and multicultural society in Korea

National identity with multiculturalism

The multiracial and multicultural phenomenon is quite a recent and unusual
experience for most Koreans who still believe Korea to be a homogeneous
country. In fact, historically, there were no national minorities or ethnic minorities in Korea. Also, foreign residents in Korea constitute an insignificant

Table 6.5 Illegal residents in Korea (unit: person)

Year	Total foreign residents	Illegal foreign residents	%*
1997	386,972	148,048	38
2000	491,324	205,205	42
2004	750,873	209,841	28
2005	747,467	204,254	27
2006	910,149	211,988	23
2007	1,066,291	223,464	21

Sources: Ministry of Justice, 2008.

Note
* Of total foreign residents.

proportion of its total population, just 2 per cent in 2008, and more than half of these foreign residents are voluntary migrant workers resident in Korea for economic reasons.

However, the population of immigrants, their second-generation children and North Korean refugees is growing very fast and pose multicultural challenges and problems. Conflicts associated with a multicultural society will arise in the near future and issues of multiculturalism will soon become predominant. Ethnic and cultural diversity will become an issue that will test democratic development in Korea. More fundamental principles and relevant institutions to deal with the issues and challenges of multiculturalism need to be discussed and introduced.

One of the principles associated with multiculturalism is national identity. Korean national identity is embodied in the display of a strong individual and group sense of belonging to Korean ethnicity, and of nationalism.[34] First of all, Korea has not been a country of immigration. Though the recent 'open door' policy promises more immigrants, the policy is mostly limited to ethnic Koreans and foreign investors. Contemporary Koreans are still known for upholding a strong sense of national identity, which is manifest in the search for 'ethnic national unity'.[35] The nationalist discourse shows that the Korean national identity has traditionally centred not around 'citizenship', that is, civic identity, but around 'race', that is, ethnic identity. As mentioned earlier, the 'belief in a racially distinct and ethnically homogeneous nation' is widely shared today on both sides of the Korean peninsula, that is, South Korea and North Korea.

Nevertheless, the South Korean national identity, which is currently challenged and contested unprecedentedly, is in the midst of a process of 'reformulation and transformation'. Korea's vision for a more competitive and multicultural country will be possible when foreign migrant workers, North Korean refugees and other racial minorities in Korea are treated as equal partners in a democratic polity. A more democratic and civic national identity could allow for diversity and equality among the people and for Korea to pursue multiculturalism for cultural diversity and social integration.

Many Koreans feel uneasy about the rush to embrace multiculturalism. They believe assimilationist policies would be realistic since there are not enough objective conditions for multiculturalism currently as migrant workers are believed to leave at the end of their contracts, and foreign spouses are expected to adapt to Korean culture. Nevertheless, many Koreans do not insist on exclusive monoculturalism. Believing that embracing a national identity is still necessary as long as it is still a world of nation states, they share the majority view of national culture and democratic patriotism. Nationalism and multiculturalism are not mutual enemies, and nationalism does not necessarily presuppose monoculturalism. Historically, multiculturalism in Western countries has not replaced their 'nationhood' or 'nation building', but only reformulated their 'nationhood', resulting in nationalism in a lively multicultural society. Many multicultural societies of advanced countries still emphasize nationalism and national culture, practise 'nation making' and maintain the sense of 'nationhood'.[36] Kymlicka puts forward an argument to theorize citizenship rights within the institutional context of the nation state.[37] He posits that minority rights are just as deserving of being viewed as 'rights' as many other social, civil and political rights to protect individuals against enduring threats.[38]

Given 'varieties of multiculturalism', 'multiple multiculturalisms' and 'many doors to multiculturalism', we can figure out society- and state-specific, but still shared, principles of multiculturalism. Specific models of multiculturalism cannot be transported directly from one country to another. Furthermore, most theories of multiculturalism deal with post-Second World War immigrants and ethnic or national minorities and, therefore, do not provide relevant explanations for the migrants resulting from globalization since the 1990s. In many Western European countries, most migrants from the 1990s are excluded from multicultural policies of equal rights and recognition. Lessons drawn from various Western countries' experiences with minority rights show that they have different goals, principles and institutions of multiculturalism, and are forming, reforming and transforming these goals, principles and institutions over time.

Multiculturalism for cultural diversity and social integration

There are not many countries that adopt multiculturalism as a policy principle. Only a few of the traditional immigration countries, such as Canada and Australia, are adopting active multiculturalism. Even New Zealand, with a multi-ethnic population, and the United States do not embrace multiculturalism as a policy principle.[39] As mentioned before, several Western European countries, which formerly adopted multicultural policies, have started to retreat from multiculturalism.[40] Recently, they argue that multiculturalism has failed and declared its demise amid rising anti-immigration feeling in Europe. The crisis of multiculturalism requires us to reconsider strategies for a multicultural society. Viewing monoculturalism and multiculturalism as mutually exclusive imperatives and thus forcing ourselves into the dilemma of having to choose either one or the other is not going to be a strategic option. Pursuing cultural diversity and social integration simultaneously could allow monoculturalism and multiculturalism to coexist.

Racially exclusive monoculturalism or national pride in being a single-race state is problematic since it ignores all who are not pure Korean, and denies any status to foreign residents. Korean values, being a form of nationalism, have been set against 'their values'. However, monoculturalism, as the majority national culture, is still strong and shared by most Koreans who are yet to endorse official multiculturalism. The policies on migration and multiculturalism provoke debates and controversies as many Koreans' perception of and attitude towards non-Koreans are not favourable. It was only recently that the government instituted proper measures that aim to improve the lives of foreigners and 'mixed-race' Koreans.

The tensions between monoculturalism and multiculturalism will best be resolved when the two are not taken to be binary opposites. The majority national culture can be conceived of as the framework within which minority cultures may be realized. In Korea, multiculturalism aims to promote mutual respect and understanding between the majority culture and minority cultures.[41] The Borderless Village, as a multicultural community, demonstrates how different nationalities can live together in one space, focusing on mutuality and cooperation as a way of life.[42]

From January 2009, the Ministry of Justice has run a Social Integration Program (SIP) that requires citizenship applicants, including foreign spouses, to take 200 hours of classes on Korean language and culture.[43] SIP is regarded as burdensome for working foreign wives and criticized as a typical assimilation policy by proponents of multiculturalism. This can be seen as an official social integration policy since many NGOs and local government agencies have already been implementing Korean language and culture education programmes. To realize a bilateral relationship between the majority culture and minority cultures, minorities should acquire resources, including an education, to attain social and economic recognition. Also, it is essential that ethnic minorities as actors must actively seek solutions to their problems. They can keep their identities and contribute to integration by helping migrant people or communities feel an integral part of Korea to avoid stereotypes of migrants, and to promote awareness of the diversity of cultures.

There are several characteristics to be noted in Korea's migration and multicultural policies. First, recently the Korean government has been developing policies for expanding migration and multiculturalism and giving more rights to multicultural families. School textbooks that describe Korea as a 'nation unified by one bloodline' are being changed to those that describe a 'multi-ethnic and multicultural Korean society'. Korea's multicultural policies can be perceived as rather progressive considering its very short history of immigration. Cultural diversity has become a central feature of Korean society, and is likely to become more so in the immediate future. Some nationalists are against making excessive changes in textbooks, warning that it is dangerous to deny Korea's singular race, which has been a source of pride for centuries. But most Koreans endorse cultural diversity as a significant element in an open and competitive Korean society.

Second, confusing, sometimes contradictory, perceptions of multiculturalism and multicultural society are evident. Many Koreans believe that a multicultural society is desirable, but they also insult migrant workers on the basis of their origins, and emphasize the superiority of Korean culture. This can be explained by Korea's economically-orientated multicultural policy. Migration is still approached mainly from an economic point of view – for its value to, and potential for, national competitiveness. However migration is not only an economic issue; it also has social, political and cultural implications. Migration is transforming society, the labour market and national culture. In this context, the issues of cultural diversity and social integration have become major challenges.

The rapid increase in the number of migrants may have negative effects, such as a rise in crime, discrimination, and human rights violations against them, which could produce serious social unrest – the dark side of a multicultural society. To limit the negative effects, multicultural polices have to be inclusive for ethnic minorities and be based on respect and redistribution even though many Koreans share unfavourable attitudes toward immigrants. Cultural diversity presents significant challenges to social integration, primarily because of the ways in which ethnic differences are linked to racial overtones and unequal economic and social outcomes.

In Korea, multiculturalism is understood as a way of meeting the legitimate equality claims of foreign residents rather than as a way to recognize any distinctive moral status of cultural groups. This kind of reframing of multiculturalism will not be problematic. Multiculturalism aims to avoid of coercion or violence and, therefore, a multicultural policy is necessary to address the unequal treatment of minority cultural groups and the 'culture-racism' to which so many are exposed. The object is to promote equality or eliminate coercion or violence.[44]

Fraser differentiates between the identity and status models of recognition, and recasts recognition struggles not as claims about collective identities but as seeking to establish the subordinated individuals as full partners in social life.[45] The key is to distance recognition politics from the exclusive call for group recognition. Recognition no longer requires any assertion about the validity of the group identity, for it is the individuals who are to be recognized as full partners, rather than the groups to which they belong. Some of the struggles for political voice may require a strong assertion of group agency, though not necessarily a strong assertion of group distinctiveness and worth. But, individuals can also mobilize recognition and redistribution for ethnic people.

Finally, the institutionalization of ethnic politics may not be impossible in Korea. Ethnic politics is involved in how issues of multiculturalism, such as redistribution, recognition and social integration, are discussed, disputed and compromised. As societies democratize and develop economically, ethnic politics will become common and many values of democracy will operate to support and sustain minority rights.[46] Therefore, the integration of foreign migrants will become one of the most pressing political issues in Korea. The solution for multiculturalism depends to a large extent on the national history, political institutions, cultures, values and principles of the host country. If Korea endorses multiculturalism to be politically correct, it may become a major political problem since there will be many groups of people who do not endorse multiculturalism.

Therefore, ethnic politics is seen as an enduring feature of a free and democratic society, and as a normal part of democratic politics, not a uniquely explosive or destabilizing issue. Many conflicts around multiculturalism will not be deep value conflicts, but political conflicts that could be solved through political practice. Particularly for the migrants in Korea, ethnic politics is more to do with political economy, and less to do with religions and values since they are voluntary migrants resulting from economic reasons. This is the reason monoculturalism and multiculturalism can be effectively reconciled and ethnic politics can be institutionalized in Korea. Minorities' demand for recognition of their identity and accommodation of their cultural difference is often regarded as the challenge of multiculturalism. In fact, in Korea, the politics of recognition has more to do with the status model than with the identity model, and the multicultural ideal is more to do with tolerating differences than with valuing diversity.

Conclusion

Recently, Korea is facing up to the multicultural challenges to its national identity and monoculturalism. For a long time, most Koreans have believed the Korean national identity to be belonging to a single-race and homogenous country. However, as global migration has become common, a greater number of non-Koreans come to live in Korea every year and the issues surrounding a multiracial and multicultural society have become a hot debate. Policies towards foreign residents are taking on increasing significance in Korea, even though most of the policies appear to favour a selected class of investors and professionals, as well as foreigners with Korean spouses.

Korean society still shows little regard for ethnic minorities' cultural identities and there is strong public unease about the society becoming increasingly heterogeneous. The government has pursued policies aimed at 'controlling and managing' foreign residents, and away from the initial purpose of cultivating a climate of promoting respect for cultural diversity. Many believe that embracing all foreigners wanting to reside and work in Korea would result in inordinate social costs, and that effective, but moderate control is necessary for social stability.

However, recently more Koreans are breaking away from these traditional sentiments and many intellectuals and NGOs are evolving ideas of multiculturalism, and developing strategies and policies to create a multicultural society and social integration. Also, the Korean government's measures are increasingly orientated towards a multicultural society and social integration. Its multicultural policy, based on inclusive democratic politics, could lead to a commitment to the sharing of power, that is, consociational politics in the near future. Also, a more flexible and accommodating position on the inflow of immigrants is likely to be achieved.

As a country with a strong ethnic national identity and a sense of having achieved a kind of sub-imperialist status, there is a growing national discourse on cultural diversity or a multicultural society in Korea. It seems that more Koreans are now embracing a civic form of national identity and such a shift from a national identity based on ethnicity toward one based on civic values will lead to the granting of equal legal rights and status to immigrants and the demanding of equal responsibilities from them in return, nudging Korea towards becoming a multicultural society. In the multicultural society of Korea, the Korean national culture – the values, beliefs and attitudes of the majority of Koreans – can coexist with other cultures. The Korean national culture, which frames multiculturalism in terms of status and redistribution, can be conceived as the framework within which minority cultures can be accommodated. This affects the nature of minority groups and the sort of relationship they desire with the larger society of Korea. Also this can resolve the tensions between monoculturalism and multiculturalism as well as multiculturalism and nationalism.

Notes

1 Lee Hye-Kyung, 'The Shift in Immigration Policy towards Expansion and Inclusion in S. Korea' (in Korean). *Korean Journal of Sociology* 42, no. 2 (2008): 104–137; Amarjit Kaur, 'Increasing Controls Stem the Tide of Migration across Southeast Asia'. *SangSaeng* 22 (Summer 2008).
2 Lee Sook-Jong, 'The Governance of Foreign Workers in Korea and Japan'. *Korea Observer* 38, no. 4 (Winter 2007): 611; In-Jin Yoon, 'The Development and Characteristics of Multiculturalism in S. Korea: With a Focus on the Relationship of the State and Civil Society' (in Korean). *Korean Journal of Sociology* 42, no. 2 (2008): 72–103.
3 Sasja Tempelman, 'Constructions of Cultural Identity: Multiculturalism and Exclusion'. *Political Studies* 47, no. 1 (1999): 17–31; Kim Namguk, 'Deliberate Multiculturalism: Cultural Rights and Cultural Survival' (in Korean). *Korean Journal of Political Science* 39, no. 1 (2005): 87–108.
4 Charles Taylor, *Multiculturalism: Examining the Politics of Recognition* (Princeton, NJ: Princeton University Press, 1994); Brian Barry, *Culture and Equality: An Egalitarian Critique of Multiculturalism* (Cambridge, MA: Harvard University Press, 2001).
5 Susan Moller Okin, *Is Multiculturalism Bad for Women?* (Princeton, NJ: Princeton University Press, 1999).
6 J. Cohen, 'Introduction: Feminism, Multiculturalism and Human Equality', in *Is Multiculturalism Bad for Women?*, edited by S. Moller Okin (New Jersey: Princeton University Press, 1999).
7 Bhikhu Parekh, *Rethinking Multiculturalism: Cultural Diversity and Political Theory* (Cambridge, MA: Harvard University Press, 2000).
8 Will Kymlicka, *Multicultural Citizenship* (Oxford: Oxford University Press, 1996).
9 Christian Joppke, 'Beyond National Models: Civic Integration Policies for Immigrants in Western Europe'. *West European Politics* 30, no. 1 (2007): 1–22.
10 Ian Buruma, *Murder in Amsterdam: Liberal Europe, Islam, and the Limits of Tolerance* (New York: Penguin, 2007).
11 Paul M. Sniderman and Louk Hagendoorn, *When Ways of Life Collide: Multiculturalism and Its Discontents in the Netherlands* (Princeton,NJ: Princeton University Press, 2007); Paul Kelly, ed. *Multiculturalism Reconsidered: 'Culture and Equality' and Its Critics* (Cambridge: Polity Press, 2002); Barbara Saunders and David Haljan, eds., *Whither Multiculturalism? A Politics of Dissensus* (Leuven, Belgium: Leuven University Press, 2003).
12 Nancy Fraser, 'Rethinking Recognition: Overcoming Displacement and Reification in Cultural Politics', in Barbara Hobson, ed. *Recognition Struggles and Social Movements: Contested Identities, Agency and Power* (Cambridge: Cambridge University Press, 2003).
13 Anne Phillips, 'Recognition and the Struggle for Political Voice', in Barbara Hobson, ed. *Recognition Struggles and Social Movements: Contested Identities, Agency and Power* (Cambridge: Cambridge University Press, 2003).
14 Ibid.; Nancy Fraser, 'Rethinking Recognition'.
15 Asia Barometer 2003 Survey.
16 Eom Han-Jin, 'Multicultural Immigration Debate in S. Korea', in *Change and Integration of Korea Society in Northeast Asian Multicultural Era* (Seoul: Korean Sociological Association, 2006); Dong-Hoon Seol and John D. Skrentny, 'S. Korea: Importing Undocumented Workers', in Wayne Cornelius, Philip Martin and James Hollifield, eds. *Controlling Immigration: A Global Perspective* (Stanford, CA: Stanford University Press, 2004), pp. 481–513.
17 Discriminatory practices against minorities have not been uncommon in modern Korea. Many Koreans have experienced discriminatory practices based on gender, region, political belief and social and economic status.

18 In 2007, the UN Committee on the Elimination of Racial Discrimination pointed out the Koreans' exclusive and racist practices, and recommended that the Korean government introduce non-discriminatory and multicultural policies for the ethnic people in Korea.

19 Seung-Jin Jang, 'Multiculturalism among Koreans: Role of Economic Self-interests and National Identities'. *Korean Political Science Review* 44, no. 3 (2010): 98–119.

20 In South Korea, nationalism can be found in conservative as well as radical groups since the two Koreas of South and North each built their own nationalist nation states in 1948: the Republic of Korea and the People's Democratic Republic of Korea, respectively. Many radical groups in South Korea do not show their opposition to nationalist North Korea.

21 Birte Siim, 'Multicultural Challenges: New [Gender] Equality Dilemmas: A Nordic Perspective', paper presented at the international conference organized by the FEMM-network, Oslo University, 10–11 January 2008.

22 The Industrial Trainees Programme, the first official government policy for foreign workers introduced in 1993, stipulated a quota of 10,000 foreign trainees recommended from the Ministry of Trade and Industry. The quota of trainees increased to 79,000 in 1997.

23 www.immigration.go.kr/HP/IMM80/index.do.

24 A foreigner who made an investment of at least $500,000 and employed at least five locals immediately became a permanent resident, regardless of his or her residence period. The Ministry says that relaxed permanent residency requirements for foreign investors are expected to boost foreign investment, job creation and economic vitality. The current regulation grants permanent residency to a foreign investor who makes an investment of at least $2 million and employs at least five Koreans; see www.immigration.go.kr/HP/IMM80/index.do.

25 An F-4 visa holder who has stayed in Korea for at least two years becomes a permanent resident, if the person has an income at least twice as much as the per capita GNI; is at least 60 years of age and receives a pension equal to the per capita GNI or more; or pays a property tax of at least W500,000. A Korean-Chinese who was born in Korea and has returned to the country after permanent departure is granted permanent residency to help their settlement back in Korea; see www.immigration.go.kr/HP/IMM80/index.do.

26 The legal status of ethnic Koreans will be significantly improved. People qualified for simplified naturalization or nationality reinstatement will be able to choose between Korean nationality and permanent resident status. In addition, even if the ethnic Koreans choose to be permanent residents, they will enjoy the same treatment as Korean nationals, in terms of being able to invite their families to Korea; see www.immigration.go.kr/HP/IMM80/index.do.

27 Lee Hye-Kyung, 'The Shift in Immigration Policy towards Expansion and Inclusion in S. Korea'.

28 The Korea Immigration Service's motto of 'policy-guided opening' means that order should be ensured as the nation deals with an influx of immigrants.

29 The Korean government policy states that universities, schools and private institutes may recruit English-language teachers only from specific 'native' English-speaking countries, that is, the United States, Britain, Canada, Ireland, Australia, New Zealand and South Africa.

30 Despite such efforts, without enough coordination, ministries appear to be competitively trying to create similar programmes, causing many of them to overlap.

31 Kim Soon-yang and Shin Yeong-gyun, 'Immigrant Brides in the Korean Rural Farming Sector: Social Exclusion and Policy Responses'. *Korea Observer* 39, no. 1 (2008): 1–36.

32 Foreign residents are able to obtain more information about life in Korea in as many as five different languages. More training programmes, including home visits and

online services, are developing to help foreign residents better adjust to their new life in Korea. See Chun-Ung Park, '"Borderless Village" for Multicultural Education'. *SangSaeng* 22 (2008).

33 Seung-Jin Jang, 'Multiculturalism among Koreans: Role of Economic Self-interests and National Identities'.

34 Nationalism is a contested concept since there is more than one concept of nationalism in contemporary South Korea. Leftist nationalism of national liberation and rightist nationalism are the most popular concepts so far.

35 Shin Gi-Wook, *Ethnic Nationalism in Korea: Geneology, Politics and Legacy* (Stanford, CA: Stanford University Press, 2005).

36 With regard to the debate on easier immigrant access to Korean nationality, in Europe, the principle of nationality based on family descent is the common form, just like in Korea.

37 Political theories of citizenship rights are theories about the sorts of rights that are appropriate in the context of Westphalian nation states.

38 Will Kymlicka, 'Multiculturalism and Minority Rights: West and East'. *Journal on Ethnopolitics and Minority Issues in Europe* 4 (2002): 1–25.

39 In New Zealand, biculturalism, recognizing the indigenous status of the Maori, has been institutionally established and this causes tension between biculturalism and multiculturalism as suitable policy frameworks.

40 Ruth Lister *et al.*, *Gendering Citizenship in Western Europe: New Challenges for Citizenship Research in a Cross-national Context* (Bristol: Policy Press, 2007). Denmark is the most restrictive of the Nordic countries in relation to migration. In terms of access to citizenship, Denmark has moved from being one of the most liberal to one of the most restrictive models for naturalization in Europe and today the Danish demand for access is nine years compared with five years in Sweden, the Netherlands and the UK. The Danish government also adopted a social benefit programme in order to integrate migrants into the labour market, but it creates poverty and is a break with universalism. The country operates several illiberal anti-immigration measures, such as restriction of the right to family unification with a spouse from abroad.

41 One of the most famous efforts is the local multiculturalism movement in Ansan, the city of migrant workers, begun by a group consisting of professors, artists, human rights activists and migrant families. The informal discussions on Korean society, immigrants and multiculturalism later became forums that eventually led to the establishment in 2006 of the Borderless Village. See Jun-Hyuk Guak, 'Multicultural Coexistence and Social Integration' (in Korean). *Journal of Korean Political Science* 15, no. 2 (2007): 23–41.

42 The movement aims to prevent discrimination against minority groups, foster positive relationships among cultural groups, change the values of Koreans regarding foreigners and migrants, and establish a multicultural community. At present, the Borderless Village has ten branches throughout the Ansan region. They hold multicultural festivals such as 'Flying Asia' and 'Migrants' Arirang'.

43 The programme is expected to reduce significantly the waiting time for naturalization, as those who complete the programme will not be required to take the naturalization exam. Less than 50 per cent of applicants pass the naturalization test. Foreign wives who have lived in Korea less than two years will also be required to take classes.

44 Jacob Levy, *The Multiculturalism of Fear* (Oxford: Oxford University Press, 2000); Anne Phillips, 'Recognition and the Struggle for Political Voice'.

45 Nancy Fraser, 'Rethinking Recognition'.

46 Choi Jong-Ryol, 'Theoretical Issues of Multiculturalism' (in Korean), paper presented at the conference on 'Prospect and Policy Response toward a Multicultural Society',

organized by the Korean Women's Development Institute, 2 October 2008; Jun-Hyuk Guak. 'Multicultural Co-existence and Social Integration' (in Korean). *Journal of Korean Political Science* 15 no. 2(2007): 23–41.

References

Barry, Brian. *Culture and Equality: An Egalitarian Critique of Multiculturalism* (Cambridge, MA: Harvard University Press, 2001).

Buruma, Ian. *Murder in Amsterdam: Liberal Europe, Islam, and the Limits of Tolerance* (New York: Penguin, 2007).

Choi, Jong-Ryol. 'Theoretical Issues of Multiculturalism' (in Korean), paper presented at the conference on 'Prospect and Policy Response toward a Multicultural Society', organized by the Korean Women's Development Institute, 2 October 2008.

Cohen, J. 'Introduction: Feminism, Multiculturalism and Human Equality', in S. Moller Okin, *Is Multiculturalism Bad for Women?* (Princeton, NJ: Princeton University Press, 1999).

Eom, Han-Jin. 'Multicultural Immigration Debate in S. Korea', in *Change and Integration of Korea Society in Northeast Asian Multicultural Era* (Seoul: Korean Sociological Association, 2006).

Fraser, Nancy. 'Rethinking Recognition: Overcoming Displacement and Reification in Cultural Politics', in Barbara Hobson, ed. *Recognition Struggles and Social Movements: Contested Identities, Agency and Power* (Cambridge: Cambridge University Press, 2003).

Hobson, Barbara, ed. *Recognition Struggles and Social Movements: Contested Identities, Agency and Power* (Cambridge: Cambridge University Press, 2003).

Jang, Seung-Jin. 'Multiculturalism among Koreans: Role of Economic Self-interests and National Identities' (in Korean). *Korean Political Science Review* 44, no. 3 (2010): 98–119.

Joppke, Christian. 'Beyond National Models: Civic Integration Policies for Immigrants in Western Europe'. *West European Politics* 30, no. 1 (2007): 1–22.

Kaur, Amarjit.'Increasing Controls Stem the Tide of Migration across Southeast Asia'. *SangSaeng* 22 (Summer 2008).

Kelly, Paul, ed. *Multiculturalism Reconsidered: 'Culture and Equality' and Its Critics* (Cambridge: Polity Press, 2002).

Kim, Namguk. 'Deliberate Multiculturalism: Cultural Rights and Cultural Survival' (in Korean). *Korean Journal of Political Science* 39, no. 1 (2005): 87–108.

Kim, Soon-yang and Yeong-gyun Shin. 'Immigrant Brides in the Korean Rural Farming Sector: Social Exclusion and Policy Responses'. *Korea Observer* 39, no. 1 (2008): 1–36.

Kymlicka, Will. *Multicultural Citizenship* (Oxford: Oxford University Press, 1996).

Kymlicka, Will. Multiculturalism and Minority Rights: West and East'. *Journal on Ethnopolitics and Minority Issues in Europe* 4 (2002): 1–25.

Lee, Hye-Kyung. 'The Shift in Immigration Policy towards Expansion and Inclusion in S. Korea' (in Korean). *Korean Journal of Sociology* 42, no. 2 (2008): 104–137.

Lee, Sook-Jong. 'The Governance of Foreign Workers in Korea and Japan'. *Korea Observer* 38, no. 4 (2007): 609–632 (Seoul: Institute of Korean Studies).

Levy, Jacob. *The Multiculturalism of Fear* (Oxford: Oxford University Press, 2000).

Lister, Ruth *et al. Gendering Citizenship in Western Europe: New Challenges for Citizenship Research in a Cross-national Context* (Bristol: Policy Press, 2007).

Okin, Susan Moller. *Is Multiculturalism Bad for Women?* (Princeton, NJ: Princeton University Press, 1999).

Parekh, Bhikhu. *Rethinking Multiculturalism: Cultural Diversity and Political Theory* (Cambridge, MA: Harvard University Press, 2000).

Park, Chun-Ung. '"Borderless Village" for Multicultural Education'. *SangSaeng* 22 (2008).Phillips, Anne. 'Recognition and the Struggle for Political Voice', in Barbara Hobson, eds. *Recognition Struggles and Social Movements: Contested Identities, Agency and Power* (Cambridge: Cambridge University Press, 2003).

Saunders, Barbara and David Haljan, eds. *Whither Multiculturalism? A Politics of Dissensus* (Leuven, Belgium: Leuven University Press, 2003).

Seol, Dong-Hoon and John D. Skrentny. 'S. Korea: Importing Undocumented Workers', in Wayne Cornelius, Philip Martin and James Hollifield, eds. *Controlling Immigration: A Global Perspective* (Stanford, CA: Stanford University Press, 2004), pp. 481–513.

Shin, Gi-Wook. *Ethnic Nationalism in Korea: Geneology, Politics and Legacy* (Stanford, CA: Stanford University Press, 2005).

Siim, Birte.'Multicultural Challenges: New [Gender] Equality Dilemmas: A Nordic Perspective', paper presented at the international conference organized by the FEMM-network, Oslo University, 10–11 January 2008.

Sniderman, Paul M. and Louk Hagendoorn. *When Ways of Life Collide: Multiculturalism and Its Discontents in the Netherlands* (Princeton, NJ: Princeton University Press, 2007).

Taylor, Charles. *Multiculturalism: Examining the Politics of Recognition* (Princeton, NJ: Princeton University Press, 1994).

Tempelman, Sasja. 'Constructions of Cultural Identity: Multiculturalism and Exclusion'. *Political Studies* 47, no. 1 (1999): 17–31.

Yoon, In-Jin. 'The Development and Characteristics of Multiculturalism in S. Korea: With a Focus on the Relationship of the State and Civil Society' (in Korean). *Korean Journal of Sociology* 42, no. 2 (2008): 72–103.

Part III

Resisting dominant narratives

7 Managing conflict in Canberra

Race relations, national identity and narrating differences

Catriona Elder

Introduction

This chapter explores the question of indigeneity and the Australian national identity. It considers the ways in which aspects of the history of Indigenous/non-Indigenous relations appear in the story of the nation that is told via the memorials and monuments of the national capital, Canberra. The basic premise of the argument is that, as a settler colonial nation, Australia subordinated the recognition of the rights of its Indigenous peoples (in particular, land rights) to a powerful story of the pioneering efforts of non-Indigenous peoples, a story that naturalized non-Indigenous claims to land and belonging. In the national capital the long-standing and popular narrative of non-Indigenous valour (martial, political, cultural and economic) is the one that is most frequently drawn on to give meaning to the spaces that commemorate or mark out Australian achievement. Yet in the space of Canberra other narratives appear. This chapter seeks to understand how stories that run counter to the dominant narrative of courageous pioneer endeavour – stories of the struggle for Indigenous rights, the history of violence towards Indigenous peoples and a recognition of Indigenous cultures – appear in this space. It considers who tells these stories, who listens, but also how these stories are managed when they threaten to disrupt the mainstream narrative.

National narratives

The Australian national capital is understood by those who manage it as a site that plays a central role in producing a story about Australian national identity. Canberra is a bustling city with commercial and suburban areas, but only a select area – known as the Parliamentary Zone – is understood as having significant symbolic value for the nation (see Figure 7.1). Within the triangle of this zone lie the Parliament House (at the triangle's apex), the High Court, Old Parliament House, the National Library, the National Gallery, Commonwealth Place, Reconciliation Place, the Gallery of Flags, Captain Cook Memorial Jet, and the Carillon. Across the lake and in a direct line with the Parliament House are Anzac Avenue and the Australian War Memorial lying at the foot of Mount

Ainslie. The Parliamentary Zone is presented as reflecting and producing a sense of national identity. Indeed, Australians are encouraged to visit this part of the city and engage with their national history. The memorials, museums, galleries, statues, thoroughfares and pathways that make up this central space are the places where Australian values are seen to be given substance.

Overall the narrative produced in the Parliamentary Zone is a quite traditional story of settler colonial achievement. It focuses on the economic, political and martial achievements of the nation. Australia is framed in terms of its imperial history (as a colony of Britain) with the goal of independence and the emergence of a unique national culture emphasized. So if the memorials and buildings in the zone are considered as a cluster, it becomes clear that they produce a story, or rather reproduce the traditional, national narrative of an Australian identity emerging from military endeavour (understood as both the support of an empire and the blooding of a new nation) and of the emergence of an egalitarian political system of democracy (the parliamentary system, the legal system).

Nations seek to produce coherent and singular narratives of identity, although, as many scholars have convincingly argued, national identities are inherently unstable and multiple. Indeed the dominance of any singular story of national

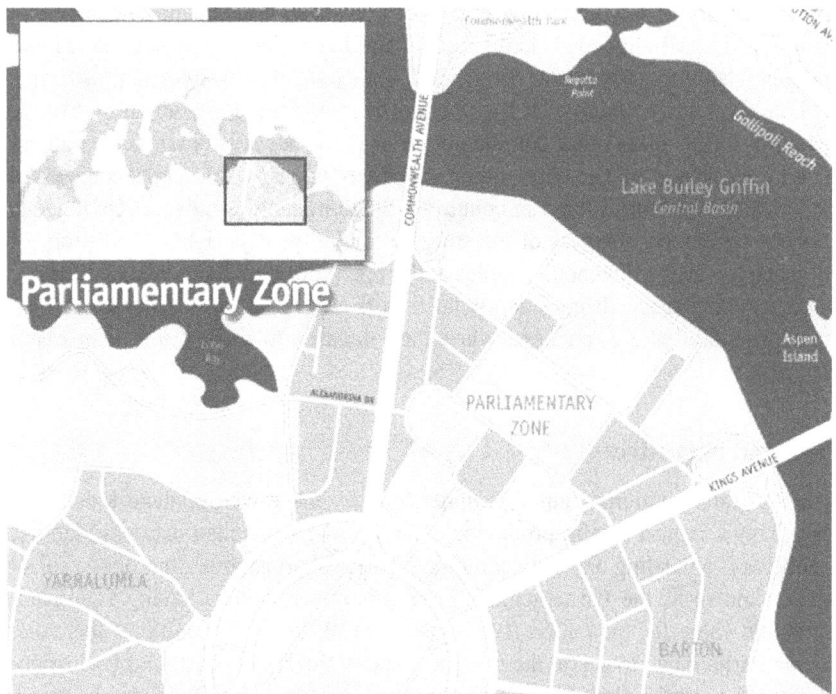

Figure 7.1 The Parliamentary Zone in the heart of Canberra is promoted as the ceremonial and tourist centre of the capital (source: image supplied courtesy of the National Capital Authority. © Commonwealth Copyright).

identity requires constant work – centralizing one story above all other available and contesting stories. In Australia one of the key conceits of this singular story of Australian national identity is based on the relationship of the non-Indigenous colonizers to the land. In the traditional story of belonging, non-Indigenous Australians arrived in Australia, peacefully settled an untouched land and shaped it into a nation, making it their own. Violence, where it was part of the Australian national story, took place overseas (in particular, in the First and Second World Wars) and worked to strengthen the nation through the valour of Australian men in the defence of their country. Within the country the story that unfolds is not one of violence, but rather of the courage of non-Indigenous people in facing a harsh land and 'taming' it. It centralizes the characteristics of mateship and egalitarianism as key to these achievements. This story has been powerfully challenged in the past 20 years and, as a result, a more nuanced story of national belonging has emerged. In this newer narrative there is a fuller recognition of the impact of the arrival of non-Indigenous colonizers on Indigenous peoples. Violence moves from something that takes place outside the nation to something internal. Furthermore, the reach of the egalitarian spirit was shown to stop short of Indigenous peoples, non-British residents, women and non-heterosexual citizens.

This chapter uses the Parliamentary Zone in Canberra as a way of analysing the ongoing tensions that exist between the various stories about the nature of being Australian that continue to circulate in the twenty-first century, focusing in particular on race relations. It considers the traditional dominant narrative, the updated version, with its more sophisticated recognition of prior and ongoing Indigenous occupation of the land, as well as other counter-narratives that continue to emerge to challenge both the standard narrative and the more liberal story. These counter-narratives suggest that the increasing recognition of Indigenous cultures never goes far enough. Indeed, the suggestion is that it works to obscure a history of violence in the colonial process, and also refuses to consider the radically alternative story of Indigenous sovereignty. The space of the Parliamentary Zone has been chosen because, as suggested above, it is understood as explicitly national – one is supposed to 'see' the nation there. But as it is a large and diverse place, it is also unlikely, even with high levels of management, that the story told within the avenues, parks, memorials and spaces of the zone will be completely under anyone's control. Indeed, the public nature of the zone invites people into it and gives them freedom to interpret or respond to the various sites in diverse ways. So it is a place where the different narratives literally clash. Indeed, this chapter focuses on the most unruly site in the otherwise highly regulated zone – the site of many clashes over 40 or so years – the Aboriginal Tent Embassy. This unauthorized memorial site in the Parliamentary Zone is explored in relation to another site – the authorized Reconciliation Place. I take these two sites – both places that seek to make visible the history of Indigenous/non-Indigenous relations – and explore the tensions between them in terms of narratives of national belonging.

Selling Canberra

Those who manage and 'sell' Canberra to overseas visitors and Australian citizens draw on much of the contents of the Parliamentary Zone to promote the city. For the bureaucrats who promote Canberra as a tourist site, their story of Canberra is that it embodies Australian-ness. The website for the National Capital Authority (NCA) – the group that oversees the development of Canberra – says of the capital:

> In the lead up to Federation [1901] and in the decades which followed the Australian people have sought to build a National Capital of which they are proud: a beautiful city a capital which represents our unity as a people; and stands proudly in the ranks of national capitals throughout the world.[1]

The blurb goes on to suggest that, 'the vision of the National Capital Authority is for a national capital which "symbolized Australia's heritage, values and aspirations [and which] is internationally recognised, and of which Australians are proud"'.[2]

In this story Canberra is a place where Australia is produced and exhibited. For example, in its *Guidelines for Commemorative Works*, the NCA states that commemorative works in Canberra should 'closely reflect the values of the Australian community'.[3] The core values that are to be reflected are listed. First and foremost comes 'egalitarianism', followed by 'freedom, civility, humour, democratic principles, civic awareness, peace, order and respect of the rule of law, mateship, diversity and tolerance'.[4] The logic here seems to be that Australian citizens viewing the monuments and sites in the Parliamentary Zone will see their own values reflected back to them.

Similarly, the Canberra Tourist Authority is quite explicit in linking the idea of visiting Canberra with ideas of being Australian. Spruiking their 2004 advertising campaign for the city, they wrote:

> The *See yourself in Canberra* brand campaign is a long-term project designed to change perceptions of Canberra by communicating that it is the only city that represents and can reflect what it is to be Australian. Canberra represents Australia's history, culture, democracy and identity. The campaign embodies these elements and carries the theme that no matter who we are or where we came from, the only place to see our true reflection as Australians is in the nation's capital.[5]

One broadcast media advertisement from this campaign finishes with the words: 'Come see your nation reflected in its capital.' It needs to be said that in this elaborate campaign the nation shown was one that was shaped by experiences of (formal) politics, war and sport.

This promotion of Canberra fits neatly with what I have called the traditional – and still dominant – narrative of the Australian identity. It draws on the notion that mateship and egalitarianism work as the foundation of Australian national character. Though, as suggested earlier, this idea has been critiqued time and time again, its currency continues. In the 1970s feminist scholars and activists mobilized powerful arguments demonstrating the absence of women from the world of mates and the inequality associated with gender relations (unequal wages, limited access to public places, the easy acceptance of violence towards women). Similar arguments demonstrating the limits of mateship and the egalitarian spirit were mounted in relation to ethnicity, race and sexuality.[6] The traditional narrative, though expanded to include citizens previously excluded, has also been curiously resistant to change as well. This chapter traces the limits of these changes and the modes of resistance in dominant national narratives in relation to Indigenous peoples' claims for equal treatment, but also in relation to sovereignty–land rights.

Planning Canberra

Canberra is a planned city and the Parliamentary Zone is the most monitored part of this planning. It is in the zone in particular that 'government planners, symbolic analysts, and local residents with economic and emotional stakes in the place' – the key managers of national remembering and forgetting – do their work.[7] One of the ways in which Canberra as a national capital is managed is in terms of landscape and vistas. One of the most majestic views of Canberra is from Mount Ainslie to the New Parliament and vice versa. From both places the viewer is on a hill or rise and sees the long avenue of Anzac Parade with either the Parliament House or the Australian War Memorial at the end of the view. War and politics sit at each end of this axis. As I suggested, in the 2004 advertising campaign, these two visions – war and politics – dominate the story of Canberra. These stories, represented by the Australian War Memorial at one end of Anzac Parade and the Parliament at the other, fit into a very powerful story of Australia as forged through a combination of democracy and individual (military) courage. They are the institutional faces of the idea of mateship and egalitarianism as national traits. Mateship in war and equality through government are powerful national narratives. The rhetoric of the role of Canberra is that the ceremonial parts of the capital represent a microcosm of the nation. These sites reflect back to the people a formal version of the national vision they have of themselves. So, for example, though most Australians have not experienced the intense mateship forged in war, they enact a watered down or everyday version of mateship in their lives.

As is the case with many nation states over the last few decades, Australian government policy has come to understand the limited nature of the dominant historical national stories and has moved to recognize cultural differences. As a result, more voices have been given a place in the nation and hence the national capital. So, with the changing national landscape, the capital needs to hold a wider variety of stories and, over the last ten to 15 years, it has. For example, the avenue that runs from the War Memorial now boasts a memorial to Australian service people who participated in the Vietnam War, and a memorial to the contribution of nurses in war. This has led to more of the stories in the Parliamentary Zone narrating conflicting stories.

Any understanding of a unified nation is always only (though not simply) imagined and is of course open to contestation. Some accommodation is made for this contestation or conflict within the imagined 'unity' of the nation. The rhetoric underpinning the role of Canberra as national capital makes room for various understandings of change and diversity. For example, the NCA in another document states: 'a good capital ... should also be a city which mirrors the nation's aspirations and conflicts' and that 'accommodate[s] generational difference'.[8] Whereas the NCA *Guidelines* recognizes that a number of sites in the capital 'are inconsistent with previous or current policies', it goes on to say that it 'accepts the presence of these "inconsistencies" as part of the unique cultural tapestry of the National Capital'.[9] After all, diversity is one of the 'values' identified as a core part of this imagined nation. I argue, however, that diversity is often accommodated in the dominant 'unified' story of the nation on the condition that it works *within* specifically prescribed limits. Diversity is easier to accept around some stories than others. Some stories still disturb the supposedly diverse national story. These stories – what could be called the counterpublic, the repressed stories – exist in tension with the dominant national story.[10]

Traditionally, given that Canberra is the formal political centre for the vision of Australian nationalism, these counterpublics were often hidden as best they could be, or removed as quickly as possible. Besides, considering the place of Canberra as the site of the coming into being of Australia as a nation, it is not surprising that one of the central points of tension is between Indigenous claims to sovereignty and the non-Indigenous counterclaim to sovereignty of the colonies that federated to create a nation. In Canberra there are two key sites that commemorate or recognize the history of colonialism in Australia. One is Reconciliation Place; the other is the Aboriginal Tent Embassy: both sit on the south side of the lake at the other end of the land axis from the War Memorial.

Remembering the colonial past

Australia is a settler colonial nation state and has a past that was at times violent since the colonizing British dispossessed the Indigenous peoples whose land they had invaded in 1788. For many years – until late in the twentieth century – this past was not very visible in the history told about Australia. It was also not recognized in the commemorative practices of the nation. History told a story of *terra nullius*. British colonization in Australia was organized around a process of Indigenous dispossession. In the 50 or so years after the British arrived in Australia in 1788, various agents of the Crown pronounced that more and more land, and finally the whole continent, was the property of the British sovereign. In the last 20 years the term *terra nullius* – land belonging to no one – has been used to describe the legal logic for this process of possession. The justification for wholesale Indigenous dispossession was the notion that Indigenous peoples were not using the land in any productive way and so the colonizers were justified in taking it themselves and putting it to 'better' use.

Twinning the process of land taking was the issue of what to 'do' about the Indigenous people of Australia. Over time, different discourses dominated – discourses of eradication, separation and self-determination – but one of the most powerful narratives was that of assimilation. In this narrative Indigenous peoples were to be 'absorbed' into non-Indigenous society over time until there was nothing remaining of their cultures except exotic artefacts and stories. The key practice for assimilation was the removal of Indigenous children from their families – especially Indigenous children who had any non-Indigenous heritage. From the late nineteenth century until the early 1970s, thousands of Indigenous children were removed from their families and raised in government or church institutions. Others were fostered to non-Indigenous families or sent to work as cheap labour for non-Indigenous families.[11]

Since 1988, the bicentenary of British colonization, in response to more vocal criticisms from Indigenous peoples and their non-Indigenous supporters (including scholars), there has been a move to recognize both Indigenous contribution to the nation, and also the history of colonization and its impact on Indigenous peoples. One of the key steps in this process was the marking of the years 1992–2001 as a decade of reconciliation in Australia. In the mid-1990s the validity and costs of the practices of dispossession and child removal were challenged by Indigenous peoples in the courts and became key points of discussion on the past and future of Australia. The process of dispossession entered the national consciousness in 1992 when the High Court of Australia recognized that the presumptions underpinning the wholesale transfer of Indigenous land to the Crown could in some cases be legally problematic. Responding to a case brought by Eddie Mabo (and known colloquially as the Mabo case), it found that the Meriam people of the island of Mer in the Torres Strait still had a native title claim to their land. A shorthand understanding of the legal finding was that the doctrine of *terra nullius* had been overturned. This finding set off both hysterical and thoughtful discussions on non-Indigenous and Indigenous peoples' claims to land ownership and to feelings of belonging.[12]

In the same decade a government report on the process and impact of the policy of Indigenous child removal was presented to the federal government. *Bringing Them Home*, the report of the inquiry into the removal of aboriginal and Torres Strait islander people from their families, enumerated the emotional costs borne by Indigenous peoples as a result of this policy of family break-up.[13] The report recommended that the government apologize to the 'Stolen Generations' and compensate them for their suffering. Again the impact of the report on non-Indigenous peoples was profound and mixed. Some wanted, as with the Mabo decision, to ignore the ramifications, claim these were issues of a past that no longer applied and get on with life without change. Others recognized the far-reaching implications of the decision and report and saw them as mechanisms to rethink the way in which the Australian nation responded to the Indigenous peoples' past, present and future.

In the late 1990s a 'history war' broke out, exemplifying these different positions and tensions of the decade. One side in the 'war' had provided a revision of Australian history that included recognition of the violence done to Indigenous people as a result of colonization.[14] This approach was challenged by counterclaims that this recognition had gone too far, was not based on sound historical evidence and painted far too negative a picture of colonizers.[15] This side made clear the resentment of many non-Indigenous Australians towards the 'black armband history' they saw as negating the worth of their forbears' lives. The tensions of the 1990s history war exemplify the ongoing tensions between national narratives – on the one hand, a resentment of what was understood as the denigration of the traditional story of non-Indigenous courage and goodness in settling Australia clashed with a new story that was underpinned by a desire on the part of many non-Indigenous people to rethink the impact of this traditional story. On the other hand, both these stories vie with the contrapuntal stories that Indigenous peoples themselves tell in response to the various non-Indigenous narratives.

The Aboriginal Tent Embassy

The first powerful narrative about colonialism in the Parliamentary Zone is not one that emerged from reflection by non-Indigenous people, but one that Indigenous people took upon themselves to introduce. It is the Tent Embassy, which sits just in front of Old Parliament House, and is made up of a changing collection of tents, lean-tos and caravans that have been on the lawns in front of Old Parliament House, on and off, for 40 years. Though the Embassy is on the Register of the National Estate as a place of special significance, it is an unauthorized building within the Parliamentary Zone. It is probably also the memorial that most 'irritates' the national story of Canberra.

The Aboriginal Tent Embassy first appeared in January 1972 when a group of Koori[16] activists made their way to Canberra to protest against a decision made by the conservative federal government that watered down earlier promises for national land rights legislation. The protestors, who brought a tent and set it up in front of the parliament, said they were protesting against the government's new approach to land rights which 'makes us aliens in our own land'.[17] Over the next few months the Tent Embassy grew, with supporters from the local university and other Indigenous peoples coming to Canberra (especially on weekends) to camp and take up space on the lawns in front of the parliament. By late autumn the Liberal government was so embarrassed and annoyed by the presence of the Embassy that it passed an ordinance making the presence of the tents in this part of parliament lawns illegal. As the authorities tried to implement the ordinance, there were violent confrontations between the activists and the police. Many people who were there remember these confrontations as some of the fiercest altercations in that turbulent era of protest. A new government (small 'l' liberal) was elected late in 1972 and in the euphoria of a more sympathetic regime, the Embassy disappeared. However, it was not gone for good. Over the next ten years it would re-emerge and disappear as a reminder to the different governments that took office of the broken promises around land rights. In 1992 the Embassy returned once more (20 years after the original protest) and has remained on the lawns ever since. So this site in the national capital is an intensely political one – marked by a history of violence, passion, opposition to its existence and precariousness.

For many Indigenous peoples this site is an important symbol of resistance. Kevin Buzzacott said of the sacred fire that burns at the site: 'We will keep this fire burning until the law makers come and talk to us about recognising our sovereignty.'[18] It is also a site that continues to accrue meaning. For example, Kevin Gilbert, a key Indigenous activist from the 1970s and 1980s, had some of his ashes scattered on the tent embassy site after he died. However it needs to be noted that the meaning of the Embassy is not the same for all Indigenous peoples. Some groups believe the Embassy should go and that the nearby Reconciliation Place should be the site of significance in this area. For some local Canberra Indigenous people, the Embassy members are regarded as outsiders – 'the Redfern mob'. As Mark Harris points out, 'any expectation that there should be a consistent voice of resistance … merely seeks to resurrect the vision of Indigenous Australians as a homogenous group reified through the projected desires of non-Indigenous spectators'.[19]

Figure 7.2 The tents that make up part of the Aboriginal Tent Embassy in the paddock across from the Old Parliament House in Canberra.

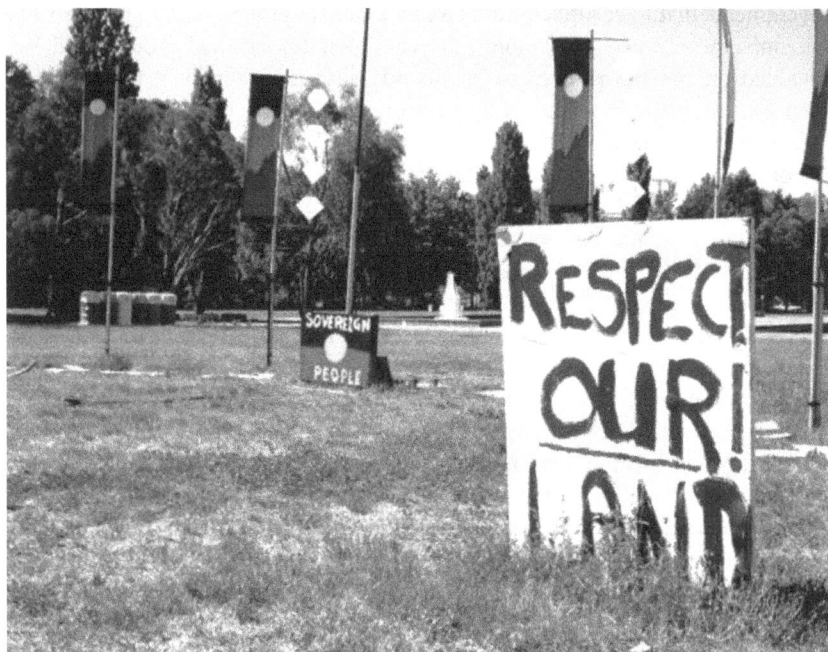

Figure 7.3 The centre of the Tent Embassy site contains a semi-circle of flags around a
        sacred fire that is kept continually burning.

The story of Australian-ness the Embassy produces is a striking one. If you
visit it, you will find a higgledy-piggledy collection of tents and mobile
housing, surrounded by various signs explaining the reason for the Embassy's
presence (see Figures 7.2 and 7.3). Many of the blogs by people who visit the
Embassy comment on it being made up of 'shacks'. There is always a fire-
place with a slow burning fire. And, depending on the day, there may be half a
dozen or hundreds of people on the site. For example, when Prime Minister
Kevin Rudd delivered the long-awaited apology to the 'Stolen Generations' in
the federal parliament in 2008, the Tent Embassy was a focal point where
people gathered to listen. The physical organization of the Embassy contrasts
with the usual stereotype of Canberra as neat, orderly and perfectly planned.
The Embassy is opposite the well-manicured rose gardens of the Old Parliament House – a striking juxtaposition. Over time, many politicians and media
commentators have complained about the 'unsightly' nature of the Embassy.
It has been called an eyesore, a disgrace and a health danger. Different government ministers over the last 40 years have threatened to remove it. Today,
since the change of government in 2008, the place of the Embassy is more
secure, but it still does not appear on official maps of the Parliamentary Zone
(see Figures 7.4 and 7.5).

Figure 7.4 The signage that marks out the buildings, memorials and monuments of the Parliamentary Zone.

Figure 7.5 The Aboriginal Tent Embassy is not marked on the Parliamentary Zone maps, although on some maps activists have hand-drawn the location of the embassy.

This official refusal to recognize the Tent Embassy in the Parliamentary Zone does not mean the Embassy is not recognized. It is on the Register of the National Estate because of its social heritage.[20] In a more popular register, the Embassy is now on the itinerary of some Canberra tourist bus routes. It also has a web presence. New technologies – the Internet, digital video – and new social formats – YouTube, blogs – mean the Embassy has an unmanaged global presence. International students studying at Australian universities come to Canberra to visit the Embassy and increase their knowledge of Indigenous politics in Australia. The Embassy has become well known overseas, through documentaries and news reports – especially from around the time of the 2000 Olympics – and is now part of an international travel route of political sites where the struggle of Indigenous peoples around the globe can be experienced and supported. In this way the Embassy is situated in terms of an 'alternative' global cultural tourism that seeks to see beyond the official story of nations. So though it is not mapped officially, it circulates via alternative maps of Canberra as a site of importance in the history of Australia. Importantly, the Embassy may be missing from national maps, but appears on global ones. So its audience is not one that is hailed by the Australian state, but one that is hailed through global networks of social justice campaigns and alternative tourism.

As stated above, the Aboriginal Tent Embassy is an unauthorized structure. No planning permission was obtained. A Koori mob simply turned up and set up shop. There are some interesting points to note here. First, that the Indigenous people of the Embassy have never asked permission for their installation. At some level there is the assumption by the protesters that they could be there and that they were on their own land. On the other hand, it is important to note the precarious existence of the Embassy. It is always being threatened with closure. The very precariousness of the rights of the Embassy to be where it is reflects the point Indigenous peoples are making. The guarantee of rights to land for Indigenous people is not automatic. In fact, it is unusual.

Reconciliation Place

One of the reasons sometimes given for the Embassy to be closed down is that across the road a new space that does exactly the same job as the Embassy exists. In the late 1990s – during the decade of Reconciliation – the National Capital Authority conducted a review of the Parliamentary Zone: it commissioned a consultancy on commemoration practices and launched a design competition for a new people's place; the federal government then announced the development of a new commemoration site in the Parliamentary Zone to be called Reconciliation Place. In many ways this renewed focus on the Parliamentary Zone led to speculation about the structures in this area. In particular, the announcement of the plans to build Reconciliation Place in 2000 led to on-and-off speculation and discussion in many different quarters – Indigenous and non–Indigenous – about the relationship of the Aboriginal Tent Embassy with Reconciliation Place. In particular, in the early years of the twenty-first century, there were ongoing suggestions that the coming into being of Reconciliation Place might mean that it was not necessary for the Aboriginal Tent Embassy to exist. The heated discussion that marked this suggestion was not surprising (and not a bad thing), given the complexity of the issue and the variety of positions available on the topic.

Former Prime Minister John Howard opened Reconciliation Place in July 2002 as a site designed:

> for contemplation and the telling and sharing of stories of reconciliation. It recognises the importance of understanding the shared history of Indigenous and non-Indigenous Australians, and reaffirms our commitment to the cause of reconciliation as an important national priority.[21]

From the outset, understandings of what Reconciliation Place would stand for and achieve have been broad and vague. This open-ended understanding of what Reconciliation Place would achieve and how it would achieve it reflects the dominant understanding of what reconciliation means and what it should achieve. That is, reconciliation is a nebulous concept that is often not clearly defined. As a result it can operate to support many different agendas. It can provide 'feel good' rhetoric without clear objectives being stated.[22] This lack of definition can be seen as far back as the original competition brief for Reconciliation Place from the NCA. Referring to the brief as 'conceptually vague', Walliss suggests it 'offered little direction regarding the specific aims of the competition, outlining a wide range of objectives and themes'.[23] This vagueness was also evident in the way people involved in the development of Reconciliation Place talked about what it would be and achieve. For example, Ian Spicer, the steering committee chair, suggested that Reconciliation Place should be 'enduring ... [and] extraordinarily respectful'. He went on to suggest that, 'it needs to honour Aboriginal and Torres Strait Islander culture as well as the shared history since European settlement ... [and] provide the opportunity for stories to be told'.[24] Around the same time, Ruddock referred to it as a 'monument to healing'.[25] While they are all worthy statements in themselves, none of these pronouncements presents any tangible or explicit indications of what Reconciliation Place and, by extension, reconciliation itself, would or could actually mean.

In contrast, the Tent Embassy is explicit in its demands and *raison d'etre*. Furthermore, it is continually occupied by Indigenous people who will tell you their demands if you ask them. However, this is not to suggest that the demands of those at the Embassy are unchanging or that there is a singular aim held by all those who occupy it. The themes that are the focus of the Embassy change over time and with personnel. What is particular about the Embassy in contrast to Reconciliation Place is that it emerged from solidly grounded hopes – land rights – rather than more nebulous hopes of improving relations between peoples.

Reconciliation Place is a beautiful, though very quiet, site. It includes a walkway divided by a grassy mound. Installations called 'slivers' are being created and placed along a pedestrian walkway over time (see Figure 7.6). The slivers highlight important aspects of Indigenous peoples' experience of colonialism and were commissioned to be completed by different Indigenous artists. When Reconciliation Place was inaugurated, only a few slivers were in place. Not surprisingly, given the timing, one of the early slivers commemorated the Stolen Generations. The cumulative effect of the slivers along the Reconciliation Place walk is to produce a sense of the achievements of individual Indigenous people and the value of Indigenous cultures artistically, politically and socially. The slivers recognize the groundbreaking contributions of individuals: Neville Bonner, the first Indigenous federal parliamentarian (senator for Queensland from 1971 to 1983 – see Figure 7.7); Dr Evelyn Scott, early advocate for Indigenous housing and legal services; and Edie Mabo. They also draw attention to the complexity and beauty of Indigenous knowledge systems – sharing ideas about Indigenous astronomy, agricultural practices, sciences and arts.

Some aspects of Reconciliation Place work to suture Indigenous peoples into the classic narratives of Australian-ness. As suggested earlier, one of the longstanding narratives of Australian identity is that of war and mateship. In one sliver titled, 'Strength, Service and Sacrifice' the role of Indigenous peoples in war is recognized. Captain Reg Saunders, the first commissioned Indigenous

Figure 7.6 This is part of artist Judy Watson's piece titled 'Fire and Water', in Reconciliation Place, which brings to mind the gathering of local indigenous peoples to feast and share during the Bogong moth season.

Figure 7.7 One of the slivers in Reconciliation Place honouring the first Indigenous federal senator – Neville Bonner.

officer, Oodgeroo Noonuccal, who served as a nurse, and Sedo Gebade, a Torres Strait Islander soldier, are all represented. (Interestingly, the other side of the sliver illustrates Indigenous contributions to another classic story of Australian-ness – sporting achievement.) Including Indigenous peoples' contribution in wars does important work in undoing the exclusion of Indigenous peoples from the national narratives (a narrative exclusion that was mirrored in political and civil exclusion). It makes clear the ways in which Indigenous peoples have been part of national life.

The official nature of Reconciliation Place and its beauty mean it has a different audience from the Tent Embassy's. One (potential) audience for Reconciliation Place is official or governmental. If one considers the audience present at the inauguration of the site, it is possible to see the nature of the audience and the role of Reconciliation Place. The site was opened by the prime minister and attended by parliamentarians and state officials from around Australia. The ceremony was also attended by Indigenous peoples, both as representatives of community and state organizations and as esteemed guests. Reconciliation Place is a place in Canberra where it is possible to show off the productive and good aspects of race relations in Australia. It is a site where enmity can be put aside and the shared future recognized.

For many Australians, Reconciliation Place, as a beautiful and serene memorial, is a far better signifier of both the past and the future of race relations in Australia than the Tent Embassy. Since they are geographically quite close, they argue the unofficial 'eyesore' Embassy should go. This is what T. C. Chang and Shirlena Huang would call an act of 'creative destruction'.[26] The important question to consider here is why there is such an insistence on only one site and why Reconciliation Place is nominated as that site. Not many Australians would argue that since there are so many war memorials in Anzac Parade, they should all be removed except one.

Some Indigenous peoples are involved in both the Tent Embassy and Reconciliation Place. Both tell stories of Indigenous survival. One is funded and recognized by the government; the other is not. This is the point of the Embassy proponents. As suggested earlier, there have been disagreements between Indigenous members of the Embassy and the Reconciliation Place committee. Indeed, playing on such divisions is a well-known ploy used by non-Indigenous peoples supposedly to demonstrate the implausibility of Indigenous political arguments (for example, 'Well, if what you say is true, then why does this Indigenous person not agree with you?'). The issue here is not which story is true, but why non-Indigenous people find one story comfortable, and the other so noxious that it is represented as detrimental to 'health'.

Reconciliation Place says to non-Indigenous peoples: consider the impact of non-Indigenous colonialism on Indigenous people. It also says: consider what we, Indigenous people, have achieved in the face of that impact. The Embassy says: 'Okay, now let's take it to the next logical step – how did you non-Indigenous people come to get our land?' So, if we return to consider the 'Strength, Service and Sacrifice' sliver, it recognizes Indigenous achievement within a particular model of the nation. The story suggests the Indigenous people can be, and have been, part of the nation. What it fails to do is explore the limits of this inclusion. So for many Indigenous peoples any narrative about war, a key story in the national repertoire, would include that of Indigenous resistance to dispossession through guerrilla warfare. This story does not and cannot appear in the narrative of Reconciliation Place. Its appearance would undo the logic of the liberal story of belonging. It is because of the potential for this story to appear and gain traction that some politicians and citizens hope to erase the Embassy. Limiting the reach of this story is easier to do in sites controlled by non-Indigenous people. But when Indigenous people turn up unannounced with their Tent Embassy and are ready to stay until justice is done, it is mostly understood as a sore that needs to be covered over or perhaps healed. But how is that healing to take place?

In the last couple of years the dissonance between the Parliamentary Zone and the Tent Embassy has not been such an issue. There is a sense that alternative, even antagonistic, narratives of the nation can still work to produce a strong sense of pleasure in national belonging. There is also a more open recognition of the social heritage value of the Tent Embassy. More Australians and tourists are willing and interested to hear this often painful story of the past. In a more recent report on the management of the landscape of the Parliamentary Zone, the NCA noted that the Tent Embassy is 'subject to an ongoing process involving a range of parties'. Some of the recommendations were that it should be:

- an evolving concept of the Tent Embassy without permanent camping;
- an educational centre for all Australians and international visitors depicting the Indigenous struggle, including the role of the 1972 protest; and
- developed as a referral point for other Indigenous issues.[27]

However, there is still a subtle condemning of the aesthetic of the Tent Embassy. There is still a sense that in the nation's capital the unplanned and makeshift nature of the Tent Embassy site (with its tents and portaloos) does not fit the 'feel' of the zone. These tensions could be understood in terms of what being a *good* citizen entails. The Parliamentary Zone, in its neatness and ambience of mostly quiet reflection, foregrounds a particular way of being Australian that the 'in your face' and 'political' nature of the Tent Embassy disturbs. Many tourists and citizens, more used to the high-quality and reflective nature of national commemoration or exhibition, find the embassy jarring and embarrassing.

It is around these issues that policymakers draw the line when imagining and planning the look of the city. By contrast the political nature of the site is coming to be seen as its strength. The site addresses the interests of a growing number of domestic and international tourists for whom colonial history and, particularly, Indigenous culture, are key points of interest. The slow recognition of the value of the site reflects policymakers coming to terms with this view. The Tent Embassy is also a site of national importance to many Indigenous peoples from around the country, who travel to the site and spend time living there with the aim of 'educating' and meeting non-Indigenous peoples and drawing strength from other Indigenous people.

Reconciliation Place and the Tent Embassy do not tell stories that are so dissimilar. What is strikingly different about them is that one is designed and constructed in the traditional manner that policymakers, architects, designers and heritage experts expect of a commemoration site. It is tranquil, informative and beautiful. The other is a mess. It is chaotic and unpredictable. It can sometimes even feel a little confronting or uncomfortable for a non-Indigenous person to be on the site. But this may not be such a bad thing. Just as some museums that commemorate trauma seek to unsettle their visitors, perhaps it might be productive for non-Indigenous people to feel a little less settled than they do in almost any other part of the Australian nation. Conflict in national stories need not be seen as negative, but can be recognized and then used to produce a more complex understanding of citizenship, sovereignty and rights, an understanding that will be more useful in the increasingly cosmopolitan and multicultural future we all face.

Notes

1 National Capital Authority, *Canberra: The Nation's Capital*, 2002. Available at www.national.capital.gov.au/plan/index/htm.
2 Ibid.
3 National Capital Authority, *Guidelines for Commemorative Works in the National Capital*, 2002, p. 6. Available at www.nationalcapital.gov.au/pubs/commworks/CommemGuidelines.pdf.
4 Ibid.
5 Australian Capital Tourism, 'Tourism Brand for Canberra', ACT Government, 2005. Available at www.tourism.act.gov.au/CA256E1D0083A261/page/Canberra+brand?OpenDocument&1=70-Canberra+brand~&2=~&3=~.
6 Catriona Elder, *Being Australian: Narratives of National Identity* (Sydney: Allen & Unwin, 2007).
7 T. C. Chang, 'Place Memory and Identity in New Asia'. *Asia Pacific Viewpoint* 46, no. 3 (2005): 249.
8 National Capital Authority, *Guidelines*, pp. 4–5.
9 Ibid., p. 5.
10 See Kurt Iveson, *Publics and the City* (Oxford: Blackwell, 2007). Iveson uses Nancy Fraser's concept in the context of Australia.
11 Link Up NSW and Tikka Jan Wilson, eds. *In the Best Interest of the Child? Stolen Children: Aboriginal Pain/White Shame*, Aboriginal History Monograph 4 (Canberra: ANU, 1997).
12 In 2012 the film *Mabo* (dir. Rachel Perkins) premiered at the Sydney Film Festival and screened not long after on ABC television. However, a few years earlier Edie Mabo's grave site was desecrated with neo-Nazi graffiti. Both events suggest the ongoing split in responses in Australia to the Mabo case.
13 Human Rights and Equal Opportunity Commission, *Bringing Them Home: Report of the Inquiry into the Removal of Aboriginal and Torres Strait Islander Children* (Canberra: AGPS, 1997).
14 Henry Reynolds, *The Law of the Land* (Ringwood: Penguin Books, 1987).
15 Keith Windschuttle, *The Fabrication of Aboriginal History (*Sydney: Macleay Press, 2002).
16 Aboriginal people from the south-east part of the Australian continent.
17 Cited in Coral Dow, *Aboriginal Tent Embassy: Icon or Eyesore?* (Canberra: Department of the Parliamentary Library, 2000).
18 Ibid.
19 Mark Harris, 'Mapping Australian Postcolonial Landscapes: From Resistance to Reconciliation?'. *Law Text Culture* 7 (2003): 86.
20 Marilyn Truscott, 'Reconciling Two Settings: Responding to the Threats to Social and Scenic Heritage Values', in *Monuments and Sites in their Settings: Conserving Cultural Heritage in Changing Townscapes and Landscapes*. Proceeding of the ICOMOS 15th General Assembly and Scientific Symposium (2006). Available at www.international.icomos.org/xian2005/papers.htm.
21 David Headon, *The Symbolic Role of the National Capital: From Colonial Argument to Twenty-first Century Ideals* (Canberra: National Capital Authority, 2002).
22 See Cath Ellis, Angela Pratt and Catriona Elder, 'Papering over the Differences: Australian Nationhood and the Normative Discourse of Reconciliation', in Mary Kalantzis and Bill Cope, eds. *Reconciliation, Multiculturalism, Identities: Difficult Dialogues, Sensible Solutions* (Melbourne: Common Ground, Altona Victoria, 2001), pp. 135–147.
23 Jillian Walliss, 'Official History and Counter Narratives: A Review of Two Competition Briefs'. *Kerb – Journal of Landscape Architecture* 10 (2001): 24.

24 Kirsten Lawson, '"Sorry" Design Unveiling; Reconciliation Place Could Replace Tent Embassy', *Canberra Times*, 16 June 2001, p. A7.
25 'Monument to Healing Feature of Plaza', *Advertiser* (Adelaide), 19 June 2001, p. 9.
26 T. C. Chang and Shirlena Huang, 'Recreating Place, Replacing Memory: Creative Destruction and the Singapore River'. *Asia Pacific Viewpoint* 46, no. 3 (2005): 267–280.
27 Mutual Mediations, 2005. Available at www.ministers.dotars.gov.au/jl/releases/2005/December/l144_2005.htm.

References

Advertiser (Adelaide). 'Monument to Healing Feature of Plaza', 19 June 2001, p. 9.
Australian Capital Tourism. 'Tourism Brand for Canberra'. ACT Government, 2005. Aavailable at www.tourism.act.gov.au/CA256E1D0083A261/page/Canberra+brand?Open Document&1=70-Canberra+brand~&2=~&3=~.
Chang, T. C. 'Place Memory and Identity in New Asia'. *Asia Pacific Viewpoint* 46, no. 3 (2005): 249.
Chang, T. C. and Shirlena Huang. 'Recreating Place, Replacing Memory: Creative Destruction and the Singapore River'. *Asia Pacific Viewpoint* 46, no. 3 (2005): 267–280.
Dow, Coral. *Aboriginal Tent Embassy: Icon or Eyesore?* (Canberra: Department of the Parliamentary Library, 2000).
Elder, Catriona. *Being Australian: Narratives of National Identity* (Sydney: Allen & Unwin, 2007).
Ellis, Cath, Angela Pratt and Catriona Elder. 'Papering Over the Differences: Australian Nationhood and the Normative Discourse of Reconciliation', in Mary Kalantzis and Bill Cope, eds. *Reconciliation, Multiculturalism, Identities: Difficult Dialogues, Sensible Solutions* (Melbourne: Common Ground, Altona Victoria, 2001), pp. 135–147.
Harris, Mark. 'Mapping Australian Postcolonial Landscapes: From Resistance to Reconciliation?'. *Law Text Culture* 7 (2003): 86.
Headon, David. *The Symbolic Role of the National Capital: From Colonial Argument to Twenty-first Century Ideals* (Canberra: National Capital Authority, 2002).
Human Rights and Equal Opportunity Commission. *Bringing Them Home: Report of the Inquiry into the Removal of Aboriginal and Torres Strait Islander Children* (Canberra: AGPS, 1997).
Iveson, Kurt *Publics and the City* (Oxford, Blackwell, 2007).
Lawson, Kirsten. '"Sorry" Design Unveiling: Reconciliation Place Could Replace Tent Embassy', *Canberra Times*, 16 June 2001, p. A7.
Link Up NSW and Tikka Jan Wilson, eds. *In the Best Interest of the Child? Stolen Children: Aboriginal Pain/White Shame*, Aboriginal History Monograph 4 (Canberra, ANU, 1997).
Mutual Mediations (2005). www.ministers.dotars.gov.au/jl/releases/2005/December/l144_2005.htm.
National Capital Authority. *Guidelines for Commemorative Works in the National Capital*, 2002, p. 6. Available at www.nationalcapital.gov.au/pubs/commworks/CommemGuidelines.pdf.
National Capital Authority. *Canberra: The Nation's Capital*, 2002. Available at www.national.capital.gov.au/plan/index/htm.
Reynolds, Henry. *The Law of the Land*. (Ringwood: Penguin Books, 1987).

Truscott, Marilyn. 'Reconciling Two Settings: Responding the Threats to Social and Scenic Heritage Values', in *Monuments and Sites in their Settings: Conserving Cultural Heritage in Changing Townscapes and Landscapes*. Proceedings of the ICOMOS 15th General Assembly and Scientific Symposium, 2006. Available at www.international.icomos.org/xian2005/papers.htm.

Walliss, Jillian. 'Official History and Counter Narratives: A Review of Two Competition Briefs'. *Kerb – Journal of Landscape Architecture* 10 (2001): 24.

Windschuttle, Keith. *The Fabrication of Aboriginal History* (Sydney: Macleay Press, 2002).

8 Renegotiating unity and diversity

Multiculturalism in post-Suharto Indonesia

Hikmat Budiman

Introduction

J. S. Furnivall once argued that because of the lack of common social will between the ethnic and racial groups of Southeast Asia, plural societies in the region faced the pressure of dissolution at the risk of nightmarish anarchy, unless some kind of formula could be devised.[1] Compared with other Southeast Asian countries, Indonesia – it is safe to say – is one of the most diverse societies in terms of ethnicity, language, custom and religion. The need for a common social platform as asserted by Furnivall is even more important today as Indonesia is now at a pivotal time after the demise of the authoritarian New Order regime of Suharto. In the wake of regional autonomy (*otonomi daerah*) and the rise of interest in local politics, the country is now at a very critical juncture where all its regions are trying to redefine themselves and their relationship with Jakarta.

Much has been said about how, when the New Order gradually took shape after 1966, the tensions between the processes of nation building and primordial attachments were no longer a threat to the nation state. Academic research has then shifted from the issue and concentrated more on the nature of the state.[2] Since Suharto stepped down, the policy on regional autonomy has created the popularly known 'little kingdoms' with 'local little kings' who are adding intricacies to the problematic relationship between the central government and its subordinates in the nascent local democratization era. The situation is exacerbated by the emergence of the (new) ethnic elite who are competing with one another for local leadership and to be the little king in their respective little kingdoms.[3]

After more than three decades of Indonesians living under the doctrine of 'national identity' and 'national unity', identity politics is now one of the crucial issues in post-New Order Indonesia. However, even when Suharto was still in power, there was a growing concern among observers about the tendency for ethnic identification in the competition for local leadership. National integration and increased contact between different groups had not eroded ethnic identities. Since the 1980s, government policies, migration and intensified competition for scarce resources have instead led to an intensification of ethnic consciousness.[4] The issue of 'native Son' (*putra daerah*, or native-born leader) – someone considered the person most entitled to serve as the head of a particular region – has, for instance, been a heatedly debated issue since the early 1990s. Meanwhile the resistance to the government's efforts to homogenize the nation and create a common culture, symbols and values based on Javanese cultural styles and values, can also be seen when people use the term *Jawanisasi* (Javanization) to refer to, and as a protest against, the imposition of the predominant cultural system throughout the country. It is nevertheless only recently that some provinces and districts have rushed out to formulate their respective local identities, based on either a particular religious teaching or a particular ethnic identity, or a combination of both.

Although not constitutionally a multicultural country like Canada, since the beginning, the modern state of Indonesia has been faced with the problem of dealing with a multicultural society. From Sukarno to Suharto to Susilo Bambang Yudhoyono, the adoption of multicultural ideas can be seen not only in the use of the official state motto of 'unity in diversity' (*Bhinneka Tunggal Ika*), but also in the enactment of some regulations, often even contradictory to one another, which are aimed at addressing the problem of diversity. On the other hand, the concept of a unitary state of the Republic of Indonesia (*Negara Kesatuan Republik Indonesia*) shows that, on top of this multicultural setting, the government places priority on preserving political sovereignty. But the need to preserve political sovereignty means that the state also has an interest in creating a unified polity.[5] More often than not, efforts at unifying polity were at the expense of ethnic and linguistic diversity, local differences, indigenous normative ordering and religious laws. The New Order of Suharto was widely known for its emphasis on unity (*Tunggal Ika*) at the expense of difference (*Bhinneka*). It should not come as a surprise that every attempt of the government now at imposing and preserving unity will clash with the interest of preserving local identities.[6] The renegotiation of unity and diversity in post-Suharto Indonesia has brought the country onto the long and winding road of problematic multiculturalism.

This chapter discusses some critical problems that Indonesia has been facing when dealing with diversity. It argues that far from having wrapped up a complete project, Indonesia still has unfinished business between the nation and its subnational nations. As will be explored in the next section, Indonesia was considered a radical departure from the old nations of the past. Now it appears to be haunted by the nations that have erupted from the ruins of the past it left behind when declaring itself a nation state. In other words, Indonesia needs to redefine and rediscover itself as it faces the great social disruptions brought about by changes in the political climate following the devastation of the old utopia of the unity of *Indonesia Raya* (the Great Indonesia) by economic and political failures of the old regime. More specifically, the government has to refine its policies regarding the multiplicity of identities and values of her citizens. The big question now is how to make it possible for seemingly incommensurable identities and values to be placed in the fledgling democratic space.

The chapter is divided into three main sections. The first section discusses Indonesia as a multicultural country, not as a descriptive reality, but more as an abstract entity depicted in some of the early notions of Indonesian nationhood. The second section sketches out some policies taken by the government of Indonesia in the realms of religion and culture. Both will show how the policies on diversity have been diverted to promote only ideas of national unity based on the 'stability approach' of the New Order regime, and how the government understood and defined diversity.

There are many forms of diversity. In *Rethinking Multiculturalism*, Bhikhu Parekh differentiates between three types of cultural diversity, i.e. subcultural diversity, perspectival diversity and communal diversity.[7] Indonesia exhibits all three types of diversity. However, the third section focuses on communal diversity, which will be narrowed down to the ethno-religious communities that can be found in various parts of the country. It assesses the impact of the state's multiculturalism policies on the life and existence of some local ethno-religious communities, and offers a brief discussion on the cultural strategies taken by these groups in their negotiations on predominant values and identity.

Early (contested) ideas on multicultural Indonesia

The problem of multiculturalism, within the context of the Indonesian nation state, can be traced back to the unfinished negotiations involved in choosing between the Indonesian word *bangsa* (nation) and the word *nasion*, which recently has often been considered by some to be a more appropriate translation of the English word, 'nation'.[8] Diverse nations (*bangsa–bangsa*), each with its own shared experiences and memories of having been subjugated by European colonialism, arrived at an agreement (or claimed to be in agreement) to converge into a new idea or – to use Anderson's terminology – an imagination of nationhood:[9] the fiction of the nation of Indonesia. The establishment of the Indonesian nation state, therefore, involved the process of augmenting the people's imagination with concepts beyond territorial claims and their previous cultures, and having a national scope. One of the intriguing questions was how the myriad of nations, each with its own culture, language, customs, traditional laws and religious teachings, could possibly be united without ignoring each of their unique characteristics.

This brings us to the discussion on the early notions of multicultural Indonesia. In October 1928, at an event called *Kongres Pemuda* (Youth Congress), some young activists representing their respective youth organizations pledged the oath of 'one country, one nation, and one language, Indonesia'. The notion of Indonesia and Indonesian nationhood preceded the dawn of the Indonesian modern state. And on that day, the work of composer W. R. Supratman, *Indonisch, Indonisch*, later to be renamed, *Indonesia Raya*, was sung and later declared the country's official national anthem. The oath is popularly known as *Sumpah Pemuda* (the Youth Oath), and this particular juncture in time is often referred to as the onset of the spirit of respecting multiculturalism in Indonesia.

The youth chose not to settle on the language of the Javanese (the largest ethnic group) or the Sundanese (the second-largest ethnic group) to represent this new nation. The Indonesian language that originated from the Malay vernacular was chosen as the *lingua franca* of the newborn nation. What united them was the sentiment of belonging to a community, the shared feeling of being united by the historical fate of being an object of Dutch colonialism.[10] Note that the youth did not even bother to discuss religion as a uniting factor for their 'imagined community'.

Early ideas on nationhood of the so-called founding fathers of Indonesia also showed how diversity had caused concern among them and how they viewed diversity as a factor that should be taken into account when forming the nation. In this chapter I will only discuss the ideas of two of them, namely, Sukarno and Sutan Takdir Alisjahbana (STA). These ideas were derived from different perspectives and arrived at different conclusions, but they obviously represented intellectual responses to cultural diversity in relation to the fate of a nation blessed (or cursed) with it.

In his first speech on the *Pancasila* state ideology on 1 June 1945, Sukarno eloquently said:

> In brief, the nation of Indonesia, *Natie* Indonesia, is not simply a congregation of people living with '*désir d'être ensemble*' (desire to unite – HB) in smaller regions such as Minangkabau, or Madura, or Jogya, or Sunda, or Bugis, but the nation of Indonesia embraces entire individuals who according to the geopolitics decreed by Allah, God the Almighty, coexist in the union of all islands across Indonesia from the Northern tip of Sumatra to the farthest end of Irian![11]

Sukarno used the word '*Natie*' to accentuate the difference between the concept of *bangsa* (nation), adopted in the phrase, '*bangsa* Indonesia', and the idea of *bangsa* that refers to the territories and cultures before the birth of Indonesia. In another part of his speech, Sukarno further elaborated on the concept of nation state in the following sentences:

> Thus, not all regions in our motherland that were sovereign territories in ancient times are *nationale staat*. We have only twice experienced the status of *nationale staat*, i.e. during the rule of the Sriwijaya and Majapahit empires. Apart from that we are never a *nationale staat*. I say with full respect that we once had our revered kings, I say with most sincere admiration to Sultan Agung Hanjokrokesumo that Mataram albeit an independent region was still not a *nationale staat*. With all deference to Prabu Siliwangi in Pajajaran, I say that his kingdom was not a *nationale staat*. With my highest regard to Prabu Sultan Ageng Tirtayasa, I say that his empire in Banten, although self-governing, was not a *nationale staat*. With tremendous respect to Sultan Hasanuddin in Sulawesi who established the Bugis Kingdom, I say that the independent land of Bugis was also not a *nationale staat*.[12]

Sukarno's conception of a *nationale staat* in the excerpt above presupposes a national state that is beyond the form of the independent nations that once existed and is, at the same time, merged from these nations into one nation state. He drew a superlative relationship between Indonesia and its subnationals. The concept of Indonesia as a national unity therefore supersedes the interests of the subnational nations. For this new nation, Sukarno strived hard to discover a platform layer that can presumably mediate the differences among pre-Indonesian nations. He named the platform, *Pancasila* (which literally means five basic principles). It is a *Weltanschauung*, a guiding principle whose values are believed to be dug and synthesized from the country's old traditions. His passion for the unity of the nation can be seen in the inclusion of the term, 'Indonesian nationality', as the first principle of the draft on the Pancasila manuscript he proposed.[13]

Is Indonesia, then, a continuation of the earlier nations? For Sutan Takdir Alisjahbana (STA), the answer is a resounding no. For him, becoming an Indonesian nation is a historical process to break free from the darkness of the past that he termed, 'pre-Indonesia *Jahiliyah*' (Age of Ignorance). In an article entitled, '*Menuju Masyarakat dan Kebudayaan Baru*' ('Towards a New Society and Culture'), published in *Pujangga Baru* in August 1935, STA wrote:

> It must be clearly stated that the history of Indonesia in the twentieth century, upon the birth of a new generation within the setting of this archipelago, has consciously embarked on a new path for the nation and the country. In earlier times, the period prior to the closure of the nineteenth century, is the age of pre-Indonesia, of Indonesia's Jahiliyah, that only recognizes the history of *Oost Indische Compagnie*, the history of Mataram, history of Aceh, history of Banjarmasin and others.[14]

The Arabic word, *jahiliyah*, adopted by STA in the above passage, refers to the period of Arabian society's existence before the advent of Islam. The term carries a negative connotation because the Arabs prior to Islam were typically depicted as people from an inferior state of civilization whose rational thoughts remained cast in darkness. Moving away from this period of gloom means that Indonesians have entered the era of enlightenment (*Aufklarung*), and are celebrating the age of modernity. STA believed that the past did not contribute to the discovery of the Indonesian nation in the twentieth century. Sukarno treated 'the earlier nations' as part of the process of forming Indonesia's *nationale staat*. In contrast, STA suggested that the people of Indonesia free themselves from such traditional binds:

> The word 'free' does not suggest that the people *are ignorant of the particulars*, the word 'free' merely means *unchained* (*tidak terikat*). This is because whoever has failed to liberate himself from the Javanese culture, will attempt to incorporate this spirit of Javaneseness (*kejawaan*) into the Indonesian culture, whoever has not set himself free from the Malay culture will

attempt to incorporate this spirit of Malayness (*kemelayuan*) into the Indonesian culture, and so forth. For these people therefore, Indonesian culture
is a slightly altered version of the Javanese or Malay culture.[15]

With this notion, STA had instigated an intellectual debate, considered to be the
most outstanding in the history of Indonesia's modern thinking, and which was
more commonly known as the *Polemik Kebudayaan* (Cultural Polemic). Unlike
several of his critics at the time, who were more inclined towards suggesting that
the development of Indonesia's culture be inspired by Eastern cultural values, as
well as the virtues of old traditions, STA, on the contrary, viewed that modern
Indonesia must construct a completely new culture, the culture of *Indonesia
Raya* (the Great Indonesia).[16] Hence, he did not recommend choosing a dominant
ethnic culture as the national culture, nor was he interested in the amalgamation
of existing cultures into a modern Indonesian container. Unlike the contemporary
multiculturalist, he was also not an advocate of a cultural mosaic either, but was
instead an exponent of the creation of a new (national) culture. It was obvious
that for STA, the pre-Indonesia empires, including Majapahit and Sriwijaya,
were not the precursors to the modern Indonesian nation state.

For both Sukarno and STA, a nation, then, is an entity that struggles to set
itself free from the cradle of the past, a rational project that betrays the past to
grasp and welcome the future. Sukarno felt that he was obligated to apologize to
the kings of ancient kingdoms because their historical role should then be immediately unseated to make way for the new generation in a newly established
nationale staat, whereas STA ascertained that the pre-Indonesia age should be
abandoned entirely to accomplish a similar goal. Both Sukarno and STA viewed
the earlier nations as being at a lower level from that of a nation state. The dis-
similarity between the two lies in their stance towards the role of these nations in
an independent Indonesia. Regardless of the differences in opinion about the
newly born nation state, Pancasila was then accepted as the state's official ideology with which the country set a foundation for dealing with diversity. No particular ethnic group, religion, race or culture was given higher status over
another. Suharto then went his own way in reshaping the country where diversity
was not only economically exploited, but also manipulated culturally and taken
advantage of politically.

Forcing unity into diversity

Since the Dutch colonial era, the composition of the populace inhabiting the East
Indies has been causing various intricate problems. To cope with such issues, the
colonial government imposed a politics of segregation, which divided the population into groups that were strictly monitored and were extremely discriminatory. In 1884, for instance, the colonial government issued the *Algemene
Baplingen van Wetgeving* (General Regulation on Legislative Principles) that
divided the population of the East Indies into two categories based on religious
orientation: Europeans (who embrace Christianity) and natives (all non-European

residents). A year later, in 1885, the colonial government issued the *Regerings Reglement* (Government Regulation), which no longer divided the population based on religion, but on race, into three groups: *Europeanen* (Europeans), *Inlanders* (indigenous population) and *Vreemde Oosterlingen* (Foreign Orientals), who included the Indians, Arabs and Chinese.[17]

In the postcolonial era, the policy of the government of Indonesia was somewhat self-contradictory: while it ceremoniously accepted and heralded diversity as a national asset for the sake of the nation's greatness, it discouraged plurality at the same time, based on the view that differences caused trouble for the state and nation. A high degree of cultural heterogeneity was viewed as an obstacle that could hinder the trajectory of national economic development. In other words, differences were seen as a threat to national stability. To handle the variety of differences, the New Order imposed control on diversity at several levels, two of which will be briefly discussed below. At the first level, it reduced the number of religions embraced by society through the imposition of a policy on '*agama yang resmi diakui di Indonesia*' (religions officially acknowledged in Indonesia). At the second level, the government set a standardized national culture by imposing the values and symbols of the dominant culture to lessen cultural differences.

Official religions

In 1965 Presidential Decree No. 1 was enacted and provided a list of the official religions recognized in Indonesia, namely: Islam, Protestantism, Catholicism, Hinduism, Buddhism and Confucianism. Confucianism was unlisted as an official religion in 1978. In the *Surat Edaran Menteri Dalam Negeri* (Internal Affairs Ministerial Circular Letter) of 1978 on the procedure for filling in the column on religion on the identity card of Indonesian citizens, the authorities would only recognize five main religions: Islam, Protestantism, Catholicism, Hinduism and Buddhism.

If the consequences of the Circular Letter of the Internal Affairs Minister of 1978 only specifically affected the followers of Confucius, the more fundamental issue actually lies in the policy of determining what is an 'official religion'. The implications of this policy have not only had a bearing on believers of Confucius, but also on other faiths outside the five 'formal' religions. Some people identify these other religions as systems of 'ethnic beliefs', which are inferior compared with the five recognized religions. Others however consider such faiths not as religions at all, but merely as traditional belief systems that have yet to be fully perfected so as to be converted into one of the five official religions.

This categorization brings forth a general perception on the concept of Indonesianness where, to become an Indonesian citizen, one must embrace one of the five religions acknowledged by the state. Beyond that, individuals or communities who observe other religions are categorized as 'non-religious' or 'heretics', or are even identified as members of the country's ex-communist party (the PKI, or *Partai Komunis Indonesia*). The category of 'non-religious' is typically used to identify followers of a belief system outside the official religion, and the label 'heretic' is attached to followers of an 'official religion' who adhere to a different interpretation and follow different rituals of the religion in question. Meanwhile the label, '*bekas PKI*' (ex-PKI), is used arbitrarily by the government to identify anyone opposing its policies. When minority identities were expressed forthrightly during the period of political openness of the post-Suharto era, they were immediately confronted by the majority (actually it was only a small part of the majority) followers of a particular official religion (particularly Islam), which resulted in the provocation of social tensions in recent years. From January to November 2007, for instance, the *Setara Institute* of Jakarta recorded at least 135 incidents that can be categorized as violations of religious freedom.[18]

Standardized cultural diversity

Much the same can be said about the New Order policies on culture. It used diversity to promote national integration and as propaganda against '*bahaya laten komunisme*' (latent threat of communism). The diversity in ethnicity, culture, language, custom, traditional attire and even local delicacies is displayed on an immense scale by the government at virtually every important state event. This parading of diversity is starkly obvious in visual representations on calendars, stamps, tourism brochures, postcards, pamphlets, schoolbooks and in television broadcasts, and the establishment of the Indonesia in Miniature Park (popularly known by its acronym, TMII – *Taman Mini Indonesia Indah*). The huge efforts to promote state cultural policies were then proven to make Indonesian citizens accustomed to equating unity with homogeneity, and equity with uniformity. As a consequence, each form of diversity that deviates from, or that does not conform to, the standard determined by the state is viewed as an anomaly and as something that should be 'tamed' or standardized to ensure its integration into the unity of Indonesia. Suharto's policy on SARA (Ethnicity, Religion, Race and Intergroup Relations) put the final nail in the coffin of the discourse on diversity in Indonesia. This policy positioned issues pertaining to ethnicity, religion, race and intergroup relations as a social taboo not to be publicly discussed because of the assumption that any mention of such matters would disrupt national stability.

The paragon of Suharto's cultural policies, reflecting the obsession of the New Order with the unity of Indonesia, is the Indonesia in Miniature Park. TMII's role is so crucial that when discussing New Order cultural policies in dealing with diversity one would almost naturally refer to it.[19] Without our recounting the numerous controversies and what intellectual critics have said about TMII's construction, it is safe to say that the park is essentially an epitome of the New Order cultural policy.[20] TMII was an attempt to represent the cultures of (at the time) 27 provinces throughout Indonesia. That the state considers it possible for the heterogeneity of diverse cultures to be encapsulated simply into 27 representations in a park enclosure indeed reflects how it interprets national culture. As noted in Acciaioli's study, TMII indeed merges both the administrative and cultural domains. Being a Batak native therefore means that you are from North Sumatra, and being a Bugisnese means that you reside in South Sulawesi.[21] Ethnicity and locality each presumes the other, and essentially turn into a single concept, identical and inseparable, becoming what Boellstorff identifies as 'ethnolocality'.[22]

Although it can be argued that the state of Indonesia had encouraged the process of dissociation of ethnicity from religion since the colonial period, the New Order cultural policy made the association of ethnicity with formal religion more apparent.[23] There is the stereotypical idea that being a Batak or Manados or Ambonese means you are a Christian, and being a Balinese means you are a Hindu. On the other hand, by diminishing cultural diversity, as can be seen in the TMII, the government has created state-monitored differences: at a certain level, diversity is indeed acknowledged, provided it has been standardized, and aligned by the state to ensure uniformity and national stability. TMII is also a place where Javanese culture is the standard culture against which all other cultures should be measured.

Impact on ethno-religious minorities

Government policies on religion and culture have also severely impacted the life of local minority communities in various parts of the country. One of these is the *ToWana* community, which will be discussed here first. *ToWana* belongs to the *Ta'* ethnic group, a minority ethnic group compared with other major ethnic groups in Sulawesi, such as the Bugis and Makassar.[24] They live in the area of the Morowali Nature Preservation Park of the Morowali district in Central Sulawesi. Like many other local communities that will also be discussed in this chapter, *ToWana* is a minority group within a minority ethnic group. For lack of a better term, I will call these communities the within-ethnic minority or ethno-religious minority, and use the two terms interchangeably. Since religion is almost inseparable from their culture, the government's policies on culture will simultaneously impact their religious life and *vice versa*.

In 2000, there was a critical moment in the park. Although it went unnoticed at the national level, it was of great importance in the context of the dynamics of multiculturalism in Indonesia. After enduring unrelenting pressures, coercion to assimilate, forced resettlement and accusations from missionaries of being pagan since colonial times, the *ToWana* community, with support from the Morowali-based NGO, *Sahabat Morowali*, made a declaration of their political stance that is critical in discussing multiculturalism in Indonesia. Their posture was encapsulated in the expression, '*Tare Kampung, Tare Agama, Tare Pamarenta*'.[25] Its literal translation is: 'No Village, No Religion, No Government.' Village, religion and government are three social institutions that are virtually inextricable from one another. They are a three-in-one package, a trident of state policies that persistently ask the *ToWana* to become part of the unitary Indonesia nation state. But to become a part of the unity, they are pressured to live in the *kampung*, and no one can live in the *kampung* without subscribing to one of the five state-sanctioned religions. An existence outside this framework insinuates that they are not citizens, but untamed human beings. Or they would be viewed as traditional societies only worthy of survival for tourism projects.[26]

Kampung is an icon of government efforts to normalize its citizens through the politics of demography and settlement. Residing in villages entails not only the physical movement from the forests to settlement areas outside the nature conservation area, but also the process of succumbing to various requisites that they are initially unfamiliar with. *Kampung*, in other words, is state-monitored settlement (through the head of a subdistrict, a village chief, and the neighbourhood association or RT/RW). To live in the *kampung*, each person also has to have a KTP (*Kartu Tanda Penduduk* or citizen ID card), on which the individual must explicitly state what official religion he or she belongs to. Without the KTP (oftentimes it also means not embracing one of the five religions), you are considered an illegal resident.

Religion in Indonesia is contained by the restricted number of official religions acknowledged by the state. During the colonial era, religion saw missionaries steering those viewed as pagans or heretics to the revelations of Christianity, and in post-colonial times, religion is part of state politics intended to exert control over its citizens. The government is considered the hub of the link between the village and religion, the ultimate authority whose powers can be wielded on behalf of all interests to force the *ToWana* into becoming part of the national unity of Indonesia. The only choice left to the people of *ToWana* to become Indonesians is to resettle to village areas beyond the conservation area, and to convert to one of the official religions.

Thus far, most members of the *ToWana* community choose the strategy of surviving in the forest to avoid forced resettlement and religious assimilation. Some others just recently moved to a resettlement location in Taronggo, a village located outside the Morowali nature preserve. The presence of the Morowali Nature Preservation Park can be a blessing to the *ToWana*, but it can also be a threat to their continued existence. A blessing because living in the enclosure allows them to inhabit a relatively safe and secure habitat, away from the intervention of people beyond their territory. At the same time, the presence of the *ToWana* is also an advantage to the management of the state-owned nature preserve because of the stereotype attached to the *ToWana* community, portrayed as a people brandishing the traditional weapon, *sumpit* (blowpipe), and still relishing slaying 'foreigners' who dare venture into their territory. Hence the area has been kept relatively safe from the possibility of further destruction. Such circumstances also make it increasingly difficult for the *ToWana* to access various public services such as health care and education. In addition, the ability to remain secure in this safe haven depends to some extent on the person who wields the authority in the nature preserve.[27]

Similar cases, but eliciting different responses and strategies of resistance, also occurred in other parts of Indonesia. The communities of *Tanah Toa Kajang* and *ToWani Tolotang* in South Sulawesi, for example, also suffered a similar dilemma in dealing with the relationship between religion, the village and the

government. The two communities revealed a distinct contrast in the local strategies they adopted to circumvent government projects to impose uniformity.
While the people of the *Kajang* community used a strategy of 'accommodation'
in dealing with the process of Islamization by formally agreeing to become followers of Islam, the *ToWani Tolotang* followed an entirely different course by
formally accepting Hinduism as their religion. The *Kajang* community resisted
and negotiated with leaders of predominant Islam by creating competing narratives and interpretations of the religious teachings that are distinctively their
own. Instead of turning to the Qur'an, *Hadith* (sayings of the Prophet) and the
Sunnah (exemplary conduct of the Prophet), as is the practice of the Muslim
majority, for instance, the people of the Kajang community normally frame their
lives based on the concept of *kamase-masea* that exhorts simple and unpreten-
tious living. They admit to being devotees of the *Patuntung* teachings sourced
from the *Pasangri Kajang*.[28] As a consequence, they are regarded as believers
whose faith in Islam needs to be perfected, and who should be forced to observe
the teachings and rituals of mainstream Islam, and obligated to discard all other
ancestral rituals and beliefs they have been dutifully performing from generation
to generation. On its part, the local government in this area has adopted policies
that are contradictory to one another. On one hand, it focuses all of its efforts on
categorizing these communities as community groups that must be developed
and and whose lives have to be improved to be on a par with other societies. On
the other hand, they are simultaneously unyielding in ensuring that these communities continue to retain the authenticity of their ancestral cultural legacy for
the benefit of local tourism projects. Diversity is encouraged not as a recognition
of difference but as a means of promoting the economics of the state's project on
tourism.

The *Wetutelu* (Islam) community in West Lombok also pursued a relatively
similar strategy (and met with a similar fate).[29] Just as in similar cases in various
parts of the country, the name that is attached to them – in their case, '*wetutelu*'
(which literally means 'three-times') – originated from outside the community.
The identity of the people of *Wetutelu* shows several distinctions that distinguish
them from the Muslim majority around them. Some presume they are known as
the *Wetutelu* community because they believe in only three of the five pillars of
Islam (*syahadat* or the declaration of faith; *shalat* or the five obligatory daily
prayers; and *puasa* or fasting in the month of Ramadhan), while mainstream
Islam observes the five articles of faith (*syahadat*; *shalat*; *zakat* or the obligation
to give alms; *puasa*; and the *haj* pilgrimage to Mecca). Others argue that the
term *Wetutelu* is affixed to the community because of their different interpretation of the obligation to perform daily prayers in Islam. If standard Islam followed by the Muslim majority contends that performing the five-time daily
prayers (*wetulima*, which literally means 'five times') is an indubitable duty, the
Wetutelu community considers it sufficient to observe only three prayers in a
year. And even this is not performed by each individual, as it is deemed adequate
if only the customary leader observes the prayers on behalf of the others. As a
result of these differences, members of this community were at one time

subjected to constant acts of violence by the followers of mainstream Islam around them, which were intended to make them cower in complete submission, and also to intensify assimilation efforts by the state through the Department of Religious Affairs. Following the G30 S/PKI tragic incident in 1965, for instance, they were indiscriminately categorized as being advocates of communism and supporters of the Indonesian Communist Party (known by its Indonesian acronym, PKI) and were faced with only two choices: be killed or accept one of the official religions acknowledged by the state.[30] Prior to this incident the size of their community had reached 20 per cent of the total population in Lombok, but afterwards, this figure plummeted drastically to a mere 1 per cent.[31] It must be clearly stated, however, that the sudden plunge in their numbers was not only attributed to the rampant killings of the *Wetutelu* people, but also due to their mass conversion to Islam or other recognized religions.

On their part, the people of *ToWani Tolotang* in the Amparita subdistrict of Sidenreng Rappang district, South Sulawesi, have still not given up the hope that their identity as followers of the *Tolotang* belief will eventually be recognized by the state, even though they are formally registered as devotees of Hinduism. Their decision to choose Hinduism rather than Islam, which is the religion most identified with by the ethnic Bugis culture, can be seen as an effort to elude an even more unpleasant possibility if they had remained adamant in not choosing one of the five religions sanctioned by the state. Becoming believers of Hinduism is therefore a strategic move that provides them with the guarantee of security from the possibility of being targeted by Islamic groups outside their community who will typically resort to forceful measures to ensure that the people of *ToWani Tolotang* forsake their ancestral belief.

By formally accepting Hinduism they have managed to free themselves from threats imposed by the religious majority outside their environment and are relatively free to practise their rituals based on the *Tolotang* teachings because of the somewhat less intense intervention from Hindu religious authorities, both in Bali and in Jakarta.[32] If they had opted for Islam, one can only imagine how they would have had to endure a similar fate to that of the *Tanah Toa Kajang* community, which is considered to have deviated from the true teachings of Islam. Or they could even have suffered a worse fate, such as the experience of the *Jamaah Ahmadiyah*, who were not only judged to be followers of 'a misleading religion', but also suffered recurring repression and acts of aggression by hard-line Islamic groups.

The cases of the *ToWana*, *Tanah Toa Kajang*, *Wetutelu* and *ToWani* communities illustrate that religion cannot be isolated from locality. Mentioning the words, *ToWani*, *Wetutelu* or *Kajang* will instinctively conjure up the conceptual connotation of their religious teachings and rituals which are different from those of the main religions in Indonesia. When religion becomes the explanatory factor for Indonesian identity or *ke-Indonesiaan* (Indonesian-ness), believers of a faith not endorsed by the state will automatically be excluded and not be fully recognized as Indonesian citizens. Simultaneously, they are also likely to be secluded and discriminated against by the rest of the population because of the social distance between a majority group (officially recognized by the state) and a minority group (whose position is viewed as problematic), and through a cultural gap arising from their being seen as heretics. These differences therefore become a form of social legitimization to ensure their separation through the discovery of 'the others', 'the minority' and 'the imperfect', in contrast to a particular collective similarity. 'The others' and 'the minority' are then secluded through the creation of a psychological (cultural) chasm that prevents them from freely participating in the exercising of the notion of a nation state and the nationhood of Indonesia.

Exclusion and seclusion also operate in the context of the social relationship between main ethnic groups and communities typically presumed to be their sub-ethnic groups, which can be explained by the process of unifying and subduing diversity. The *Tanah Toa Kajang* and *ToWani Tolotang* communities in South Sulawesi, the *Parmalim* community in Medan and the *Wetutelu* community, for instance, experience one of the following two possibilities: they can either be considered different from the more dominant ethnic group (such as in the case of the *Parmalim* community in North Sumatra, or *Sedulur Sikep* in Central Java), or the religion they embrace is considered to be a lesser religion, misleading or even evil (as in the case of the *Wetutelu, Ahmadiyah* followers, or *ToWana* community). Not only are they treated as separate citizens in the same country (discrimination), but practically all of them also experience what is commonly known in the glossary of social science as marginalization.

ToWana, ToWani Tolotang and several other communities mentioned earlier are minority groups in terms of their numbers when compared with the remaining population in Indonesia. Even if the total number of people in these groups is aggregated as a statistical figure, their ratio in the whole population will still be insignificant compared with the remaining majority. The concept of ethnic minority may not be accurate in attempting to categorize them because, in essence, they are part of a larger ethnicity in their respective regions. These groups are within-ethnic minorities, although their own ethnicity is not necessarily a minority. They do not demand special rights, nor do they wish for political representation in parliament, but they insist that their people be treated as citizens with equal rights despite practising a faith, culture and social reasoning different to those of the majority population around them.

With reference to the discussion above, the problem with multiculturalism and, at a certain level, also the issue of minority rights, at least within the context of Indonesia, does not lie mainly in the fact that there are indeed differences between one particular community and another, but rather in the ongoing practices of distinction carried out by one group in relation to the other. If the concept of difference means a description that each community group has a set of characteristics and identity different from others, then the concept of distinction refers more to the process of determining the uniqueness of each characteristic that is then used as a reference to ascertain the form of social relationship that exists among them.

As a result of numerous historical processes, the *Kajang* community and *ToWani Tolotang*, for instance, are in many respects different from the majority of Bugis or Makassar ethnic people in general. And the Wetutelu community is different from the other Lombok inhabitants. The difference becomes the source of problems when it serves as the basis for distinctions in treatment of the respective groups. Ironically, such distinctions also occur as a result of the process of seeking similarities and integration through the process of assimilation. Those who are not the same are (forcefully) made to merge into 'the same', 'the majority', and thus those who choose to remain different will become 'the others', 'the minority'. Therefore, the minority issue in this context refers not only to the population ratio, but also the social (and discursive) process causing the distinctions.

The *Sedulur Sikep* community in Central Java is part of the largest ethnic group in Indonesia, but it is also part of a minority group, not because 'they are non-Javanese' but because they choose to live a life that is culturally (and religiously) different from that led by the Javanese majority. The choice causes them to be viewed as being 'lesser Javanese' than the rest of the Javanese. They are a minority within the ethnic majority. The *ToWani* community in South Sulawesi is a part of the Bugis ethnic group, who despite being smaller in number compared with the Javanese or Sundanese ethnicity, is still considered to be a major ethnic group in Indonesia. They experience minoritization not because they are not 'Bugisnese', but because they comprehend and practise their 'Bugis-ness' in a manner different from the rest of the Bugis community, on the basis of which they are then treated unequally. On the other hand, statistically, the Indonesian Chinese as an ethnic group in Indonesia at present probably exceeds the population of the Bataks ethnic group, but while the Batak community is a minority group compared with the Javanese or Sundanese, they have never been perceived as a minority group in the national context in the way that the rest of society perceives the Indonesian Chinese to be a minority group. In the same manner we can also say that the minority issue does not initially refer to the presence of a group with a relatively smaller population in comparison with the populace outside, but instead refers more to the process through which they have become a group that is constantly perceived as a minority. This is an illustration of how the concept of minority that is solely based on numerical numbers is always problematic.[33]

Conclusion

Since the dawn of modern Indonesia, the country has formally attempted to negate the notion that diversity is a threat to social cohesion and can cause trouble to the integrity of the nation. It is also worth noting that the current tourism board, which is under the state department of tourism and culture, used the tagline 'ultimate in diversity' to promote the so-called 'Indonesia Visit Year 2008' programme. Once again, the state utilized diversity to promote its own agenda (in this case, an economic agenda through tourism projects). The motivation behind this was also essentially the same: the state attempted to exert centralized control over its citizens through 'standardized' diversity.

There are at least two contradictory issues that emerge from the above observation. First, national unity that had been excessively enforced by an authoritarian regime resulted instead in the tendency to search for local particularities following the downfall of the regime. In the New Order era, unity was widely criticized as it was considered to be masking and yet legitimizing the practices of state violence. At the time, it was perceived that the concept of unity ded not allow room for differences. The *Bhinneka Tunggal Ika* slogan was diverted into placing more emphasis on '*Tunggal Ika*' (unity), with total disregard for the aspect of '*Bhinneka*' (diversity). The Pancasila ideology, particularly manifested in the form of state policies on '*demokrasi Pancasila*' (Pancasila democracy), was accused of being a justification for encumbering freedom and public participation. Second, when the democratic space opened up, and diversity was celebrated in every corner of the country, the discourse that then surfaced was instead on the necessity to protect national unity. Pancasila, which was initially suspected of being the legitimization of repressive measures against the people by the state, has now been recommended for revitalization. The irony in the wake of identity politics in the democratization of Indonesia is that the emphasis on differences has turned out to be the process that tends to become anti-diversity.

If the New Order era was characterized by its preoccupation with uniforming diversity under national imperatives, the subsequent years have instead been marked by an obsession of similar magnitude with the reinforcement of identity through ethnic and/or religious distinction. There is an urgency to conduct critical studies on the process of exclusion and seclusion of ethnic/religious minority groups to delve into possible scenarios for a better future for Indonesia. At least two things need to be taken into serious consideration.

First, it is inevitable that a nation needs unity as the foundation for its establishment. However, unity is not identical to uniformity as exercised by the New Order. Rather it is the attitude of accepting that, to maintain the common purpose of one nation, there must be a set of shared values. Through the youth who pledged the Oath in 1928, Sukarno and his contemporaries had given the perfect illustration of how, to build a nation from a myriad of differences, they had to find the common denominator to bind the diversity within the nation. They had to let go, at a particular moment, their attachment to their primordial roots to find something in common with others. They still had their own roots but they realized that these roots alone were not enough on their own to hold together the entire nation in their quest to liberate the people from foreign occupation. This is where Sukarno played his best role as a solidarity maker in the struggle against colonialism.

The problem with multiculturalism that has increasingly been discussed after the downfall of Suharto is that it is mostly focused on the idea of granting special rights to a particular group. As with the cases of Aceh and West Papua provinces, the conferring of special rights on a particular region, based on cultural and/or religious distinctiveness, has the potential of prompting dozens of other regions that are also eligible to demand the same privilege. In the province of Bali, for example, where local residents are mostly Hindus, there is a strong possibility of them insisting on being given equal treatment. This will defeat the purpose of the regulation: what is so special about being given a special status if every other region is given the same status? The cases of *ToWana, ToWani Tolotang* and other ethno-religious minority communities have also shown us that what they really need is not special status as a particular group within society, but a recognition that they have their own right to decide what is good and bad for their life. As citizens of Indonesia they have the same right to access public services. Providing them with basic public facilities is a must in a democratic country. They do need education and health services, but this does not necessarily mean that they want classical education in modern schools, or to be forced to go to a public health service miles away from their homes. Providing public services that are designed according to the specific conditions of the people is more justifiable than treating them as minority groups entitled to special rights.

The discourse on multiculturalism in Indonesia can also easily entice people into believing that, for local cultures or identities to survive, we have to abandon the concept of shared values and loyalty to the nation, and instead give priority to ethnic and local differences, as if the nation could be replaced with an aggregation of a large number of diverse minorities. If this is what multiculturalism tries to offer, what makes it different from the practices of segregationism during the Dutch colonial era? When translated into government policies, multiculturalism without a strong commitment to the nation is rampant multiculturalism, unbounded multiculturalism that will be of no benefit to the country.[34] It puts emphasis on particularity by ignoring altogether the need to share something in common to make the nation possible in the first place. In the context of democratization in Indonesia, it can also bring about a reverse reaction that is anti-democratic, such as ever-increasing religious fundamentalism and anti-minority tendencies. Paradoxically, it also tends to be anti-culture in that it denies the cultural dynamics that naturally involve the process of sharing, borrowing and even the stealing of certain elements of one culture by other cultures. It draws thick borders among identities and cultures, and is suffocated by the illusion of cultural purity.

Second, democracy undeniably necessitates national unity. Establishing democracy presupposes the presence of the integrity of a nation state. However, the national integration approach enforced through excessive coercion can no longer be maintained for it has steered Indonesia into a situation of turmoil that exists up to the present day. The national integrity of a nation state will, of course, require the loyalty of its citizens towards their nation. Citizen loyalty, however, can only be accomplished if the state is capable of giving back all that has been given to it by the people through their improved well-being, prosperity, freedom, guarantee of social and political rights, and security. The problem with the New Order was that, while it persistently demanded the people's loyalty to the nation and, in doing so, often used militaristic coercive power, it was not capable of delivering prosperity and justice to the people because of rampant corruption and collusion between Suharto's cronies and their families. The unity was not threatened by primordialism from below, but by criminality from above.[35] That was the case with the Aceh struggle against the so-called 'Indonesia Jawa' (Javanese-dominated Indonesia), and that is also the case with West Papua province.

As Indonesia is now in the process of renegotiating with its subnational nations through regional autonomy, local democratization and decentralization, it is worth mentioning that, in the absence of justice, prosperity, freedom and security, not only will democracy be crippled, but the search for a nation will also become irrelevant for the existence of the people.

Notes

1 J. S. Furnivall, *Netherlands India: A Study of Plural Economy* (New York: Cambridge University Press, 1967), p. 447. See also, Azyumardi Azra, 'An Islamic Perspective of Religious Pluralism in Indonesia: The Impact of Democracy on Conflict Resolution', in K. S. Nathan, ed. *Religious Pluralism in Democratic Societies: Challenges and Prospects for Southeast Asia, Europe, and the United States in the New Millenium* (Singapore and Kuala Lumpur: Konrad Adenauer Stiftung and Malaysian Association for American Studies, 2007), p. 288.

2 Henk Schulte Nordholt and Gerry van Klinken, *Renegotiating Boundaries: Local Politics in Post-Suharto Indonesia* (Leiden: KITLV Press, 2007), p. 3.

3 Gerry van Klinken, 'Indonesia's New Ethnic Elites', in Henk Schulte Nordholt and Irwan Abdullah, eds. *Indonesia: In Search of Transition* (Yogyakarta: Pustaka Pelajar, 2002), pp. 68–72.

4 Henk Schulte Nordholt and Gerry van Klinken, *Renegotiating Boundaries*, p. 23.

5 Bryan S. Turner, 'Religious Renewal and Social Diversity: Sources of Citizenship, Conflict and Cooperation in Multicultural Societies', in K. S. Nathan, ed. *Religious Pluralism in Democratic Societies*, p. 257.

6 See, Arskal Salim, 'Dynamic Legal Pluralism in Modern Indonesia: The State and the Sharia (Court) in the Changing Constellations of Aceh', paper presented at the First International Conference of Aceh and Indian Ocean Studies, organized by the Asia Research Institute, National University of Singapore and Rehabilitation and Construction Executing Agency for Aceh and Nias (BRR), Banda Aceh, Indonesia, 24–27 February 2007.

7 Bhikhu Parekh, *Rethinking Multiculturalism: Cultural Diversity and Political Theory* (Basingstoke: Macmillan, 2000), pp. 2–4.

8 The concept of *bangsa* in the Indonesian language oftentimes fails to represent fully the meaning of the English word 'nation'. *Bangsa* can blur the understanding of the notion of Indonesia as a new 'nation' because the concept of *bangsa* also refers to nations that have existed even before Indonesia became a nation state. Therefore, the term 'nasion' has recently been used to produce a closer match with the phonetics of the English version and to represent the clear departure from the concept of *bangsa*. This is to emphasize that Indonesia as a *nasion* is widely different from the idea of the earlier *bangsa* that existed in pre-nation state Indonesia. Mochtar Pabottingi of the Indonesian Institute of Sciences has pioneered the use of the term 'nasion' in place of *bangsa*. Without disregarding the reasons of those who prefer to adopt the two expressions in different ways, I have opted for the word *bangsa* as the synonym of the English word, 'nation', for the purposes of this chapter.

9 Benedict Anderson, *Imagined Communities: Reflections on the Origin and Spread of Nationalism* (London: Verso, 1991).

10 M. Guibernau, *Nationalisms, The Nation-state and Nationalism in the Twentieth Century* (London: Polity Press, 2005), p. 47.

11 Sukarno, 'Pidato Lahirnja Pantja Sila' [Speech on the Birth of Pancasila], in *Lahirnja Pantja – Sila. Pidato pertama tentang Panca sila yang diucapkan pada tanggal 1 Juni 1945 oleh Bung Karno* [*The Birth of Pantja – Sila: The First Speech on Pancasila Declared on 1 June 1945 by Bung Karno*] (Jakarta: Yayasan 17–8–45, n.d.), p. 22. The words in italics are not meant to emphasize a particular part of the sentence, but are instead intended to highlight the fact that these words are not English words but the vocabulary of the Indonesian language.

12 Ibid., p. 23.

13 The text of Pancasila formulated by Sukarno was slightly different from what was then officially accepted as the ideology of the Republic of Indonesia. In Sukarno's formulation, Pancasila consists of: (1) The Indonesian nationality; (2) Internationalism and humanity; (3) Consensus or democracy; (4) Social welfare; and (5) Belief in the one and only God. However the official Pancasila text that remains until today reads: (1) Belief in the one and only God; (2) A just and civilized humanity; (3) The unity of Indonesia; (4) Democracy guided by the inner wisdom in the consensus arising out of deliberations/ representation; and (5) Social justice for the whole of the Indonesian people.

14 This article was reprinted in *Horison*, in July 1986. The words in italics were originally from STA.

15 Ibid.

16 Sanusi Pane was the first to respond to STA's writing in his article, 'Persatuan Indonesia' [The unity of Indonesia], featured in the *Harian Umum* daily newspaper, 4 September 1935. Pane rejected STA's dichotomy of Indonesia and pre-Indonesia, and stated that rather than imitating the West, the culture of Indonesia should be rooted to the past and the virtues of Eastern cultural values. He suggested that Indonesia embrace as many sources as possible for its cultural advancement, including Western cultural elements. However, he repudiated values that were considered to be 'harmful' in Western culture, such as materialism, individualism and intellectualism. Refer to Sanusi Pane, 'Persatuan Indonesia', in *Polemik Kebudayaan*, pp. 13–24.

17 Sudargo Gautama and R. N. Hornick, *An Introduction to Indonesian Law: Unity and Diversity* (Bandung: Alumni, 1974), pp. 3–4.

18 *Koran Tempo* (Jakarta), 19 December 2007.

19 Patricia Spyer, 'Diversity with a Difference: Adat and the New Order in Aru'. *Cultural Anthropology* 11 (February 1996): p. 26.

20 John Pemberton, *On the Subject of 'Java'* (Ithaca and London: Cornell University Press, 1994); G. Acciaioli, 'Pavilions and Posters: Showcasing Diversity and Development in Contemporary Indonesia'. *EIKON* 1 (1996): 27–42; Tom Boellstorff, 'Ethnolocality'. *Asia Pacific Journal of Anthropology* 3, no. 1 (2002): 24–48.

21 G. Acciaioli, 'Pavilions and Posters': 38.

22 Tom Boellstorff, 'Ethnolocality': 25.

23 Rita Smith Kipp, Disassociated Identities: Ethnicity, Religion and Class in an Indonesian Society (Ann Arbor: University of Michigan Press, 1993).

24 *ToWana* literally means 'people from (or who live in) the forest'. The name comes from a mix of a native word '*To*', which means 'people', and a Javanese word, '*Wana*', which means 'forest'. There is no clear explanation for the use of the name, *ToWana*, to identify them despite the fact that they prefer to be called the people of *Ta'* ethnicity (*orang suku Ta'*). Some say that the name was given to them by the Dutch missionaries; others point to the tendency of the New Order regime to name something based on the Javanese vernacular. However, these people then internalized the name of *ToWana* and made it their own.

25 Based on a conversation with Jabar Lahadji, director of the Sahabat Morowali Foundation, Kolonedale, Morowali, Central Sulawesi, on 4 February 2008, in Puncak, Bogor, West Java.

26 Hikmat Budiman, 'Hak Minoritas, Multikulturalisme, Modernitas' [Minority Rights, Multiculturalism, Modernity], in Hikmat Budiman, ed. *Hak Minoritas: Dilema Multikulturalisme di Indonesia* (Jakarta: Interseksi Foundation, 2005), p. 2.
27 Ignatius Yuli Sudaryanto, 'Kesukuan dan Pertentangan Agama di Cagar Alam Morowali. Kasus Orang-orang Wana di Kayupoli, Sulawesi Tengah' [Ethnicity and Religious Conflict in the Morowali Nature Preserve: Case of the Wana people in Kayupoli, Central Sulawesi], in Hikmat Budiman, ed. *Hak Minoritas*, pp. 223–255.
28 Syamsurizal Adhan, 'Islam dan Patuntung di Tanah Toa Kajang: Pergulatan Tiada Akhir' [Islam and Patuntung in Tanah Toa Kajang: A Never-ending Struggle], in Hikmat Budiman,ed. *Hak Minoritas*, pp. 257–323.
29 Heru Prasetia, 'Masyarakat Adat Wet Semokan: Di Tengah Ketegangan Ujaran dan Ajaran' [The Adat Society of Wet Semokan: In the Midst of Friction between Statement and Teaching], in Hikmat Budiman, ed. *Hak Minoritas*, pp. 107–167.
30 G30 S (*Gerakan 30 September*, or the 30th of September Movement) was an abortive *coup d'etat* by a self-proclaimed group of Indonesian Army personnel in 1965. On 1 October 1965, the group kidnapped and assassinated six generals and one first lieutenant of the Indonesian Army. The aftermath of the coup claimed hundreds of thousands of alleged communists throughout the country in 1965. Suharto's New Order regime referred to the incident as G30 S/PKI to associate it with the Indonesian Communist Party (PKI) so as to accuse them of attempting to topple the government. For more details on the incident, refer to Benedict Anderson and Ruth T. McVey, *A Preliminary Analysis of the October 1, 1965 Coup in Indonesia*. Interim Report Series (Ithaca, NY: Cornell Modern Indonesia Project, 1971). For an analysis of the mass murder of the alleged Indonesian communists, see John Roosa, *Pretext for Mass Murder: The September 30th Movement & Suharto's Coup d'Etat in Indonesia* (Madison: University of Wisconsin Press, 2006).
31 Heru Prasetia, 'Masyarakat Adat Wet Semokan: Di Tengah Ketegangan Ujaran dan Ajaran', p. 133.
32 Heru Prasetia, 'Lintas Batas Identitas: Posisi dan Artikulasi Komunitas Tolotang Sulawesi Selatan' [Cross-border Identity: Position and Articulation of Tolotang Community in South Sulawesi], in Mashudi Noorsalim and M. Nurkhoiron, eds. *Hak Minoritas: Multikulturalisme dan Dilema Negara Bangsa* (Jakarta: Interseksi Foundation, 2007), pp. 59–106.
33 Perhaps for the same reason, the Minority Rights Group International (MRG) does not limit its scope to numerical minorities, but instead gives particular attention to the 'non-dominant' (be it ethnically, religiously or linguistically) category to differentiate the minorities from the majority groups of society. MRG also recognizes that for various reasons these communities may not wish to be classified as minorities, and that these groups are not homogeneous. See Minority Rights Group International, 'Who are Minorities?'. Available at www.minorityrights.org/?lid=566.
34 For a brief discussion on this topic, see The Communication Network, 'The Diversity Within Unity Platform'. Available at www.gwu.edu/~ccps/dwu_positionpaper.html.
35 Henk Schulte Nordholt and Gerry van Klinken, *Renegotiating Boundaries*, p. 6.

References

Acciaioli, G. 'Pavilions and Posters: Showcasing Diversity and Development in Contemporary Indonesia'. *EIKON* 1 (1996): 27–42.
Adhan, Syamsurizal. 'Islam dan Patuntung di Tanah Toa Kajang: Pergulatan Tiada Akhir' [Islam and Patuntung in Tanah Toa Kajang: A Never-ending Struggle], in Hikmat Budiman, ed. *Hak Minoritas: Dilema Multikulturalisme di Indonesia* (Jakarta: Interseksi Foundation, 2005).

Alisjahbana, Sutan Takdir. 'Menuju Masyarakat Baru dan Kebudayaan Baru', Indonesia-Prae-Indonesia', in Achdiat K. Mihardja, ed. *Polemik Kebudayaan: Pokok Pikiran St. Takdir Alisjahbana, Sanusi Pane, Dr. Poerbatjaraka, Dr. Sutomo, Tjindarbumi, Adinegoro, Dr. M. Amir, Ki Hajar Dewantara* (Jakarta: Pustaka Jaya, 1977).

Anderson, Benedict. *Imagined Communities: Reflections on the Origin and Spread of Nationalism* (London: Verso, 1991).

Anderson, Benedict and Ruth T. McVey. *A Preliminary Analysis of the October 1, 1965 Coup in Indonesia.* Interim Report Series (Ithaca, NY: Cornell Modern Indonesia Project, 1971).

Azra, Azyumardi. 'An Islamic Perspective of Religious Pluralism in Indonesia: The Impact of Democracy on Conflict Resolution', in K. S. Nathan, ed. *Religious Pluralism in Democratic Societies: Challenges and Prospects for Southeast Asia, Europe, and the United States in the New Millenium*(Singapore and Kuala Lumpur: Konrad Adenauer Stiftung and Malaysian Association for American Studies, 2007).

Boellstorff, Tom. 'Ethnolocality'. *Asia Pacific Journal of Anthropology* 3, no. 1 (2002): 24–48.

Budiman, Hikmat. 'Hak Minoritas, Multikulturalisme, Modernitas' [Minority Rights, Multiculturalism, Modernity], in Hikmat Budiman, ed. *Hak Minoritas: Dilema Multikulturalisme di Indonesia* (Jakarta: Interseksi Foundation, 2005).

Communication Network, The. 'The Diversity Within Unity Platform'. Available at www.gwu.edu/~ccps/dwu_positionpaper.html.

Furnivall, J. S. *Netherlands India: A Study of Plural Economy* (New York: Cambridge University Press, 1967).

Gautama, Sudargo and R. N. Hornick. *An Introduction to Indonesian Law: Unity and Diversity* (Bandung: Alumni, 1974).

Guibernau, M. *Nationalisms, The Nation-state and Nationalism in the Twentieth Century* (London: Polity Press, 2005).

Klinken, Gerry van. 'Indonesia's New Ethnic Elites', in Henk Schulte Nordholt and Irwan Abdullah, eds. *Indonesia: In Search of Transition* (Yogyakarta, Pustaka Pelajar, 2002).

Minority Rights Group International. 'Who are Minorities?'. Available at www.minorityrights.org/?lid=566.

Nordholt, Henk Schulte and Gerry van Klinken. *Renegotiating Boundaries: Local Politics in Post-Suharto Indonesia* (Leiden: KITLV Press, 2007).

Pane, Sanusi. 'Persatuan Indonesia', in Achdiat K. Mihardja, ed. *Polemik Kebudayaan: Pokok Pikiran St. Takdir Alisjahbana, Sanusi Pane, Dr. Poerbatjaraka, Dr. Sutomo, Tjindarbumi, Adinegoro, Dr. M. Amir, Ki Hajar Dewantara* (Jakarta: Pustaka Jaya, 1977).

Parekh, Bhikhu. *Rethinking Multiculturalism: Cultural Diversity and Political Theory* (Basingstoke: Macmillan, 2000).

Pemberton, John. *On the Subject of 'Java'* (Ithaca and London: Cornell University Press, 1994).

Prasetia, Heru. 'Masyarakat Adat Wet Semokan: Di Tengah Ketegangan Ujaran dan Ajaran' [The Adat Society of Wet Semokan: In the Midst of Friction between Statement and Teaching], in Hikmat Budiman, ed. *Hak Minoritas: Dilema Multikulturalisme di Indonesia* (Jakarta: Interseksi Foundation, 2005).

Prasetia, Heru. 'Lintas Batas Identitas: Posisi dan Artikulasi Komunitas Tolotang Sulawesi Selatan' [Cross-border Identity: Position and Articulation of Tolotang Community in South Sulawesi], in Mashudi Noorsalim and M. Nurkhoiron, eds. *Hak Minoritas: Multikulturalisme dan Dilema Negara Bangsa* (Jakarta: Interseksi Foundation, 2007).

Roosa, John. *Pretext for Mass Murder: The September 30th Movement & Suharto's Coup d'Etat in Indonesia* (Madison: University of Wisconsin Press, 2006).

Salim, Arskal. 'Dynamic Legal Pluralism in Modern Indonesia: The State and the Sharia (Court) in the Changing Constellations of Aceh', paper presented at the First International Conference of Aceh and Indian Ocean Studies, organized by the Asia Research Institute, National University of Singapore and Rehabilitation and Construction Executing Agency for Aceh and Nias (BRR), Banda Aceh, Indonesia, 24–27 February 2007.

Smith Kipp, Rita. *Disassociated Identities: Ethnicity, Religion and Class in an Indonesian Society* (Ann Arbor: University of Michigan Press, 1993).

Spyer, Patricia. 'Diversity with a Difference: Adat and the New Order in Aru'. *Cultural Anthropology* 11 (February 1996): 25–50.

Sudaryanto, Ignatius Yuli. 'Kesukuan dan Pertentangan Agama di Cagar Alam Morowali. Kasus Orang-orang Wana di Kayupoli, Sulawesi Tengah' [Ethnicity and Religious Conflict in the Morowali Nature Preserve: Case of the Wana people in Kayupoli, Central Sulawesi], in Hikmat Budiman, ed. *Hak Minoritas: Dilema Multikulturalisme di Indonesia* (Jakarta: Interseksi Foundation, 2005).

Sukarno. 'Pidato Lahirnja Pantja Sila' [Speech on the Birth of Pancasila], in *Lahirnja Pantja – Sila. Pidato pertama tentang Panca sila yang diucapkan pada tanggal 1 Juni 1945 oleh Bung Karno* [*The Birth of Pantja – Sila: The First Speech on Pancasila Declared on 1 June 1945 by Bung Karno*] (Jakarta: Yayasan 17–8–45, n.d.).

Turner, Bryan S. 'Religious Renewal and Social Diversity: Sources of Citizenship, Conflict and Cooperation in Multicultural Societies', in K. S. Nathan, ed. *Religious Pluralism in Democratic Societies: Challenges and Prospects for Southeast Asia, Europe, and the United States in the New Millenium* (Singapore and Kuala Lumpur: Konrad Adenauer Stiftung and Malaysian Association for American Studies, 2007).

Index

Page numbers in *italics* denote tables, those in **bold** denote figures.

Ma, E.K. 128, 130–2
Mabo, E. 175, 182, 186n12
McLeod, J. 124
Madanipour, A. 114
Malayan Historical Society 42
Malayan Independence 30; celebrations
42, 51n56; pre-Independence 51n71
Malaysia 14, 18, 25n22, 30, 33–4, 37–40,
48n3, 50n42, 50n47, 51n60, 59–60, 73;
capital city 32; creation of heroes 41;
first prime minister 46, 48n6; Greater
Malaysia 31, 47; Indian-Malaysian 125;
industrializing economy 112; kinship
links 66; Malaysian Federation 60;
Malaysian Malaysia project 60–1;
mosaic approach 60–1; multi-racial
49n28; New Economic Policy 32, 46;
patronage politics 62; postcolonial
multicultural system 68; post-
independence government 4; Second
Malaysia Plan 32
Maori 85–6, 88–9, *93*, 99; activists 84;
children 87; indigenous status 5, 61, 98,
100–2, 164n39; marginalized 5; non-
Maori 5, 89, 98; society 103n17;
tangata whenua 85, 87, 101–2; treaty
partner 5, 99; urban migration 91
marginalization 113, 201; social 102;
socio-economic 68
marginalized 145; Malay community
62–3; Maori 5, 86; non-White ethnic
minorities 6
marriage 42, 153; early 76; failed 154;
inter-ethnic 122–3; inter-marriage 6;
international 142–3, 151, 153; migrant
brides 143, 149–50, 152–4; teenage
pregnancies 76; Transnational Marriage
and Family Support Centers 154; *see
also* spouses
Merdeka Historical Exhibition 42, 44,
51n57
migrant workers 6, 142, 148–9, *150*,
152–3, 156–7, 159, 164n41; illegal 155;
Thai 117
Migrant Workers' House 156
military heroes 20; Singaporean 4, 11, 14,
16, 19–21, 23–4, 24n1
Minority Rights Group International
207n33
modernist 13; architecture 33–6
multicultural 114, 145–8, 156–7, 161, 185;
Australia 101; Canada 101, 190;
challenges 142, 157, 161; communities
159, 164n42; country 157, 190–1;

families 153–4, 159; global landscape
77; governance 71; Indonesia 191;
Korean society 159; neoliberal solution
72; pedagogy 67; policies 71, 77, 142–3,
148, 150, 153, 158–61, 163n18, 191;
Support Centres 154
multiculturalism 57, **69**, 70, 73–4, 77n1, 89,
92, 98–9, 101, 114, 123, 142–4, 146–7,
158; death of 145; facile 100; in Indonesia
197, 201, 203–4; in Korea 147–8, 151,
156–7, 159–61, 164n41; liberal 59–61,
144; neoliberal **71**, 72–7; in New Zealand
5, 100, 164n39; non-Western 57;
offensive 133; postcolonial 59, 61, 64,
68–9, 73, 77; problematic 160, 190;
protective 133–4; Singaporean 5, 57, 59,
68; state policies 191; Western 5758
multicultural liberal systems 58, 62–3,
66–9, 72, 75; nation 5; postcolonial
systems 58–60, 63, 66–8, 71, 73, 75–7;
social fabric 92; society 5–6, 134,
142–3, 147–9, 153–4, 156–9, 161, 190;
states 4–5; systems 5, 63, 65–6, **69**, 73;
utopias 5, **69**, **71**, 76
mural competition 49n25; entry **39**
Muslim
Muslims 62, 128, 130; Association of
Muslim Professionals in Singapore 62;
community 61, 130; ethnic minorities
129; headscarf 144–5; kindergartens 68;
majority 7, 199; Malay-Muslim
community 62–3, 74; minorities 73,
126, 129–30; orthodoxy 146; patients
121; representations 52n79

National Humiliation 129–30
nationalism 1–4, 112, 130, 148, 161; Asian
143, 147; in Australia 7, 174;
expansionary 147; in Korea 156–8;
Malay 30–2, 41, 51n68, 52n78; Malayan
41; native 113; postcolonial 75; in South
Korea 163n20, 164n34
national narratives 1, 3–8, 14, 16, 18, 30,
176, 183; Australian 169–70; dominant
173; legitimacy 12; scripting 21, 47;
Singaporean 11, 13, 17, 19–20, 22–3,
25n17; Southeast Asian nations 41
National Service 4, 1819, 23; national
servicemen 23, 24n1
nation-building 11–12, 19, 24, 73–4, 112,
157, 189; efforts 13; imperative 57, 59;
internal dynamics 72; post-
independence 21; projects 1, 3, 11, 60;
second phase 70

For Product Safety Concerns and Information please contact our EU
representative GPSR@taylorandfrancis.com
Taylor & Francis Verlag GmbH, Kaufingerstraße 24, 80331 München, Germany

www.ingramcontent.com/pod-product-compliance
Lightning Source LLC
Chambersburg PA
CBHW062021270326
41929CB00014B/2276

9 7 8 1 1 3 8 6 5 3 5 5 9